Strategic Human Resource Management

Corporate Rhetoric and Human Reality

LYNDA GRATTON, VERONICA HOPE HAILEY,
PHILIP STILES, AND CATHERINE TRUSS

OXFORD
UNIVERSITY PRESS

OXFORD
UNIVERSITY PRESS

Oxford University Press, Great Clarendon Street, Oxford OX2 6DP

Oxford New York
Athens Auckland Bangkok Bogotá Buenos Aires Calcutta
Cape Town Chennai Dar es Salaam Delhi Florence Hong Kong Istanbul
Karachi Kuala Lumpur Madrid Melbourne Mexico City Mumbai
Nairobi Paris São Paulo Singapore Taipei Tokyo Toronto Warsaw
and associated companies in Berlin Ibadan

Oxford is a registered trade mark of Oxford University Press

Published in the United States
by Oxford University Press Inc., New York

British Library Cataloguing in Publication Data
Data available

Library of Congress Cataloging in Publication Data
Strategic human resource management: corporate rhetoric and human
reality / Lynda Gratton . . . [et al.].
    p. cm.
  1. Personnel management.   2. Strategic management.   I. Gratton,
  Lynda.
  HF5549. 884 1999 658.3—dc21   98-40754
ISBN 0-19-878204-7 (Hbk)
ISBN 0-19-878203-9 (Pbk)

10 9 8 7 6

Typeset in Utopia
by Best-set Typesetter Ltd., Hong Kong
Printed in Great Britain
on acid-free paper by
Bookcraft (Bath)
Ltd, Midsomer
Norton, Somerset

Dedicated to Michael, John, Jan, and Norvald

ACKNOWLEDGEMENTS

THE authors would like to extend their thanks to the many organizations and individuals who have contributed to the writing of this book. The members of the Leading Edge Consortium—BP, BT, Citibank, Glaxo Pharmaceuticals UK, Hewlett Packard, Kraft Jacobs Suchard, Lloyds-TSB, the Chelsea & Westminster Healthcare Trust, and W. H. Smith—and their human resource directors have all contributed resources both financial and intellectual and we are greatly indebted to them for their willingness to share the downside as well as the upside of their experiences. Investors in People have also played an important role in resourcing the project. Arthur D. Little Inc. sponsored Patrick McGovern's research fellowship at London Business School, and Peter Scott-Morgan kindly allowed us access to his Unwritten Rules of the Game© methodology.

The authors would also like to thank the following for permission to reproduce previously published material: the editors of *Journal of Management Studies* for Chapter 2, 'Soft and Hard Models of Human Resource Management' by Catherine Truss, which is a version of an article published in the January 1997 issue, 34/1: 53–73; Professor John Storey for Figure 6.2; and the editors of *Human Resource Management Journal* for Chapter 7, 'HRM Policies and Management Practices' by Patrick McGovern, which is an extended version of an article published in 1997, 7/4.

We have benefited enormously from the constructively critical insights of many colleagues, especially Nigel Nicholson, Sumantra Ghoshal, Ann Huff, Randall Schuler, Rob Goffee, John Hendry, David Guest, Andrew Pettigrew, and Patrick Flood.

We were lucky enough to have invaluable research assistance from Peter Moore, Rose Trevelyan, Annie Lucas, Björn Haring, and many others from the companies themselves. Edel Conway and Simon Bacon brought their statistical skills to bear on the mass of data generated by the project. Anthony Senior and Jayne Ashley both took on the administrative load of the project with consummate professionalism and good humour. Simon Bird's eagle-eyed editorial skills finally brought the book together, and we owe him an enormous debt of gratitude for his help in getting us to press. Finally, we must thank our long-suffering families, especially all the Leading Edge babies, for their forbearance during long periods of writing.

Of course the usual disclaimer applies, and the responsibility for any errors, omissions, or oversights remains that of the authors alone.

L. G.
V. H. H.
P. S.
C. T.

CONTENTS

List of Figures   x

List of Tables   xi

1. Introduction   1

2. Soft and Hard Models of Human Resource Management   40
   Catherine Truss

3. Performance Management in Fast-Changing Environments   59
   Philip Stiles

4. The Rhetoric and Reality of 'New Careers'   79
   Lynda Gratton and Veronica Hope Hailey

5. Managing Culture   101
   Veronica Hope Hailey

6. Contextual Diversity for the Role and Practice of HR   117
   Veronica Hope Hailey

7. HRM Policies and Management Practices   133
   Patrick McGovern

8. Transformation at the Leading Edge   153
   Philip Stiles

9. People Processes as a Source of Competitive Advantage   170
   Lynda Gratton

10. The Emerging Themes   199

References   227

Index   239

LIST OF FIGURES

4.1 The new career   81
6.1 The evolutionary cycle   119
6.2 Types of personnel management   120
6.3 The evolutionary cycle   130
9.1 The People Process Map: embedding transformational change   185
10.1 An emergent model of initiative transfer within organizations   215

LIST OF TABLES

1.1	Data collection and assimilation	19
1.2	Participating companies	21
1.3	Participating companies and questionnaire data collection	22
2.1	Reported number of days' training received by employees per year (%)	46
2.2	Employees' perceptions of training (%)	46
2.3	Respondents agreeing/strongly agreeing with the statement, 'I do not have the opportunities I want to be promoted' (%)	49
2.4	Communication between management and staff (%)	50
2.5	Respondents agreeing/strongly agreeing with the statement, 'I do not have a great deal of trust in my manager' (%)	50
2.6	Integration of HR factors and strategy at corporate/group level	52
2.7	Control over setting work targets (%)	55
2.8	Organizational flexibility (% agreeing/strongly agreeing)	56
3.1	Performance management practices: Citibank	72
3.2	Performance management practices: Glaxo Pharmaceuticals UK	73
3.3	Performance management practices: Hewlett Packard	74
3.4	Performance management practices: Lloyds Bank UK Retail Banking	75
4.1	Shifts in the career paradigm	80
4.2	Theme 1: Architectures enabling the 'new career'	86
4.3	Theme 1: Architectures enabling the 'new career' (%)	89
4.4	Theme 2: Individual perceptions of self-management (%)	92
4.5	Impact on commitment (respondents agreeing/strongly agreeing with these statements, %)	95
4.6	Theme 3: Line management support	98
7.1	'How frequently is your performance at work appraised?' (all respondents, %)	137
7.2	Constraints on HRM practice	140
7.3	'How important a factor is it in your performance appraisal that you successfully implement personnel policies?' (line managers only, %)	141

7.4 'Which of the following have the greatest influence on the development of your people management skills in your organization?' (line managers only, %)   142

7.5 'Please rank the following in order of what motivates you to be involved in personnel activities in your organization' (line managers only, %)   144

7.6 'Which of the following personnel activities do you carry out for your subordinates as part of your job?'—career planning (line managers only, %)   149

8.1 Major changes within the companies: BT Payphones (1994)   156

8.2 Major changes within the companies: Chelsea & Westminster Healthcare Trust (1995)   156

8.3 Major changes within the companies: Citibank (1994)   157

8.4 Major changes within the companies: Glaxo Pharmaceuticals UK (1993)   158

8.5 Major changes within the companies: Hewlett Packard (1994)   159

8.6 Major changes within the companies: Kraft Jacobs Suchard (1994)   159

8.7 Major changes within the companies: Lloyds Bank Uk Retail Banking (1994)   160

8.8 Major changes within the companies: W. H. Smith News (1994)   160

9.1 The short-term cycle   181

9.2 The long-term cycle   182

9.3 Feedback and redirectional elements   184

1

Introduction

This is a not a book about the rhetoric of senior managers, embodied in such statements as 'people are our most important asset' or 'career development is the core of our relationship with our employees'. It is not a set of idealized descriptions of how Hewlett Packard manages performance or a wish list of change management practices at Glaxo Pharmaceuticals UK.

This is a book about the reality of people management in large, complex companies. Some of the companies in the research project on which this book is based are considered to be world class in their management of people, others are not. All are commercially successful, generally one of the top five performers within their business sector. In their diversity, they represent the type of large companies found throughout the Western world and face the challenges which are discussed in executive boardrooms from London to Stockholm to Cincinnati. The many hundreds of thousands of people these companies employ voice concerns and aspirations you can hear in the local bar or on the evening news.

This book represents the culmination of a collaboration between academics and senior managers to study, analyse, reflect, and discuss the challenges they face in people management. It also represents an attempt to reflect the experience, concern, and aspirations of people at all levels in these companies.

How can we characterize our understanding of people management practices in large companies? Back in 1992, a discussion with Hewlett Packard's human resource group in the UK crystallized what some of us had felt from our own perspectives as academics in the field and advisers to companies. Too often our understanding was based on glamorized case studies presented by personnel directors at industry conferences, describing how they had introduced complex human resource systems which had been applauded throughout the company and quickly adopted as a company standard, or detailing the survey responses of senior managers who agreed how important human resource management was in their company, and attested to the continual or rising importance it would have in the future.

It all looked so straightforward, but we knew the reality was different. Data from confidential surveys conducted by London Business School and others mapped the feelings of isolation and bewilderment created by changes in the nature of the psychological contract between employer and employee. The rhetoric may have been about human resources partnering with line managers, but privately human resource managers spoke of the 'clerk of works' role they played, trying to tie together companies changing faster than we had ever imagined. Even in Hewlett Packard, seen by practitioners and academics as a people management benchmark, concerns were raised about integrating the rapidly changing business imperatives with the human resource systems to create a measure of continuity and consistency. Yet, with a few important exceptions, our shared knowledge of how companies managed people in the late 1990s was not sufficient to create a bedrock of solid understanding from which to build.

We began to realize that a close collaboration between industry and academia with a well-honed methodology would have the potential to make a real, significant contribution. During 1992 we approached the personnel directors of a number of large companies, either with headquarters in the UK (BP, BT Payphones, Glaxo Pharmaceuticals UK, Lloyds Bank UK Retail Banking, W. H. Smith News) or with headquarters outside the UK but with significant UK operations (Citibank, Hewlett Packard, Kraft Jacobs Suchard, General Motors). We also spoke to senior executives from one of London's large and newly created trust hospitals. Our mission was clear, to create and share a base of research capable of shedding light on the people issues they faced. Our proposals were met with excitement and understanding. Bill Proudlock from Glaxo (now Glaxo Pharmaceuticals UK), Clive Dilloway and Peter Moore from BP, and Mike Haffenden from Hewlett Packard created an early triumvirate with which we hammered out the basic values and philosophy of the endeavour. They were joined over the following year by Gillian Arthur from Citibank, John Kick from Hewlett Packard, Rodney Buse from W. H. Smith News, Peter Bareau from Lloyds Bank (now Lloyds TSB), Mike Anscombe from Kraft Jacobs Suchard (a business of Philip Morris), and Bruce Warman from Vauxhall (a business of General Motors). All participated actively through the following years, although we were never able to negotiate the depth of research access we required to conduct research in BP or Vauxhall.

THE BASIC PHILOSOPHY

About what the research would be . . .

As the research consortium took shape we developed a set of beliefs about what the research would and would not be.

- We would gain access to highly sensitive data about the true nature of human resource management in these companies, looking at rhetoric and reality through discussion and observations right through the business.
- We would partner with industry and provide a forum in which this information could be reported and debated. The series of Leading Edge Forum meetings which stretched from 1993 until the present day embodied our wish to build long-term research relationships with practising managers.
- We would make the research findings available to a wider practitioner and academic community, and by doing so create a platform for a deeper and more informed debate about people management issues.

The research consortium has remained true to these beliefs right up to the present day: by providing the research team with access to everyone we wanted to see, and allowing us to debate and discuss sensitive issues; by entering into the Forum meetings with enormous curiosity and respect for their own colleagues and those in the other consortium companies; by encouraging wider debate of the findings and allowing the research team to prepare a series of papers which represent one of the most open and honest evaluations of what human resource management really means in large, complex companies.

About what the research would do . . .

In the first report to the Leading Edge, prepared in 1992, we made four key points. First, that strategic human resource management (SHRM) is undoubtedly a concept of fundamental interest to both practitioners and academics alike, but research carried out to date had been very inconclusive. At that time there were few empirical studies and as a consequence the commentary was highly prescriptive and presented an idealized view of how people should be managed. Secondly, we identified several questions which arose from the existing literature which we believed needed to be answered if we were to improve our knowledge of how human resource strategy works within organizations, and how to assess best practice. These included the following questions: what are the features of the external and internal contexts which impact on the human resource strategy process? What is the link between intended business strategy, intended human resource strategy, and the realized interventions? What is the impact of human resource strategies at an individual and an organizational level? And finally, how does human resource strategy influence everyday managerial behaviour? To answer these questions we began to map the HRS process which we aimed to test empirically. We were aware that there are a number of influences on HRS formulation and implementation, which include the external environment, the strategy pursued by the organization, and what we termed leverage factors such as structure and culture. We concluded early in our investigation that the methodology we pursued would be central to the success of the endeavour. We described the methodology in the following way:

This would consist of three elements: the collection of 'hard' data from written sources, such as mission statements, company reports, and HR documents; interviews with key executives and HR directors; a questionnaire survey over defined areas of the population.

This first methodology report to the Leading Edge Forum was discussed extensively during the spring of 1993 and formed the foundation of much of the subsequent work. We may have later extended the methodology to include focus groups and the 'Unwritten Rules of the Game' interviews, and drawn out emerging themes, but our philosophy remained essentially the same. We would undertake a research study which was empirical in its nature, and we would keep asking the hard questions.

About the research team . . .

We were, and remain, a diverse research team, representing many of the disciplines and approaches which are at the centre of the study of human resource management. It has been our experience that this diversity brings with it enormous strengths. It encourages us continually to question long-held dogmas and disciplinary truisms, to consider the findings from many perspectives, and to push our thinking stronger and harder. Our search for a 'common voice' which transcends our individual perspectives is apparent in the themes which dominate our research and which are represented in the chapters of this book. The way we examine and describe these themes is essentially from the individual author's perspective. In this book we have allowed these individual voices to be heard.

DEVELOPING THE INITIAL RESEARCH QUESTIONS AND MEASURES

We developed a set of research questions which created the basis of the methodology and framed the emerging themes. There were four research questions which appeared to be critical if the field of study was to be moved forward substantially. These research questions created a framework of research measures which are listed below.

The research questions:

1. What contextual features impact on the human resource strategy process? What is the precise nature of these internal and external variables and how do they impact upon the process of both devising a human resource strategy and implementing it?

2. What is the link between intended business strategy, intended human resource strategy, and realized human resource interventions?
   What is the relationship between the business strategy of a company and its human resource strategy: is there a strong relationship or do strategies emerge? What is the link between espoused human resource strategy and the reality of day-to-day human resource activities?
3. What is the impact of strategic human resources on particular outcomes, both at an individual and an organizational level?
   What is the impact of specific human resource interventions on individual or organizational outcomes?
4. How does human resource strategy influence everyday managerial behaviour?
   In particular, what roles do the line manager and the human resource professional play in delivering human resource strategies, and how is their behaviour influenced by these strategies?

What contextual features impact on the human resource strategy process?

The significance of environmental and contextual factors has been long acknowledged in shaping human resource strategy, and in the ability of the company to realize these strategies. The growth of the concept of a strategic approach to managing people can be attributed to rapid environmental changes that have taken place over the last two decades (Baird and Meshoulam 1988; Tichy *et al.* 1982). These environmental influences operate at a general level, and at a more specialized level concerned with the organization's own significant environment. The more general influences operate in four main areas: at the societal level, particularly changes in demographics and the shape and education of the workforce; changes in technology, for example the profound impact of information technology on the way in which people work; changes in the structure of the economy, for example changes in the balance between the public and private sector, inflation, or the shift from manufacturing to service industries; and at the political and legal level, changes in employment legislation can also impact on human resource strategies.

It is through the mediation of the 'organizational environment', however, that broader environmental changes are made meaningful to individual organizations. It is these 'experienced relevant business conditions' which impact on the formulation and enactment of human resource strategy. These business conditions include 'stakeholders' in the organization, who can influence the strategy depending on their power. These stakeholders can include the organization's competitors and suppliers, the government, the media, environmentalists, local community organizations, and consumer advocates (Freeman 1985; Tsui 1988).

What elements internal to the organization may exert an influence on strategy formulation and implementation? These 'levers' form the inner context and include such aspects as technology, culture, management philosophy and style, structure, and the 'dominant coalition' (Lundberg 1985; Milkovich and Boudreau 1991). Culture involves a set of taken-for-granted assumptions or rules for being in the world (Adler and Jelinek 1986). In our methodology we attempted to understand the culture of the organizations through the 'Unwritten Rules of the Game' interview process. Internal stakeholders play a significant role as levers. These include employees, managers, professional staff, the HR department itself, and owners, who hold a stake in the way human resources are managed in the organization. These 'strategic constituents' can have different and often conflicting needs (Tsui 1988). Related to these constituents are the dominant coalitions or management groups that exercise the most power in the organization.

In the description of the companies later in this chapter we explore some of the dominant contextual factors which have influenced the prioritization and implementation of human resource strategies.

In focusing on this research question we developed a number of research measures, which are described below.

The research measures: external environment:

- level of maturity of the industry; nature and extent of the competition, intensity of competitive pressure; environmental restrictiveness; extent and rapidity of technological change; perceived turbulence, hostility, and complexity; type, extent, and predictability of change.

The research measures: organizational-specific environment:

- management style and philosophy:
  level of individualistic decision-making; importance of participative decision-making; importance of management by objectives;
- employee climate:
  trust, commitment, risk-taking, morale, team working; level of criticism vs. level of praise; perceptions of senior management; perceptions of success of the organization; pride;
- administrative heritage:
  vision of founder; major successes/failures that are legendary in organization; leadership style of founders; philosophy, values;
- structure:
  extent of formal definition, centralization, and formal communication; use of informal structures such as project teams; extent of horizontal processes;
- culture:
  shared vision and common understanding of organizational goals; values, attitudes, and beliefs; style of decision-making.

What is the link between intended business strategy, intended human resource strategy, and realized human resource interventions?

Over the last two decades there has been a profound shift in thinking about the role that people play in the success of the business, with a growing view that the management of people is a key organizational capability and one which should be highly integrated with the strategic aims of the business. A cornerstone of this notion of strategic human resource management (SHRM) is the creation of linkage or integration between the overall strategic aims of the business and the human resource strategy and implementation. In principle, the processes and people within the company are managed in such a way as to foster the aims of the business strategy (Beer and Spector 1985; Devanna *et al.* 1982; Evans 1986; Miles and Snow 1978; 1984) and create an integrated approach to managing the various human resource interventions, such as selection, training, reward and development, so that they complement each other (Hendry and Pettigrew 1986; Storey 1992). In short, to create a 'set of interrelated practices with an ideological and philosophical underpinning' (Storey 1989: 3). Thus the emphasis is on vertical integration (integration between the business strategy and the human resource strategy) and horizontal integration (integration within the various human resource interventions). This strategic approach to human resource management emphasizes the delivery of business strategy and the impact on 'bottom-line' performance through the way in which people are managed (Lengnick-Hall and Lengnick-Hall 1990).

There have been a number of conceptual attempts to understand more fully the nature of this integration between business strategy and human resource strategy. At the broadest level is the notion that integration occurs when the human resource strategy is 'matched' with the organization's stage of development or strategic orientation or management style. So, start-up businesses require a rather different approach to human resource management from companies in decline (Baird and Meshoulam 1988); similarly multi-divisional companies have rather different needs from those of less complex organizational forms (Fombrun *et al.* 1984). The key business strategies of innovation, quality enhancement, and cost reduction require specific sets of role behaviours, which, in turn, suggest different HRM policies in relation to job design, employee appraisal, development, reward, and participation (Schuler and Jackson 1987).

From an empirical perspective, there is some evidence that organization or product life cycle is a determinant of HR practices, and that an appropriate fit between life cycle and HR practices may be associated with better firm performance (Butler *et al.* 1991).

How realistic is this broad concept of integration between business strategy and human resource strategy? From a conceptual position it could be argued that the concept of a top-down, unitarist planning process is overly simplistic, ignoring the political processes, the fact that organizations do not move sequentially from one predictable stage to another, and that many pursue multiple rather than single strategies. This 'classical' top-down approach to strategy development may fail to take into consideration the realities of organizational decision-making processes. There are other ways of considering the process of strategy creation. For instance, the 'evolutionary' approach is based on the notion that it is the market that selects winners, and the environmental fit is the main goal; strategy is therefore emergent. According to the 'processual' perspective, strategy is a word used to describe the way in which managers seek to simplify and order a complex world; it is discovered in action, not specifically formulated through rationalistic processes. The 'systemic' perspective emphasizes the role of social systems in shaping strategic goals, and challenges the notion that any single model of strategy can be universally applicable (Legge 1995b; Whittington 1993). As Legge (1995b: 103) comments:

Clearly, the feasibility and even what is meant by integrating HRM policies with business strategy will very much depend on which perspective on strategy and strategy-making one adopts. Arguably the act of consciously matching HRM policy to business strategy is only relevant if one adopts the rationalistic 'classical' perspective.

How prevalent is strategic human resource management in the reality of large, complex businesses? Whilst commentators have set out to provide a working definition of the term, relatively few empirical studies have been carried out. In examining the evidence of the uptake of SHRM, we kept two points in mind. First, there is a relative dearth of empirical data, whilst many assertions concerning the presence and nature of human resource management have been made on the basis of either one or two case studies, surveys of personnel managers, or simply no empirical data at all. Secondly, as Storey has noted, 'the seductive power of the concept means that it is all too easy to fall into the trap of distorting reality by relaying the often incomplete and indeed amorphous character of everyday managerial practice by attributing to it a spurious coherence' (1992: 17). Thus we must bear in mind that we as researchers may well be keen to find evidence of SHRM in the organizations we study, and could perhaps tend to interpret our findings in a way that supports our views about changes that have taken place in the management of people at work.

Despite these two caveats, it was clear that a number of interesting and thorough empirical studies of human resource management had been carried out which provided some evidence of the way it is being applied within organizations, and which also provided insight into what we might expect to observe in our study. In developing our own research methodologies and thinking we were particularly influenced by Storey's study of 40 large UK companies (Storey 1992; Storey and Sisson 1989); by Devanna et al.'s study of 168 large American companies (1982); and by Stace and Dunphy's study of the strategic orientation of the HR function in 13 Australian organizations (1990).

These empirical studies had indicated that moves towards a strategic approach to human resource management were not as common as the normative or descriptive literature would lead us to believe. Storey reported considerable evidence of a change in rhetoric within the companies he studied. There was a move away from talking about rules and regulations towards a language based on a more strategic approach involving ideas of culture, mission, and commitment. However, whilst the rhetoric was strategic, in reality the change was messy and incomplete, with organizations presenting characteristics of both the old and new approaches. He argued that many of these changes are not necessarily a move towards wholesale SHRM, but are often piecemeal initiatives formulated in response to certain situations. Devanna *et al.* (1982) found a similar trend in their study of strategy and related HRM practices. They report that the majority of organizations used formal strategic planning, but that 53 per cent said that human resource considerations had a less than moderate effect on strategic formulation. They also discovered that the majority of HR activities took place at the operational level, with hardly any taking place at the strategic level.

Related to the question of the link between business strategy and human resource strategy is the means by which intended human resource strategies are realized. There have been various attempts to model the strategic human resource management process. A number, such as Lundberg's (1985) model, are derived from investigations in one, or several, organizations, whilst the conceptual models (Storey 1992) are derived from the literature and then tested within organizations. Lundberg's model is derived from a case study carried out within the Reynolds Corporation in America. At the core of the model is the notion that strategy and tactics are influenced by the 'dominant coalition', usually consisting of the management operating team, which is the most powerful group in the organization on a day-to-day basis and in terms of governing long-term strategy. The nature of this dominant coalition is influenced by a number of factors, including organization history (such as the vision of the founder), values and attitudes, marketing, finance, competition, and regulation. It is also influenced by the chief executive's leadership role or style, and by external stakeholders (such as major suppliers, customers, and equity holders). Various environmental factors also influence the dominant coalition, such as the market and the state of the industry. Organization strategy is formulated by the dominant coalition and the HR strategy flows from and supports this strategy. In Storey's model (1992) the trigger for changes in the human resource process is enhanced competition, leading to a strategic response which impacts on the organizational beliefs and assumptions, the role of line management, and other key factors such as communication and the psychological contract.

What was clear was that one of the most interesting areas remaining to be fully explored was the interlinkage between articulated human resource strategy and particular HR activities. What is planned may not be what is implemented. We saw this as a major question for this research study.

In focusing on this research question we developed a number of research measures, which are described below.

The research measures: intended business strategy:

- articulated strategic objectives; strategic type of stated business goals.

The research measures: intended human resource strategy:

- strategy creation and implementation:
  formal strategic planning processes; performance aspirations; clarity of corporate vision; extent of communication and understanding of strategy; perceived commitment of senior managers to strategic goals;
- human resource strategy:
  strategy documents; human resource goals; integration between goals; current major human resource initiatives.

The research measures: realized human resource interventions:

- type of intervention:
  strategic linkage; major interventions; future plans; future challenges;
- process outcomes:
  recruitment and selection; induction; performance management; training and development; career and succession planning; equal opportunities; employee relations.

What is the impact of strategic human resources on particular outcomes, at both an individual and an organizational level?

A key question for practitioners and researchers is the extent to which human resource interventions impact on the financial performance of the business. The case for the advantages of implementing a strategic approach to managing people has been made by a number of commentators including Schuler and MacMillan (1984) and Lengnick-Hall and Lengnick-Hall (1988). They argue that a strategic approach to human resource management increases profitability, lowers turnover, increases product quality, lowers production costs, and increases flexibility and innovation. But is this true? Certainly during the mid-1990s there was no conclusive evidence of a link between a strategic approach to managing people and the financial performance of the firm. This in part reflected the difficulty of measuring organizational performance, which can be assessed at different levels, at different times, and using different indicators (Hrebiniak *et al.* 1988); the difficulty of measuring the success of the human resource intervention (Walker 1980); and the difficulty of measuring the impact of an intervention over time. In summary, as Storey (1992) has argued, the demonstration of this causal link is fraught with immense difficulty because of the vast range of confounding variables.

In debating our own approach to this question we have argued against a central role for financial performance as a desirable outcome of human resource strategy. It may well be a strategic objective of the organization, but human resource strategy is there to ensure that the organization's human resources are deployed in such a way as to support the organization's aims; financial performance is not synonymous with organizational strategy, and its outcome measures are not the same. So what can we measure? First, concerning levels of analysis, there are two orders of outcomes: organizational (for instance flexibility or innovation) and individual (for instance the ability to hire certain skill sets). Unlike the desired outcomes of strategy, most human resource strategy outcomes are at the individual level. Second, although it is true that outcomes will be evaluated differently depending on the perspective of different stakeholders, it would appear most appropriate to concentrate on the organization itself. Thus, there are two levels of outcome to consider: outcomes from the individual human resource interventions (such as the hiring of certain types of people) and general outcomes from the overall human resource strategy (such as levels of commitment and trust).

In focusing on this research question we developed a number of research measures, which are described below.

The research measures: outcomes:

- organizational commitment:
  ambience of the organization in terms of morale, conviviality, satisfaction, and shared commitment;
- profitability and growth:
  level and stability of profitability; growth rate of sales or revenues;
- adaptability:
  flexibility;
- competence:
  employees' competence to take on new jobs and skills as needed; attitude towards change and learning.

How does human resource strategy influence everyday managerial behaviour?

Between the 1980s and the mid-1990s we saw profound changes in the rhetoric concerning the roles of the human resource function and the line management. In this study we set out to examine the current reality of these roles and to investigate the extent to which the strategic role is changing.

The human resource function in the 1980s had been associated primarily with the 'clerk of works' role of negotiator in collective bargaining agreements and administrator of policies and procedures (Anthony 1986; Armstrong 1984; Legge 1978; Watson 1977). By the 1990s there was an increasing awareness that culture, people, and processes rather than capital or technology could form the basis for sustained competitive advantage within the firm (Barney 1991). With this realization came a profoundly different way of looking at the roles of the human resource function and line management in supporting and enabling the people aspects of the company to assume this central importance. For the human resource function the exhortation was clear: balance the administrative role with the strategic role of business partnership or architect, and actively engage in understanding and developing this source of sustained competitive advantage (Tyson and Fell 1986; Ulrich 1987; 1997; Walker 1994).

A similar shift in role was expected of line managers. It was no longer appropriate for line managers to delegate responsibility and decision-making for the management of people to an administrative platform service, the personnel function; it was no longer appropriate for line managers to 'abrogate responsibility for people; instead they were expected to be accountable for how their staff behaved, performed, were selected and dismissed' (Anthony 1986). They had a key role to play in supporting the new psychological contract, creating commitment and trust, and focusing the people resources of the company onto the business strategy. The management of people was perceived to be too important to be left to operational personnel specialists, and it was felt that decisions about people should be made closer to the point of service or product delivery. This changing role for managers has been noted by those writing about managerial practice in general (Kanter 1989b; Mintzberg 1973; Scase and Goffee 1989; A. Stewart 1989), and their writing supports the changing role of line managers implied in the HRM literature, namely that effective line managers should have strong interpersonal skills and the ability to influence and negotiate with other people. Kanter (1989b) in particular identified a set of core competencies for line and general managers which included the ability to manage ambiguity, complexity, and uncertainty, and to manage without authority. The message was clear: line and general managers must develop excellent people management skills.

Was this shift in thinking paralleled by a shift in practice? Was the HR function assuming a more strategic 'architect' or 'business planner' role, and were managers developing sophisticated people management skills? In practice, research was showing transitional stages in these developments and highlighting some of the underlying structural obstacles to creating these roles.

With regard to the HR function, the findings were not wholly supportive of the shift. In a study conducted in the UK in the mid-1980s Storey (1992) described the supposed strategic role of HR in a small sample of organizations. He found few HR functions actually fulfilled the strategic criteria. Other case descriptions have suggested that the more strategic role has been adopted in some cases, particularly in high-technology and innovative companies (Yeung *et al.* 1994).

What of the sophisticated people management role for line managers? Storey's work carried out in the late 1980s, reported in 1992, indicated that there was an intention that line managers would indeed become far more important in determining how human resources should be used. However, these changes had not arisen from a formal redivision of HR responsibilities between the specialist function and the line. Instead, they reflected changes in manufacturing processes, in the labour management generally, and the assertiveness of line managers themselves. These structural and market changes had brought with them expectations of a new management style which required line managers to be more involved with employees and their development, and to engage more in communication.

However, whilst there may be an intention on the part of the company for line managers to take a more active role in people management, in reality there seemed to be a number of blocks to this occurring for all line managers. Research had shown that some were not being adequately consulted about the new devolution of responsibilities; they were unclear about their roles, or did not believe it was a legitimate part of their job (Bevan and Hayday 1994). Company case studies undertaken in the late 1980s revealed that for some companies devolution to line management was severely constrained by the short-term pressures of business, and by the low educational and technical skill base of the managers (Kirkpatrick *et al.* 1992; Lowe 1992). This hampered their ability to focus on the developmental or 'soft' approach to people management. This lack of training and competence amongst line managers has been supported by a more recent research report by Hyman and Cunningham (1995).

It was our intention in this study to survey and interview line managers and HR professionals across all the sample companies to understand their roles, and the sources of support and the impediments to moving to a more strategic role. As the following list of research measures shows, they included the characteristics of the human resource function, their level of expertise, the skill and role of line management, and the manner in which human resource interventions were realized.

In focusing on this research question we developed a number of research measures, which are described below.

The research measures: influences on managerial behaviour:

- characteristics of the human resource function:
  structuring of tasks; organization of department; acquisition and use of knowledge; nature of HR information systems; processes to identify and plan for the future; size of HR department;
- level of expertise:
  knowledge and expertise; perceived credibility; type of people employed;
- design and implementation of HR interventions:
  participation of HR director in strategic decisions; level of HR expertise; linkage between strategy and HRS; employees' perceptions of the strategy of the HR department; senior managers' expectations of HR function; measures of success; main stakeholders in HR policy formulation and implementation; change facilitation skills of HR department;

- involvement of line managers:
  participation in the policy formulation and implementation; level of competencies; commitment to implementation; managerial involvement metrics;
- human resource philosophy:
  psychological contract; level of investment in human resource activities.

DEVELOPING THE RESEARCH METHODOLOGY

Our primary aim was to examine how people are managed in certain large companies in the UK in the mid-1990s. We wanted to take into account intentions, or the organization's espoused approach, and the realized or enacted reality. This gap between rhetoric and reality (or espoused and enacted theories) essentially means that there may be a number of different views or angles concerning particular phenomena. It was our intention to capture the richness of these organizational phenomena through in-depth analysis designed to track both convergence and divergence of the elements of the people management process. Further, by using this triangulated methodology we were attempting to confront the view expressed by Jackson *et al.* (1989) that the field of human resource strategy has been ill served by empirical analyses:

A lack of longitudinal in-depth case studies in the American work, combined with a penchant for small-scale, low response rate surveys, gives only fragile empirical support—if that—for a weighty prescriptive superstructure. (1989: 117)

During the autumn of 1992 and the spring of 1993 we discussed and agreed our philosophy for the research methodology, knowing that much of the strength of our subsequent work would be generated by the research method. Central to the project's approach would be the case study method. This was well suited to an endeavour like our own which is predominantly exploratory, with emergent paradigms rather than a single dominant paradigm or unifying theory, and where the focus is building rather than testing theories. Given the fragmented nature of the human resource management literature, the problems over HRM's conceptual status, and the relative youth of the subject, an exploratory, theory-building approach was the logical path to take.

It was our view that the use of multiple methods of field study would enable us to obtain a richness of data. This triangulation (Jick 1979) uses a combination of methods to study the same phenomenon, the basic premise being that the particular limitations of a given method will be compensated by the counterbalancing strengths of another (Snow and Thomas 1994). We used two field methods—interviews (including an ethnographic study) and surveys—together with the extensive gathering of internal documents and external data. These methods allowed us to triangulate policy, or the intended strategy or human resource process; practice, or the realized human resource interventions; and impact.

Interviews and focus groups

In contrast to earlier studies that had focused their data collection solely on the human resource function, we took a vertical slice through the organization's strategic apex, middle line, and operating core (Mintzberg 1983) to consider the reality as well as the rhetoric. Specifically, we interviewed at four different levels within each organization: senior managers, line managers, non-managerial staff, and human resource staff. This has allowed us to gain within-method triangulation—examining the same phenomena from a number of different angles. There were three distinct types of interview undertaken in the study.

Semi-structured interviews

Building upon the literature review, we designed a set of semi-structured interview formats to elicit the opinions of employees over a range of issues, including the nature of the business strategy, the role of the HR function, and the nature of various HR activities within the organization (for example, recruitment, appraisal, pay, career management). These interview formats were focused on both policy (for example, this question to human resource managers: 'What is the policy on succession planning?') and practice (for example, this question to middle managers: 'Tell me about how succession planning occurs in your department'). A total of 287 hour-long semi-structured interviews were carried out within the period of study. In most of these interviews two researchers were present, and the majority of interviews were tape-recorded. The tapes were subsequently transcribed and compiled under the broad headings described under the research measures. These were then content-analysed across a number of themes and used to illustrate our broad conclusions.

Ethnographic interviews

We were conscious that the semi-structured interviews would elicit factual information about policies and practice. But what could they really tell us about the culture of a place, about people's deep-seated motivations, about 'the way that people behave around here'? For this we had to turn to deeper and more prolonged face-to-face interviews to uncover the sense-making activities of employees concerning their organization in general and HR policies and processes in particular.

We debated this need within the research team as well as with others. Clearly survey questionnaires would provide useful information about commitment and satisfaction, but how much would they reveal of people's inner workings?

At this time we began to speak to Dr Peter Scott-Morgan, a director of Arthur D. Little, an American consultancy firm. He was in the process of completing a book about what he had termed 'the unwritten rules of the game'. Like us he was fascinated by rhetoric and reality, by what was espoused and what was enacted. For him the 'unwritten rules of the game' were about the reality of organizational life—'what you have to do around here to get on', in other words, what behaviours really are rewarded. There were close parallels between his views and our aspirations for our research. These parallels were sufficiently close for Arthur D. Little to create a two-year research post to enable us to add the 'rules' methodology to our own. As well as gathering important data concerning the interpretative schema of employees, the 'Unwritten Rules of the Game' interviews were also intended to provide an audit of the culture of each company.

The Unwritten Rules work is built on an analytical framework which consists of three concepts: Motivators, Enablers, and Triggers. Motivators are those things which are important to individual employees in the context of the organization. Enablers are important to them given these motivators. They typically correspond to the unwritten, or informal, organization structure. Finally, Triggers, which are frequently performance measures, link Motivators and Enablers. Triggers reflect how individuals satisfy or impress the enabler in order to get what they want. The 'sensible ways' individuals behave in order to satisfy their Motivators, Enablers, and Triggers are what Scott-Morgan calls unwritten rules. It should be noted that the Motivators, together with their unwritten rules, drive all of the other unwritten rules. A Motivator, for example, might be 'to climb the corporate ladder', in which case a related unwritten rule might be to 'job hop'.

There are no 'good' or 'bad' unwritten rules. They are instead either 'appropriate' or 'inappropriate' for the organization, depending on their side effects. Side effects are the unintended consequences of the behaviour encapsulated in unwritten rules. These can have positive or negative implications for the organization. For example, if it is an unwritten rule that sales managers should change their jobs every two years in order to climb up the organization hierarchy (and become labelled as 'high fliers' in the process), then one of the side effects may be that the firm's sales activity is undermined by chronic short-termism. This short-termism will be the result of a lack of continuity in the sales organization brought about by a high incidence of job hopping.

Focus groups

We broadened the interview methodology by using a focus group of members of the human resource function (with an average of five members in each focus group) prior to commencing the detailed field study. The aim of this was to gather information on the key organizational concerns and the major challenges for the HR function. This information would help frame the subsequent questions within the interviews and provide an initial understanding of the structure and nature of HR interventions.

Employee survey

In order to increase validity further, the qualitative methods highlighted above were complemented by the use of quantitative techniques, specifically a number of questionnaires. The employee survey contained measures on communication, organizational strategy and values, satisfaction with HR activities and the HR function, employee relations, and standard scales on job satisfaction, commitment, trust, and morale.

In addition to this main instrument, two other questionnaires were used: one for senior managers on the nature of strategic decision-making and change, and one for senior HR staff on the role of the corporate centre in the design of policy. The percentage response rates for the key questions are used throughout this report.

Archival data

Internal documents were analysed and an extensive analysis of external data (including newspaper cuttings, analysts' reports, research reports, and historical writings) was also carried out to provide a check on the validity of the field findings.

COLLECTING AND ANALYSING THE CASE DATA

In 1993 we piloted the methodology with Glaxo Pharmaceuticals UK, reviewed our findings, and then broadened the sample. The data collection occurred company by company between 1993 and 1995. Data were collected by the research team with people seconded from the consortium companies. The Leading Edge Forum had agreed at an early stage that transferring learning from the research team to the participating companies would be a major challenge. We created a series of Forum workshops to discuss the findings, but realized this might not be sufficient. To increase the transfer of learning we asked each company to second to the research team a member of the human resource function. This person would work as a member of the research team, primarily engaged in conducting the semi-structured interviews in a company other than their own. They typically worked for two or three days a week over the four weeks of company data collection. The feedback for this team of seconded researchers has been enormously positive and we will certainly continue this practice.

By July 1994 we had completed the studies for Citibank, Glaxo Pharmaceuticals UK, and Hewlett Packard, and later that year we prepared an academic progress report. In this report we reviewed the methodology against the original aims of the research and came to a number of conclusions. First, we had hoped to chart the evolution of human resource management by asking people to describe the evolution over the previous five years. The idea of charting this was abandoned after the Glaxo Pharmaceuticals UK pilot, when we discovered that historical data were difficult to obtain, relying heavily on people's memories (which tended to be patchy) or archive material (which often did not exist). We realized that only a truly longitudinal study would create the data we required to examine questions of evolution, and that this data would always be insubstantial in a 'snap shot' study. Secondly, we had hoped to examine the relationship between business strategy and human resource strategy and how it had evolved over time. We found it more difficult than we had anticipated to pin down a 'human resource strategy' in the sample companies, and came increasingly to support Mintzberg's view that these strategies emerge over time. We had augmented the interview data on business strategy by designing a questionnaire for directors about the content and process of business strategy. However, we found that directors rarely agreed on the core business strategy, or the business strategy process. On the other hand, our data on intended and realized human resource interventions was comprehensive, both from interview data concerning individuals' experiences of human resource management and from the focus groups which studied intentions. Finally, we planned to explore how human resource management influences everyday managerial behaviour, in particular to examine the devolution of responsibility to line managers and away from the human resource function. Our triangulated methodology looked likely to provide a rich source of data about this devolution.

For each company we collected an enormous set of data about the policies, practices, and impact of the human resource management strategies. Now began the task of assimilating and creating threads of meaning.

As each company was researched we prepared a full case description. As Pettigrew notes, 'the discipline of producing an executive summary of these diagnostic cases also forces closure in the pattern recognition process' (1992: 110). The empirical data gathered within each company were analysed using content analysis, patterns were established within and across employee levels, and finally, key themes were identified. To some extent, the empirical findings would be set in the context of the existing literature and theoretical debates. Once completed each case study was circulated, first to the managers within the company (to establish any factual errors), and later for dissemination to all members of the Leading Edge Forum. Forum workshops were held with all Leading Edge participants to discuss the company case and draw conclusions and recommendations. This became an enormously important element in the process of understanding the data. These discussions provided valuable opportunities to receive feedback from the companies and to increase our under-

Table 1.1. Data collection and assimilation

Phase 1	Focus group with members of the HR community. Archival data collected about the history of the organization and the key external factors.
Phase 2	Semi-structured interviews conducted with sample of senior managers, line managers, HR staff, and operating core (at least 24 in each organization). 'Unwritten Rules of the Game' interviews conducted with middle managers (12 in each organization).
Phase 3	Employee survey sent to 20% of the population in each target organization; 60% response rate achieved with a total of 2,200 survey questionnaires analysed. Strategic questionnaire sent to 10 senior executives at business and corporate level.
Phase 4	Extensive case report prepared for each organization describing the survey results with interview quotes structured around key HR processes. One-day workshop run for each organization in which representatives of all participating organizations and the research team discuss the data and conclusions.
Phase 5	A series of five themed, comparative workshops held in which HR and other senior executives from all the organizations discuss the differences between the organizations against a set of emerging themes.

standing of these organizational phenomena. An overview of the five phases of data collection and assimilation is presented in Table 1.1.

CONTEXT AND THE LEADING EDGE COMPANIES

The eight companies studied in this research were chosen because they were all amongst the top five performers in their sectors—none were industry laggards. The industrial sectors they operate in range from telecommunications to banking to consumer foods and distribution. They are in non-competing sectors, since the level and sensitivity of data they shared precluded the possibility of including competitors in the sample.

We are aware that the choice of companies has certain weaknesses; specifically, the need for confidentiality removed the possibility of within-sector comparisons. Clearly this is a self-selected sample, and may not be representative of a wider sample of major companies. However, we have attempted throughout the research to compensate for this, by ensuring we use identical methods in all the organizations; by concentrating our analysis on a vertical slice through the core activity of each organization, thus ensuring we are covering comparable elements; and by creating broad groupings, for example around sector (such as service industry) or contextual features (such as level of industry competition). A brief overview of these companies and the businesses we examined is presented in Table 1.2, and a more detailed description of the companies follows later in this chapter.

Some of the companies were the UK businesses of American multinationals (Citibank, Hewlett Packard, and Kraft Jacobs Suchard), others were UK-based multinationals (BT and Glaxo Pharmaceuticals), whilst Lloyds Bank and W. H. Smith operate primarily in the UK market place. All were experiencing the UK and global context of the mid-1990s. Some factors of this context had profound implications for the way these companies were competing in their markets and the stance they had taken to the management of people.

A major theme of this book is that organizations are products not only of their strategy, structure, and capabilities, but also of their culture, their history, and the economic, social, technological, and political forces which impact upon them. The relationship between the organization and its environment has been the subject of much theoretical debate, with some models, notably institutional theory and population ecology (Hannan and Freeman 1989), treating the organization as a black box and assigning primacy to environmental forces, while other models, notably strategic choice theory (Child 1972), emphasize organizational forces. Our view is that a combination of the two forces is required, with organizations choosing strategies in response to environmental changes and, through adaptation, changing the environment in which they operate (Dutton and Dukerich 1991). In this section, we shall highlight some of the major environmental trends which have impacted on the Leading Edge companies as a basis for understanding how the organizations have reacted and adapted.

The external context 1993–1995

Central amongst these trends are various macro-economic issues. We shall describe five factors: (1) recession, (2) the liberalization of markets, (3) globalization, (4) technological advances, and (5) changes in labour markets. We shall also examine the importance of administrative heritage as both an enabling and a constraining influence on organizational responses.

Recession

The economic context of the early 1990s was dominated by recession, in both the UK and the USA. The UK recession was the longest in post-war history (OECD 1994) and, unlike previous recessions, the service sector as well as manufacturing was badly affected. Unemployment rose to 2.87 million in the UK in October 1992, and unlike the recession of 1979–81, the impact of job losses

Table 1.2. Participating companies

	Organization/type	Area studied	Product activity	Total employee number in area studied
BT	UK/utility	BT Payphones	Telecommunications	2,800
Chelsea & Westminster Healthcare Trust	Public sector	Chelsea & Westminster Healthcare Trust	Health services	1,870
Citibank	US/TNC	Global Finance Europe	Corporate banking	1,790
Glaxo Pharmaceuticals	UK/TNC	GP UK	Pharmaceuticals	1,400
Hewlett Packard	US/TNC	Computer Service (sales and marketing)	Office equipment	2,000
Kraft Jacob Suchard (Philip Morris)	US/FMCG	KJS UK headquarters	Consumer goods (food)	500
Lloyds Bank UK Retail Banking	UK/chain	Thames Valley and East Region	Clearing bank	3,200
W. H. Smith	UK/chain	News Distribution	Distribution	4,300

Table 1.3. Participating companies and questionnaire data collection

	Date of data collection	No. of questionnaires analysed	No. of managers in questionnaire sample	Response rate (%)	Typical line manager roles[a]	Typical operating core roles
BT Payphones	1994	294	111	50	Field managers; regional managers; team leaders	Engineers
Chelsea & Westminster Healthcare Trust	1995	126	37	39	Clinicians; general managers	Nurses; junior doctors
Citibank	1994	177	82	59	Relationship managers; departmental managers; project leaders	Traders; dealers; administrators
GP UK	1993	178	27	71	Marketing managers; team leaders	Administrators; sales; marketing
Hewlett Packard	1994	215	92	56	Marketing managers; team leaders	Sales people; engineers
Kraft Jacobs Suchard	1994	164	63	70	Marketing managers; IT managers; team leaders	Sales people; marketing professionals
Lloyds Bank UK Retail Banking	1994	610	255	51	Cluster managers; branch managers; assistant branch managers	Branch staff
W. H. Smith News	1994	456	156	46	House managers; supervisors	Warehouse staff

[a] Line managers: responsible for managing/supervising employees.

was felt throughout the country. In the USA, the 1990–1 recession saw similar hostile conditions and a sharp rise in the unemployment rate—to 7.75 per cent (OECD 1991–2). A major effect of the recession was to dampen consumer confidence, and high interest rates and falling asset prices saw households reduce spending in favour of increased saving. Organizational responses were to reduce stocks and manning levels and to focus on restructuring and cost reduction (OECD 1993). The Leading Edge companies were not immune to the effects of recession. For example, Citibank had a 'near death experience' in 1991 when the combined effects of the recession and large exposure to bad loans almost forced the bank out of business. Hewlett Packard, though remaining the only company to stay profitable during the recession, nevertheless had enough of a profits scare in 1991 to force the founders of the company, Bill Hewlett and Dave Packard, to return to make root and branch cuts and restructuring. For many of these companies cost reduction and downsizing were dominant business goals during this period.

Deregulation

The period of the study was also characterized by the continuing government drive in the UK for privatization and the deregulation of markets. The Conservative government began its privatization programme in 1979 to bring improved efficiencies in organizations which were, at the time, in the public sector, and to increase share ownership (OECD 1993). There was a perception of over-manning and large-scale inefficiencies in public sector organizations. BT was hived off from the Post Office in 1984 and its monopoly replaced by a duopoly with the granting of a licence to Mercury, which led to 'significant competition in the business and long-distance markets, but had little impact on local residential services' (OECD 1996: 63). The entry of two mobile telephone operators added to competition in local areas. The government also introduced market-based reforms in core public sector activities, including education, local government, and, most controversially, the health service, as part of the ideological drive to increase efficiencies. In the health service this included the introduction of a Patients' Charter, the creation of semi-autonomous trusts, the forcing of a split between purchasers and providers of health care, and introduction of competitive tendering. Hospitals now competed with other providers for contracts from health care purchasers, and were responsible for delivering financial targets to the NHS. The liberalization of markets, already well entrenched in the USA, also occurred in the UK outside the privatized sector through deregulation, notably in the financial services industry, which was opened up in 1989, removing the barriers between types of financial institution so that, for instance, building societies could sell current accounts, while banks could offer insurance. This transformed the industry, bringing many new entrants and a bewildering variety of product and service innovation, necessitating large structural changes for the major players. The two banks in our sample, Citibank and Lloyds Bank UK Retail Banking, faced large change programmes as they sought to compete in this new environment. Governments in the UK and the USA have been vigilant on anti-trust issues. In the UK, the Monopolies and Mergers Commission has been central to increasing competitiveness in the UK. Among their many interventions, the report into the news distribution industry in 1992 prompted widespread change in W. H. Smith News.

Globalization

The removal of trade barriers, primarily through successive GATT rounds and the introduction of the single European market in 1992, has brought a significant movement towards a global economy. Other forces which have supported this trend are a greater sophistication in communications and information systems, the emergence of international financial dealing, advances in distribution, and the growth of the multinational form of corporation (Northcote 1991). The three multinational firms in our sample, Citibank, Hewlett Packard, and Kraft Jacobs Suchard (owned by Philip Morris), have had to consider how best to configure and coordinate activities and how best the control process, *vis-à-vis* the parent company, is managed.

Technological advances

Advances in technology have dramatically altered the basis of competition in many industries. The rate of technological change—that is, the introduction of new technology such as 'personal computers, cellular phones, fibre optics, the Internet, massive databases, LANs (local area networks), artificial intelligence, virtual reality, satellite transponders and teleconferencing' (Bettis and Hill 1995: 9)—has shortened product life cycles and development cycles. The speed of technological diffusion—the rate at which technological information is absorbed into the industry—is also increasing, encouraging copying and increased competition in the form of 'me too' players. These issues have large implications for organizations which are technology-intensive, for example BT Payphones, Glaxo Pharmaceuticals UK, and Hewlett Packard, as well as those which use technology to a great extent, such as Citibank and Lloyds Bank UK Retail Banking.

Increases in technology have resulted in increased skill levels for some practices and processes, and deskilling in others (OECD 1996). In BT Payphones, new telephone box technology requires fewer traditional engineering skills for installation and repair staff, for when a unit breaks down it is simply lifted out and replaced with a new one. At Hewlett Packard, engineers must move from repairing individual personal computers and printers to working on networks, a significant jump in skill level.

Labour market conditions

Both the UK and the USA have little formal regulation concerning labour markets in comparison to other OECD countries (OECD 1996), in particular over such issues as terms and conditions, working hours, and recruitment and dismissal practices. In the UK, this has been exacerbated by the reform of the trade unions, introduced in the 1980s by the Conservative Party under Margaret Thatcher, which encouraged the breaking up of national bargaining arrangements and made strike action more difficult—in particular by imposing a requirement for postal strike ballots. Union membership, already ravaged by the high unemployment following the recession of 1982, was hit even harder and is now at its lowest figure since 1946, down to 9 million. (Union density is now down to 31 per cent: see P. Bassett 1994.) The result was a high degree of decentralization in wage determination and a widespread use of performance-related pay. Pay flexibility has been accompanied by labour market flexibility: about 25 per cent of the workforce is in part-time jobs, self-employment has increased, and there is wide diversity in working hours (OECD 1996). In addition, short-term jobs were increasing (from 5 per cent in 1984–91 to 7.5 per cent by mid-1995), adding to the perception of job insecurity in this period. In the Leading Edge companies union activity, even in the face of large lay-offs, was minimal (BT did not lose a single day to union activity when implementing its downsizing programme), and pay was determined, to a large extent, on an individual basis. Only Chelsea & Westminster Healthcare Trust (the only organization in the sample still in the public sector) remained largely tied to the central pay negotiation process carried out through the Whitely Councils, the Pay Review Boards, and the Royal Colleges.

Organizational context: administrative heritage

These contextual factors have had major implications for the Leading Edge organizations. But in responding to these pressures, they do not have a completely free hand; they are constrained by what has been called their 'administrative heritage'—the cultural and physical constraints on an organization (Bartlett and Ghoshal 1989). The degree of discretion, or strategic choice, an organization has will be determined to a large extent by leadership style, national culture, commitment to past and continuing strategies, the success of certain symbolic actions, and the nature of its systems and processes. The Leading Edge companies illustrate different administrative heritages and we describe them briefly below.

BT Payphones

BT, with a stock market value of £26 billion in 1996, dominates the UK telecommunications market, and with a workforce of 150,000 people is the country's largest private sector employer. The company has 87 per cent of the UK business market for telephone calls, 97 per cent of the UK residential market, and 76 per cent of the market for international calls (BT Annual Report and Accounts 1994). Although 98 per cent of the group's turnover arises from UK activity, BT has a stated aim of becoming a global telecommunications company. As part of the Post Office, the business enjoyed a monopoly and, in common with many public sector organizations, there was tolerance of over-manning and other inefficiencies. The civil service mindset also brought a paternalistic culture, long-term job security, and a strong internal labour market. In 1984, with privatization, the liberalized market brought new competition and BT rationalized and reoriented itself. Its still dominant position in the market is in part due to its core technological capabilities, but also due to increases in the quality of service. The research was conducted in BT Payphones, which acts as a shop window for the organization. The Payphones business is responsible for all aspects of payphones in the UK, both public and private, and has a workforce of 2,800. Traditionally the payphone service was perceived as a 'social obligation', and a condition of privatization was that BT maintained the service in spite of the fact that it was a drain financially. Problems with the serviceability of payphones and with vandalism led to a poor image for the service, an image which was highlighted prominently in the media and which led to BT's reputation as a whole suffering. In order to focus change, BT Payphones was set up as a business unit four years ago, and is part of Personal Communications, a division which is highly cash generative. Changes in phone box design, new technology, new working practices, and changes in organizational structure have led to a dramatic turnaround: in four years, the Payphones business has turned a £40 million loss into a £60 million profit.

Chelsea & Westminster Healthcare Trust

Chelsea & Westminster Healthcare Trust acquired trust status in 1994. The hospital, built at a cost of £133 million in 1993, is widely regarded as a flagship for the National Health Service and provides acute care and other services for large areas of west London. The restructuring of the NHS in 1991, which separated the purchase of health care from its provision to form an internal market, created trusts, which severed links with district authorities to become independent bodies. Though trusts are supposed to be free-standing, they operate within a centrally determined framework which regulates financial performance and operating cost. The Chelsea & Westminster Healthcare Trust is successful on these fronts, and its status as a teaching hospital has been boosted by a merger with the Imperial College teaching school. Its reputation in research and teaching is essential in attracting funds for the Trust. The values of the NHS have remained constant even following the reforms—principally, the drive to deliver patient care. The NHS is one of the clearest examples of a professionally dominated organization (Pettigrew and Whipp 1991) and the dominance of the medical professions, chiefly nurses and doctors, remains a central feature of the Trust. The introduction of a general management cadre following the report of the Griffiths Inquiry (1983) raised suspicions among the clinical staff early on, but in the Chelsea & Westminster this concern is now easing, primarily because clinicians were given senior roles in the management of the Trust, and because the chief executive David Highton was well respected by all staff. Though patient care is the main priority, there is concern that meeting budgets (a requirement following the purchaser–provider split) will lead to conflicting values. The Trust is organized along directorate lines (similar to business units), being divided into five clinical areas and four support directorates. A concern for the Trust is the high turnover of staff, since career advancement is based on frequent moves between hospitals to gain experience of new specialisms and environments. Allied to a shortage of nurses, this is a major problem for all health care trusts.

Citibank

Citibank is the largest bank in the USA, and with operations in ninety-eight countries is arguably the world's leading global bank. The Leading Edge research was conducted in 1993 in a commercial part of the bank, Global Finance Europe, with headquarters in London, a business which includes capital markets, foreign exchange, futures and options, and derivatives trading. Citibank's guiding philosophy was to 'let a thousand flowers bloom'—to have interests in all aspects of banking. The vision of Walter Wriston, chief executive, was responsible for the growth of the bank globally and the development of an aggressively individualistic, and some say arrogant, culture. The rapid expansion of the bank was halted in 1991 when loans to Latin American countries and real estate deals had proved disastrous, causing a 'near death experience'. The new chief executive, John Reed, tightened financial management, improved risk control procedures, and installed tougher internal control systems. Costs have been ruthlessly driven out: the payroll was reduced by 14,000 and operating expenses were cut by $1.5 billion. The bank has now regained an AA credit rating from US agencies.

The removal of national barriers to financial services provision meant that Citibank's country-based structure become inappropriate to the needs of its multinational clients. A new structure as a 'global relationship bank' was introduced in 1994, targeted on customers rather than geography. The heritage of its global network has helped considerably in this change process.

Glaxo Pharmaceuticals UK

Glaxo Pharmaceuticals UK is the world's largest pharmaceutical company by sales, with turnover of £10.5 billion, and employs 57,000 people worldwide. The merger with Wellcome in a £9.1 billion deal in 1995 gave the combined company a leading 5.1 per cent of the fragmented world market. The focus of our research was in the pre-merger Glaxo Pharmaceuticals UK business, which is the sales and marketing division of the UK operation, with headquarters at Stockley Park, Middlesex, and employing 1,400 staff nationwide. Glaxo, founded in the nineteenth century, has always been associated with innovations in drug development. But its growth into a major international player came with the development and marketing of the blockbuster anti-ulcer drug Zantac. The marketing strategy under Richard Giordarno was to place a premium price on Zantac and promote it extensively. Glaxo's reputation as a provider of high-quality, premium-priced drugs was thus reinforced. Glaxo Pharmaceuticals UK had formerly been run on functional lines, organized around major product groupings, with each product 'silo' having a strong hierarchy dominated by the marketing function. Though this structure had brought the company success, it had a limitation in that it encouraged high internal barriers and gave little incentive to work in cross-functional teams. Also, it was essentially a product market structure rather than a customer service structure, which meant it was increasingly out of touch with the large-scale changes occurring in the UK health service. The expiry of its patent, the emergence of biotechnology, and the fragmented nature of the market led Glaxo into the merger with Wellcome in order to bring greater clout as a supplier in a highly competitive market.

Hewlett Packard

Hewlett Packard is the world's leading producer of test and measurement instruments and the world's third largest computer company. It has become a major player in the personal computer market, and at the time of our research was the sixth biggest in terms of market share, having moved up from fourteenth largest in 1992. It is also the second largest player in the computer workstations market, and holds the dominant position in the laser printer business. The company was the only major computer manufacturer which remained profitable during the recession. For the Leading Edge research the sales and marketing organization in the UK Computer Systems Organization was examined. The corporation employs 96,200 staff worldwide, of which 20,200 are employed in Europe and 2,000 in the UK (in the UK Computer Systems Organization). Underpinning the Hewlett Packard culture is the HP Way, developed by founders Bill Hewlett and Dave Packard, which emphasizes clearly stated and agreed overall objectives but gives people the freedom to work towards these goals in ways they determine best for their own areas of responsibility. Other pillars of the HP Way include an emphasis on selecting individuals on the basis of their creativity and their enthusiasm, and the need for cooperation between organizational levels. A sophisticated performance management process and clear organizational values, together with a single status culture, has brought strong identification with the company on the part of employees. The organization has traditionally had a decentralized structure, but with the growth of the computer business a more centralized approach was taken to reflect the systems nature of the business. In 1991 a combination of the recession, the entry of low-cost clone manufacturers into the personal computer market, and increasing bureaucracy in Hewlett Packard led to poor organizational performance and an enforced voluntary redundancy programme. New products, cost-cutting measures, and the return of the founders Bill Hewlett and Dave Packard turned the business around, and in 1993 the UK increased turnover by 43 per cent and generated profits of $85 million compared to a break-even position the year before.

Kraft Jacobs Suchard

Kraft Jacobs Suchard is part of Philip Morris, which is the world's largest packaged consumer goods organization, the world's number one tobacco company, the world's second largest food company, and the world's third largest brewer. The Philip Morris Group has 165,000 employees manufacturing and marketing more than 3,000 products in over 170 countries. Kraft Jacobs Suchard is the European division of the Philip Morris food business, the name deriving from the merger in 1993 of Kraft General Foods Europe and Jacobs Suchard. The focus of our research was on the head office function of Kraft Jacobs Suchard UK, the fourth largest business within the European region with a turnover of £700 million, 9 per cent of the total European revenue, and 4,000 employees. The head office of KJS, in Cheltenham, coordinates the company's central activities including sales, marketing, human resources, finance and information systems, distribution, and planning, and has 500 employees. The three names of Kraft, Jacobs, and Suchard stand for the company's core categories of cheese, coffee, and confectionery. They also reflect the acquisitive nature of the Philip Morris Organization. The company manages such major brands as Bird's, Café Hag, Dairylea, Kenco, Maxwell House, Maxpax, Philadelphia, Vitalite, Milka Chocolate, Suchard, Terry's of York, Toblerone, and Twilight. The culture of KJS UK is based on the concept of continuous improvement, providing clear objectives and strategies and supporting a strong results-oriented approach to the business. A process-oriented management style has developed as a result. Clear financial targets, detailing growth figures in turnover and profit, are agreed by KJS in Zurich and each country devises its own broad strategy to fulfil them. The ambitious level of the targets, together with a strong emphasis on driving costs out of the business, has brought a culture which stresses short-term payback. (The targets set by Europe are for twelve months.) Once targets have been agreed, KJS UK has a large degree of autonomy in the setting of its strategy to meet those targets.

Lloyds Bank UK Retail Banking

Lloyds Bank is the most profitable of the UK clearing banks, with pre-tax profits of £1,031 million and a post-tax return on shareholders' equity of 21 per cent (Lloyds Bank Annual Report 1994). The bank is structured into five major business units: Lloyds Abbey Life, Private Banking and Financial Services, UK Retail Banking, Corporate Banking and Treasury, and International Banking. Lloyds has a strong bureaucratic culture, with a direct command and control style built upon a rigid hierarchical structure with clear elements of paternalism and authoritarianism. The focus of this research was in the Thames Valley and East region of the UK Retail Banking business. UK Retail Banking forms 'the front line' of the bank's services, responsible for the branch network which retails a large range of financial services. It is responsible for many of the principal processing activities of the bank, including money transmission, and for the development and operation of the bank's IT systems. The division has more than 6 million personal and business customers, 1,800 branches, and 37,900 employees, making it by far the largest business in the group. Major structural changes in banking, including new technology, deregulation, and overcapacity, prompted Lloyds to adopt a strategy which focused on selective market leadership rather than global growth, and to place shareholder value as the governing objective of the business. Traditional banking aims of maximizing size in terms of assets and market share were viewed as poor measures of success. Instead, the measures of market value and share price were adopted. Since 1984, Lloyds has doubled the stock market value of the business every three years. The embracing of shareholder value as a governing objective had strong repercussions for the structure of the business. Previously, the processes of the bank, such as marketing, manufacturing, and retailing, tended to be tightly bundled together, with the branch as the main economic unit and profit centre. The 'unbundling' of the bank's processes produced increased focus and a reduction in overheads, since the bank could centralize many activities which had previously been carried out by branches. The segmentation of the business has also had a marked effect on the activities undertaken by branches. Traditionally the branch was a complete provider of products and services; now many processes have been centralized and the branch has become a delivery system for products designed centrally. The focus has shifted away from employees in the branch network as generalists in the delivery of a number of products, towards developing people who have strong sales and service abilities. The management structure of branches has also changed with the introduction of a segmented management structure, whilst a downsizing programme means that the bank now employs 25 per cent fewer people than it did five years ago.

W. H. Smith News

W. H. Smith News, founded over 200 years ago, is the market leader in the distribution of newspapers and magazines in the UK by market share and by turnover. W. H. Smith is divided into two broad divisions: Retail, which encompasses the W. H. Smith high street chain, Do It All, Paperchase, Playhouse Video, Virgin/Our Price, and Waterstone's; and Distribution, which includes

Heathcote Books, W. H. Smith Business Supplies, and W. H. Smith News. The focus of our research was in W. H. Smith News. This division has 4,300 employees in 72 wholesale houses and over 22,000 retail customers. The 72 wholesale houses in the News Division are split geographically into four areas. Each wholesale house has a house manager and each region a regional manager. The houses are run as autonomous businesses, with the house manager responsible for meeting tight financial performance targets set by the group. Since the News Division is the cash-rich division within W. H. Smith, effectiveness in achieving financial targets is paramount. In the News Division there are three main customer groupings: (1) newspaper publishers (30 per cent market share), (2) magazine publishers (42 per cent market share), and (3) retailers (News Division supplies 22,000 out of 40,000 retailers in the UK). According to the Annual Report and Accounts 1993, W. H. Smith group's turnover in 1993 was £2,442.4 million, of which Distribution (not including Business Supplies) accounted for £825.9 million. Operating profit for the group was £115.9 million, with Distribution accounting for £33.2 million. This is impressive given the small asset base of the Distribution operation—£20.7 million net assets compared to net assets of the Retailing Division of £490.7 million in the UK and Europe. The prevailing style of management was characterized by a former chief executive as 'Autocratic, tempered by paternalism. The values of the business were hierarchy, loyalty, security, and obedience to orders.' The nature of the work has also brought strong traditions. The business runs 24 hours a day, 7 days a week, 364 days a year (only Christmas Day is not worked). The hours are long, deadlines are tight, and much of the work, particularly in the warehouse, is physically demanding, but the pace and deadline-driven nature of the business, together with clear success criteria, generates a high level of excitement and the satisfaction of achieving goals is almost immediate. In 1989, the W. H. Smith group instigated a process of corporate renewal. This was prompted in part by the effects of the recession and also by the decision taken a year earlier by News International to switch its distribution from W. H. Smith News to the non-unionized rival firm TNT. W. H. Smith News lost £40 million of business overnight. Major initiatives were introduced to improve both productivity and customer service. Compulsory redundancies were made. The need for enhanced customer focus intensified in 1994 with the publication of the Monopolies and Mergers Commission's investigation into the industry structure and the basis upon which newspapers are supplied, which may result in retailers having less dependence on W. H. Smith News for the delivery of titles.

Organizational responses

The presence of significant external pressures has brought an imperative for the Leading Edge organizations to adapt to the new environment. Their administrative heritages ensured that each organization had unique constraints on the process of adaptation, but nevertheless there were several general responses which were common to many of the companies. These were: (1) downsizing, (2) restructuring and re-engineering, (3) partnerships, and (4) mergers and acquisitions.

Downsizing

The most widespread response to the recession was to effect large-scale redundancies—euphemistically referred to as downsizing or 'right-sizing'. As discussed earlier, the recession affected the service sector as well as manufacturing. At BT, the downsizing has 'touched every part of what we do' (according to one senior manager), and over 100,000 jobs have gone since privatization in 1984. In BT Payphones, the redundancy package has been used 'very aggressively' and the numbers in the business unit have dropped from 4,000 to 2,800. In banking and the financial services in general, the shedding of labour has been a conspicuous feature of the industry following deregulation and technological change. Lloyds has reduced the number of employees by 25 per cent and Citibank has cut 14,000 staff worldwide. Even Hewlett Packard shed employees to remain competitive. Such large-scale restructuring and redundancies were made easier by the lack of resistance from organized labour.

Restructuring and re-engineering

In order to remain competitive, firms have had to increase performance dramatically whilst heavily reducing costs. There were a number of common initiatives which were widely used and which quickly became known by standard terms in the management jargon. Following the US lead, business process re-engineering (BPR), with its promise of cutting out unnecessary stages from organizational processes and using information technology to improve efficiency, was used by the majority of UK companies during this period. BPR, in various guises, took place at BT, the Chelsea & Westminster Healthcare Trust, Citibank, Glaxo Pharmaceuticals UK, Lloyds Bank UK Retail Banking, and W. H. Smith News. Restructuring of the firm was a common theme. Moves were made from geographic structures to business units (at BT Payphones), from functional structures to business units (at the Chelsea & Westminster Healthcare Trust, Glaxo Pharmaceuticals UK, and Kraft Jacobs Suchard), and variants on 'hub and spoke' working were introduced (at Lloyds Bank UK Retail Banking and W. H. Smith News). Total quality management (TQM) also promised to improve performance while reducing the cost base. BT, Hewlett Packard, and Kraft Jacobs Suchard have had fully fledged TQM programmes, while the other Leading Edge companies espoused quality through vision and values statements.

There has also been a redefinition in core businesses, producing a spate of divestments to ensure strategic focus. Citibank now focuses on a select number of clients and has jettisoned the 'supermarket' approach to banking; Lloyds has scaled down its international operations; Kraft Jacobs Suchard has divested its yellow fats business; Chelsea & Westminster Healthcare Trust is now looking beyond acute care to encompass community care activity; Hewlett Packard moved out of the provision of support for individual stand-alone personal computers and printers in favour of large clients with networked facilities; W. H. Smith News, following the report of the Monopolies and Mergers Commission, has shifted its marketing effort towards retailers rather than solely concentrating on publishers; Glaxo Pharmaceuticals UK is now no longer content to be the end of the pipeline for Glaxo R & D, and is actively exploring the possibilities of marketing other firms' drugs under licence. These examples indicate the range of reorientation initiatives and, in light of the changing nature of the environment, these look set to continue.

Partnerships and alliances

The formation of partnerships has become widespread in recent years, particularly in technology-related industries, and is now seen as an important element in the competitive strategies of firms (Movery *et al.* 1996). The reasons behind the increasing rate of formation of partnerships include the need to spread the costs and risks of innovation, the chance to acquire new skills or technical capabilities from a partner firm, access to new markets, and strategic coordination amongst competitors to increase market power. BT's aspirations for alliance with companies such as MCI are intended to secure BT's aim of becoming a global player, and also to develop its technological capabilities. Glaxo Pharmaceuticals UK has developed a series of partnerships with leading biotechnology firms to explore new products, while Hewlett Packard has developed an alliance with the microchip manufacturer Intel.

Mergers and acquisitions

Two of the largest mergers in UK corporate history—Lloyds Bank and TSB, and Glaxo and Wellcome—took place during the period of our research. It is clear that increased size, market dominance, and technological capability are major drivers in reducing strategic uncertainty and increasing competitive advantage. Even in the public sector, Chelsea & Westminster Healthcare Trust is seeking a takeover of a community trust in what could be termed vertical integration between primary and acute care providers.

Conclusion

The features of the external context are changing constantly and the organizations in the Leading Edge have had to adapt rapidly to their new environments.

This has involved downsizing, large-scale restructuring and reorienting of their businesses, and engaging with other firms in the market, either through partnerships or through mergers and acquisition. What is also crucial is that by and large organizations take their people along with them through all this change, so that changes can be implemented and learning can occur. In a broad sense, this book is concerned with how employees are managed in this environment of uncertainty and turbulence. For organizations which do not learn and which are unresponsive to change, the future will indeed be bleak.

OVERVIEW OF THE BOOK

At the beginning of this research we developed a set of broad questions which began the framing of the methodology and focused on the type of interview and survey data we should be collecting. We were interested in the impact of a company's context (both internal and external); in the ability to deliver a strategic approach to people; in the relationship between what was intended and what was realized; in the ways in which human resource interventions impact on the individual and the manner in which human resource strategy influences everyday managerial experience. These broad themes have remained central to our endeavour throughout the six years in which the project has operated. We have also been aware of the 'emergence' of themes and the increased interest in a number of issues of which we were initially only tangentially aware.

Chapter 2: Soft and hard models of human resource management

In this chapter Catherine Truss describes two conceptual models which frame much of our understanding of human resource management. She isolates a tension which we returned to many times during our research, the philosophical dichotomy between soft and hard models of human resource management. The soft model emphasizes individuals and their self-direction and places commitment, trust, and self-regulated behaviour at the centre of any strategic approach to people. In contrast, the hard model stresses the rationalism of strategic fit and places emphasis on performance management and an instrumental approach to the management of individuals. She argues that to incorporate both elements within one working model is highly problematic since they rest on diametrically opposed assumptions about human nature and managerial control. In her interpretation of the data she asks, 'Do organizations practise either soft or hard HRM, and if so, under what conditions?' Her conclusions are clear: no single company adopted either a pure soft or pure hard approach to human resource management. At the level of rhetoric, many embraced the tenets of the soft version, but the underlying principle was invariably restricted to the improvement of bottom-line performance. She argues that we should be moving to a more empirically grounded model which recognizes that the rhetoric of HRM is concerned with hermeneutical man and commitment-based strategic control, whereas the reality of HRM as experienced within organizations today is based on concepts of modern man and tight strategic direction towards organizational goals. This distinction between rhetoric and reality is a critical aspect of this book and a subject we return to in our concluding chapter.

In the next three chapters we focus on three key organizational levers: performance management, career development, and culture.

Chapter 3: Performance management in fast-changing environments

Performance management is a central tool used to align employee behaviour and organizational objectives, especially in the hard model, and in this chapter Philip Stiles examines how this process works in those four companies in the sample which operate in high-velocity environments. Processes such as performance management tend to be inflexible, highly resistant to change, and subject to rapid ossification. How do we balance the need to embed processes with the need to be flexible and adaptive to changing circumstances? Interestingly, he found that the objectives and design of the formal performance management processes in the four organizations were largely similar, intended to create vertical linkage between corporate and business objectives and employee performance. He reports that goals were set participatively, often supplemented by competency frameworks; appraisal was more frequently conducted through multiple perspectives; rewards decisions were more likely to be decentralized; and formal training was supplemented by coaching and self-development activities. He concludes that the application of performance management is influenced by the degree and experience of change, the involvement and commitment of line managers, and the transparency and perceived fairness of the process.

Chapter 4: The rhetoric and reality of 'new careers'

Performance management processes are a well-established and relatively robust part of organizational life. In this chapter Lynda Gratton and Veronica Hope Hailey discuss another core human resource process, one which is much less robust. In incorporating the rhetoric and reality concept into the title they return to a proposition which Catherine Truss described earlier. When it comes to career development and the psychological contract, the rhetoric of the new career deal of 'employability' is far from employee reality. The organizational upheaval and downsizing described in the organizational context section is played out in no greater way than in career development, where many of the old certainties have been destroyed. They argue that there are three related pillars which have to be in place if the rhetoric of the new employment contract is to become a reality: enabling systems architecture, individual perceptions of self-management, and line management commitment and capability. They report that few of these pillars are intact and describe the anxiety and cynicism felt by employees. They conclude that we are witnessing a transition which will require fundamental adjustments in career tracks and opportunity structures. We await with great anticipation the longitudinal study, which we will report on in 1999, really to understand the speed and depth of this transition.

Chapter 5: Managing culture

In the soft model of human resource management, culture has a key role to play in the creation of a high-commitment workforce. A common assumption is that the effective management of culture is central to the performance of the organization and that, manipulated correctly, a culture can help to make employees committed and compliant. The management of culture can be seen as moving away from a command and control style of management, with formal rules ensuring compliance, towards gaining adherence to organizational values and placing a premium on individual responsibility. In this chapter Veronica Hope Hailey describes the experiences of Hewlett Packard and Glaxo Pharmaceuticals UK in their attempts to manage culture. She contrasts a company in which cultures have emerged (Hewlett Packard) with one in which a cultural change has been more actively managed (Glaxo Pharmaceuticals UK). She concludes that these companies manage behaviours rather than values, and where strong values do exist they are assimilated by osmosis, rather than inculcated by management.

In the next two chapters we consider two of the major stakeholders in the delivery of people management: the human resource function and line management.

Chapter 6: Contextual diversity for the role and practice of HR

In the first of these chapters, Veronica Hope Hailey studies the HR function in four of the case companies. She argues that models of the HR function have been too simplistic and have failed to address the diverse and complex roles that are required of it. In practice the roles are diverse, with both internal and external context and organizational transition playing a key part. In describing this diversity she proposes an evolutionary model for the work of the function which is cyclical rather than linear and which places greater emphasis on context.

Chapter 7: HRM policies and management practices

In the second of these chapters we examine the rhetoric of line managers' roles in HRM. Patrick McGovern focuses on the existing state of management practice by considering line management involvement in performance management. His analysis of the case data shows that there is wide variety both within and across organizations in the extent of line management involvement and commitment. Such variances in practice are not systematic; they do not reflect a conscious policy to have different types of involvement for different groups of employees. Rather the variance reflects the configuration of incentives and constraints which shape management involvement. Four constraints are identified: the institutional reinforcement of human resource practices, the policies and traditions of trade unions and professional associations, managerial short-termism, and de-layering. Against this backdrop we ask, 'Why do managers bother?' It is clear from this research that managers do not feel strong institutional pressure, and neither are they all supported by systematic training. So whilst the institutional recognition of the role of line managers is necessary, it is not sufficient without the goodwill of the managers themselves. Patrick McGovern concludes by arguing that the prospects for full-blown devolvement to the line are not promising given the current priorities of businesses.

In Chapters 8 and 9 we move to a systemic view of the whole human resource arena. In Chapter 8 we consider how these companies have faced up to the major transformations and challenges they face, whilst in Chapter 9 we construct a model to describe the key people processes against a temporal frame of both the short and longer term.

Chapter 8: Transformation at the Leading Edge

One of the most enduring memories of this study has been the sheer volume and intensity of change in the external and internal contexts of the companies we studied. In this chapter Philip Stiles describes the ways in which the companies have faced these changes, the methods they have used to effect transitions, the role which people processes have played, and the impact these methods have had on employees. He speaks of adjusting the hardware and the software of an organization and looks at the impact of creating new ways of working, focusing on new behaviours and bringing middle managers on board. He sets out a number of propositions, which form the basis of the longitudinal study that follows this research, and highlights the central role played by organizational identity as a key variable in the reaction to change.

Chapter 9: People processes as a source of competitive advantage

It became very clear during this research that the key people processes do not operate in isolation, but rather are part of complex networks of decisions and leverage points. The people process model is an attempt to describe the key processes in a systemic manner. Lynda Gratton highlights the key role played by these clusters of processes and the vertical, horizontal, and temporal linkages which serve to create a connection between the business goals and the behaviours of individual members of the organization. She describes how these processes operate in the organizations we observed and provides broad descriptions of the processes operating at the highest level of linkage. She then goes on to describe those processes where companies are focused in their efforts, and those which are underdeveloped. Like Catherine Truss, she draws attention to the underdevelopment of processes associated with the creation of a human resource strategy and calls for greater focus on this key part of organizational life.

Chapter 10: The emerging themes

This final chapter provides an opportunity to review the three overriding themes of the book. These include not only responses to our initial questions, but also our lasting impressions, those moments of illumination and clarity. In the first theme we summarize what we have learnt about the nature of human resource strategy in large contemporary organizations and return to our initial four research questions. We highlight the importance of context and in particular the impact of downsizing on many of the companies we studied. We discuss the importance of long-term thinking, but report the reality of underdeveloped and under-functioning strategic approaches to the management of people, the relatively limited strategic and 'architectural' role for the HR function, and the gap between the intention and reality of line management involvement.

In the second theme we draw together threads which have run throughout our research concerning the nature of commitment and trust in contemporary organizations. The findings are clear and highlight the importance of self-development and career opportunities, involvement and communication, and the establishment of just and fair HR practices in the creation of high-commitment workforces. Against this backdrop of change and turbulence we acknowledge the difficulties of maintaining trust and commitment as the very fabric of the organization is fundamentally transformed. We return to Catherine Truss's initial thoughts on the nature of the hard and soft models and discuss the quandary of creating ever more complex monitoring and control systems on the one hand, and the proposition of 'developmental humanism' on the other. The challenge is to create a 'light hand' capable of supporting these activities without embroiling managers in a web of bureaucracy.

In the third theme we return again to our basic guiding principle in this research, that we are interested in rhetoric and reality, in that which is espoused and that which is realized. The gap is clearly articulated throughout this book. In this final piece we attempt to understand and describe it and set out a number of propositions to guide our own future work and provide some pointers for management practice. We observed that the gap between rhetoric and reality is potentially influenced in four broad ways: by the credibility of senior management and its relationship with employees; by the organizational context, with large, transforming, political organizations most prone to creating a gap; by the persuasiveness of the rhetoric; and finally, by the interpretation of employees, with sense-making and commitment particularly critical. We conclude that there is more than one type of gap, and describe the three that we have seen. The first we call 'slip-up', where the content of the rhetoric is particularly complex or ambiguous. The second is a 'structural' gap, which essentially reflects the complex nature of organizations. We also saw examples of a 'stretch' gap, where the gap between rhetoric and reality is created to introduce stretch goals and encourage managerial discretion.

These three emerging themes, with the emphasis on process fairness and the role of the line manager, set the scene for the continued longitudinal research in our case companies.

Soft and Hard Models of Human Resource Management

CATHERINE TRUSS

Human resource management has frequently been described as a concept with two distinct forms: soft and hard. These are diametrically opposed along a number of dimensions, and they have been used by many commentators as devices to categorize approaches to managing people according to developmental-humanist or utilitarian-instrumentalist principles (Legge 1995*b*).

The terms have gained some currency although, from a theoretical point of view, the underlying conflicts and tensions contained within the models have not been sufficiently explored and, from a practical perspective, available empirical evidence would suggest that neither model accurately represents what is happening within organizations (Storey 1992; Wood 1995). This leads us to question the value of these dimensions for defining normative forms of human resource management. In this chapter, we first analyse the conflicts and tensions both between and within the soft and hard models, and then report on the findings of an in-depth empirical study which will enable us to review and challenge the theoretical foundations upon which the soft and hard models are based.

CONFLICTS AND TENSIONS BETWEEN SOFT AND HARD MODELS OF HUMAN RESOURCE MANAGEMENT

The soft–hard dichotomy in HRM exists primarily within normative, or prescriptive, models of human resource management, rather than in what Legge (1995*b*) terms the descriptive-functional or critical-evaluative traditions. The earliest examples where this terminology is used are in the work of Guest (1987) and Storey (1987; 1992). Guest (1987), in seeking to define HRM, identifies two dimensions, soft–hard and loose–tight. Similarly, Storey (1992) plots existing interpretations of HRM along the two dimensions of soft–hard and weak–strong. Although these two commentators draw heavily on the work of American HRM academics in drawing a distinction between the two forms—the Harvard model for the soft version (Beer *et al.* 1985) and the Michigan model for the hard version (Fombrun *et al.* 1984)—the terms 'soft' and 'hard' have not been used in the American literature, and the debates surrounding them have taken place exclusively in a British context (Hendry and Pettigrew 1990).

Guest (1987) and Storey (1992) in their definitions of soft and hard models of HRM view the key distinction as being whether the emphasis is placed on the *human* or the *resource*. Soft HRM is associated with the human relations movement, the utilization of individual talents, and McGregor's (1960) Theory Y perspective on individuals (developmental humanism). This has been equated with the concept of a 'high commitment work system' (Walton 1985*b*), 'which is aimed at eliciting a commitment so that behaviour is primarily self-regulated rather than controlled by sanctions and pressures external to the individual and relations within the organization are based on high levels of trust' (Wood 1996: 41). Soft HRM is also associated with the goals of flexibility and adaptability (which themselves are problematic concepts, as we shall see in more detail later), and implies that communication plays a central role in management (Storey and Sisson 1993).

Hard HRM, on the other hand, stresses 'the quantitative, calculative and business-strategic aspects of managing the "headcount resource" in as "rational" a way as for any other factor of production', as associated with a utilitarian-instrumentalist approach (Storey 1992: 29; see also Legge 1995*b*). Hard HRM focuses on the importance of 'strategic fit', where human resource policies and practices are closely linked to the strategic objectives of the organization (external fit), and are coherent among themselves (internal fit) (Baird and Meshoulam 1988; Hendry and Pettigrew 1986), with the ultimate aim being increased competitive advantage (Alpander and Botter 1981; Devanna *et al.* 1984; Lengnick-Hall and Lengnick-Hall 1990; Miles and Snow 1984; Storey and Sisson 1993; Tichy *et al.* 1982; Tyson and Fell 1986).

These two perspectives on human resource management are viewed as opposing: 'what is striking is that the same term [HRM] is thus capable of signalling diametrically opposite sets of assumptions' (Storey 1992: 26). However, both Guest and Storey, whilst explicitly acknowledging this dichotomy, incorporate both perspectives when constructing their own human resource management 'models' or 'theories'.

For example, in his 1987 paper, Guest draws on both hard and soft dimensions in constructing his theory of human resource management which contains reference to four HRM 'policy goals', including 'strategic integration', which is clearly associated with his interpretation of the hard model, and 'commitment', which is associated with his view of the soft model. Thus, Guest acknowledges a difference between the concepts and assumptions of soft and hard HRM, but abandons the distinction when embarking upon theory-building. Similarly, Storey (1992) identifies his four key features of an HRM approach as incorporating both soft elements such as commitment, and hard elements such as strategic direction.

The incorporation of both soft and hard elements within one theory or model is highly problematic because each rests on a different set of assumptions in the two key areas of human nature and managerial control strategies. Many of these assumptions can, in fact, be traced back to the work of McGregor (1960), who even used the terminology 'hard' and 'soft' to characterize forms of managerial control. McGregor was concerned with how to foster an organizational environment conducive to innovation. He concluded that most managerial control strategies were based on views of human nature contained in Theory X (such as, that people dislike work), leading to tight managerial control through close direction. This has overtones of the emphasis within the hard model on strategic direction, integration, and the use of performance management techniques such as appraisal.

Theory Y, on the other hand, opens up the notion that 'man will exercise self-direction and self-control in the service of objectives to which he is committed' (McGregor 1960: 326). If people are assumed to be in pursuit of self-fulfilment through work, then management's aim should be to foster individual growth and development in order to realize the potential of its 'human resources' (*sic*). He continues, 'The principle of integration demands that both the organization's and the individual's needs be recognized' (McGregor 1960: 329). This has a surprising degree of similarity to today's soft version of human resource management, resting on the notions of commitment and self-direction, with the dual aims of meeting the needs of the organization and of the individual.

McGregor's argument was that it is our view of human nature (Theory X or Theory Y) which ultimately influences management control strategies. Echoes of this can be found in Noon's argument that definitions of human resource management contain contradictory elements of 'modern man', who is influenced by physical, psychological, and social laws, and 'hermeneutical man', who is self-bound and '*creates* organizational reality and structures rather than *responds* to them' (1992: 27; see also Sullivan 1986).

Soft models of HRM can be compared with the Theory Y approach or notions of 'hermeneutical man'. The soft version assumes that employees will work best (and thereby increase organizational performance) if they are fully committed to the organization (Beaumont 1992; Dunham and Smith 1979; Guest 1987; Legge 1995a; Lundy 1994; Walton 1985a). Hope notes that 'the employee working under an HRM system would not merely comply with the organization's wishes, but positively and affectively commit themselves to the aims and values of their employers, and thereby give added value through their labour' (1994: 3). The soft model emphasizes that this commitment will be generated if employees are trusted, if they are trained and developed, and if they are allowed to work autonomously and have control over their work (Guest 1987; Hendry and Pettigrew 1990; Kamoche 1994; Mahoney and Deckop 1986; Purcell 1993; Purcell and Ahlstrand 1994; Tyson 1995a). In other words, the strategic premise of the soft model, in contrast to the hard model, is that control comes through commitment (Purcell 1993).

Under the hard model, on the other hand, control is more concerned with performance systems, performance management, and tight control over individual activities, with the ultimate goal being to secure the competitive advantage of the organization (Guest 1995). This implies that the individual is managed on a much more instrumental basis than under the soft model, where *both* competitive advantage *and* employee commitment are accorded equal importance.

Ultimately, then, there is a tension and conflict between elements of self-expression and high trust contained within the soft model, and of direction and low trust within the hard model (Noon 1992). Although hard and soft models of human resource management therefore are derived from very different intellectual traditions, and incorporate diametrically opposed assumptions about human nature and managerial control, both have been incorporated within the same theories or models of human resource management. Thus, for instance, Storey's model contains elements of modern man (or Theory X) when he states that 'people-management decisions ought not to be treated as incidental operational matters or be sidelined into the hands of personnel officers' (1992: 26), in other words, people management needs to be controlled and directed 'from above', and elements of hermeneutical man (or Theory Y) when he states, 'it is human capability and commitment which . . . distinguish[es] successful organizations . . . The human resource ought to be nurtured' (1992: 26). The opposing nature of the models' underlying assumptions leads us to question the validity of constructing models of human resource management on the basis of both soft and hard elements.

CONFLICTS AND TENSIONS WITHIN SOFT AND HARD MODELS OF HUMAN RESOURCE MANAGEMENT

These conflicts between soft and hard versions of HRM are further compounded by the conceptual difficulties contained within them, particularly concerning the notions of strategic integration and commitment.

Strategic integration has been defined by Legge as having three dimensions, 'the integration or "fit" of human resources policies with business strategy; the integration or complementarity and consistency of "mutuality" employment policies aimed at generating employee commitment, flexibility and quality; [and] the internalization of the importance of human resources on the part of line managers' (1995*b*: 96). Integration with business strategy can be concerned with developing HR policies that 'fit' either the organization's stage of development (life cycle models) or its strategic orientation, such as models which build on Porter's three generic strategy types (Schuler and Jackson 1987). 'The fundamental strategic management problem is to keep the strategy, structure and human resource dimensions of the organization in direct alignment' (Tichy *et al.* 1982: 48).

The problematic nature of this concept has been identified by a number of commentators. For instance, whilst fit between strategy and HRM implies that HRM policies should be *contingent* upon business strategies, fit amongst HR policies themselves would imply 'an *absolutist* approach to the design of employment policy' (Legge 1995*a*: 38). Further, there is no evidence that a tight fit leads to positive outcomes, and the concept of fit implies inflexibility and rigidity which could, in themselves, be detrimental to organizational outcomes (Lengnick-Hall and Lengnick-Hall 1990). Legge (1989) and Keenoy (1990) both argue that fit might not be attainable, or desirable, in a diversified organization.

An underlying assumption of some 'matching models' of hard human resource management, which argue that an appropriate human resource strategy can be found for any business strategy, is that there is a simple, linear relationship between strategy and human resource strategy, particularly where it is argued that typologies of linkages, such as a one-way or reciprocal linkage, can be established (Baird and Meshoulam 1988; Butler *et al.* 1991; Dyer 1984; Golden and Ramanujam 1985). This fails to acknowledge the complexities both between and within notions of strategy and human resource management, such as the Mintzbergian contrast between 'emergent' and 'intended' strategies (Dyer 1985; Truss and Gratton 1994), and is based on a rational model of individuals and organizations, which takes no account of the significance of power, politics, and culture (Kamoche 1994; Purcell and Ahlstrand 1994). The matching model is based on a narrow, classical view of strategy formulation which assumes that formulation and implementation are separate activities and, consequently, that strategies in the HR area can simply be 'matched' to business strategies at the formulation stage. However, Whittington (1993) has identified three other perspectives on strategy formulation—evolutionary (the market selects the winners and environmental fit is the main goal; strategy is therefore emergent), processual (strategy is a means used by managers to codify a complex world, and is discovered in action rather than formulated), and systemic (social systems have a key role to play in shaping strategic goals)—none of which would allow for a process of 'matching' with HR strategies to take place. Human resource management can also be non-strategic and reactive (Miller 1987).

The soft model of HRM is founded on the concepts of commitment, flexibility, and quality, although these are similarly ambiguous and open to debate (Purcell 1993). Keenoy (1990) argues that the goals of quality, flexibility, commitment, and integration presented in Guest's (1987) soft model of HRM may well not be mutually compatible and, in practice, may be difficult to achieve. The assumption that committed workers are necessarily more productive has also never been proven (G. Bassett 1994).

Prieto (1993) notes that there are three types of flexibility: numerical (flexibility in the number of people in the workforce), wage (where wage adjustments can be linked to profits), and functional (where there is a broadening of skills).

These three types of flexibility, he argues, are all very different and may even be contradictory. Whilst flexibility is frequently presented as a desirable attribute for both organizations and individuals, Prieto (1993) argues that the more coercive side has been downplayed. For instance, numerical flexibility may include the use of short-term contracts or temporary assignments as a means to alter the size of the workforce, at the expense of more permanent forms of employment that may be more attractive to employees. This can therefore affect levels of commitment. There is also confusion surrounding the notion of commitment itself, and it is unclear whether the desired form of commitment is to the organization, work group, immediate supervisor, union, or occupation, and the interaction and potential conflict between these different forms of commitment has not been addressed within the HRM literature (Legge 1995b).

Thus, as we have seen, conceptualizations of human resource management along the soft–hard dimension are plagued with inconsistencies and ambiguities. At a theoretical level, the principal problem with using them together as elements to construct a 'theory' of human resource management is that they are founded on opposing assumptions regarding human nature and, consequently, the legitimacy of managerial control strategies. Noon's (1992) observation that theories of human resource management lack the requisite criteria of parsimony and completeness also applies, particularly where such complex notions as 'strategic integration', 'commitment', and 'flexibility' are concerned.

If such conceptual weaknesses exist within models of HRM, how valid can they be as the basis of normative theories? Do organizations practise either soft or hard HRM and, if so, under what conditions? How can these practices, in turn, inform theories of human resource management? We have differentiated between soft and hard models in terms of two criteria: first, underlying perceptions of human nature, and secondly, managerial control strategies. The soft perspective is characterized by a developmental-humanist stance and the hard perspective by a utilitarian-instrumentalist stance. We shall analyse our data along these two dimensions. In particular, we shall make reference to the views and experiences of the employees to contrast company rhetoric with individual perceptions.

HUMAN NATURE

First, we consider perceptions of *human nature*. The soft perspective implies that individuals are viewed as a resource worthy of training and development, whereas the hard perspective implies that individuals are a cost to be minimized. We would therefore expect minimal training to take place within organizations adopting a 'hard' perspective, with a greater emphasis on training under 'soft' HRM.

Table 2.1 shows that most of the employees surveyed, in all organizations except W. H. Smith News, received at least some training in the current year. However, the vast majority of employees received between 1 and 10 days

Table 2.1. Reported number of days' training received by employees per year (%)

	20+ days	11–20 days	1–10 days	None
BT Payphones	3	11	56	29
C&W NHS Trust	12	11	51	24
Citibank	2	2	55	40
GP UK	6	13	72	9
HP	3	8	75	13
KJS	2	7	57	33
Lloyds	2	9	59	28
WHS News	2	2	41	53

Note: Data for all tables in this chapter collected 1993–5.

Table 2.2. Employees' perceptions of training (%)

	'I receive the training I need to do my job well.' (agree/strongly agree)	'The organization does not encourage me to develop new skills.' (disagree/strongly disagree)
BT Payphones	41	31
C&W NHS Trust	36	46
Citibank	30	49
GP UK	56	71[a]
HP	46	69
KJS	51	63
Lloyds	29	37
WHS News	36	43

[a] The question used at GP UK (the pilot study) was reversed, i.e. the statement was positive. The percentage given represents those agreeing with the statement. There is the possibility that this led to a higher score for GP UK.

training, with only a minority being trained for more than 20 days. Most training took place within Glaxo Pharmaceuticals UK and Hewlett Packard.

Table 2.2 shows that, although employees may be receiving training, the quality and usefulness of that training cannot be taken for granted. In only two of the organizations, Kraft Jacobs Suchard and Glaxo Pharmaceuticals UK, did more than half the respondents indicate that they thought they received the training they needed to do their jobs well. In Lloyds Bank UK Retail Banking and Citibank, fewer than one third of respondents felt they received enough training, and it was only in three of the organizations that most respondents felt they were encouraged to develop new skills. One Lloyds Bank UK Retail Banking senior manager said, 'People's perceptions of development would be that it is inadequate. But of course they are looking at being developed as generalists and I want them to be specialists more and more.' This implies a tension between individual aspirations and company needs that is ultimately resolved, as the hard model would suggest, at the expense of the individual.

These views contrast sharply with company rhetoric. All the companies placed great emphasis on training and development, with most having a number of large-scale training initiatives either in place or being developed, sometimes as part of a broader cultural change programme. There was clear evidence that all the organizations were increasing their investment in training, sometimes from a very low base. This was particularly true at Lloyds Bank UK Retail Banking and W. H. Smith News, where training initiatives were being put in place at the time of the research that represented a marked improvement on earlier provisions. We may therefore expect that levels of training and skill development will increase within both these organizations.

Significant qualitative differences emerged between the types of training offered. It was clear that even where training opportunities were provided, these were not necessarily equated with a soft, developmental HRM perspective. For instance, the training offered by Citibank was felt by most interviewees to be of excellent quality, but its primary focus was on creating a workforce with the skills the bank needed in specialist technical and professional banking matters, with management and other skill development training hardly figuring in the programme offered. The training manager stated that the training programme's primary aim was broadly to support the bank's three-year plan and, secondly, to ensure that each course met a particular business objective. There was no explicit aim within the training of increasing individuals' skill levels or broadening their experience. The technical bias of this training programme implies a somewhat different view from the long-term individual development suggested by the soft model, although it does not suggest a cost minimization strategy indicative of a hard approach. This raises the point that workforce skill levels will always need to be high in such knowledge-based organizations.

Similarly, at Kraft Jacobs Suchard one internal brochure stated, 'We believe that outstanding people, more than physical assets, financial resources or brands, make the difference in achieving superior business results,' and another document concluded, 'Individual development, when managed effectively, leads to increased productivity and growth.' Thus, at Kraft Jacobs Suchard, training and development were regarded as necessary investments in human capital aimed at improving competitive advantage and the bottom line rather than developing the individual, although this is likely to be an additional outcome.

BT Payphones was putting through a programme of cultural change, entitled 'Involving Everyone', with the purpose of developing an achievement orientation in individuals and fostering a sense of shared purpose. A portfolio of management development programmes was on offer. The aim behind this was described in one document as 'to increase our people's potential to achieve [our] business goals'. The focus was on 'get[ting] people to become responsible for their own development', in the words of one senior manager. Thus, at BT Payphones, training and development were again linked to competitive advantage.

Another form of individual development within organizations is career management. Upward progression may be one of the rewards given by organizations to their employees in return for their labour (Mumford 1971). One of the most characteristic features in all the companies studied was a shift in responsibility for career management from the organization to the individual. For example, at Citibank internal documentation noted, 'No one at Citibank is guaranteed a career. What you are offered is the chance to pursue one.' At Kraft Jacobs Suchard, one member of the HR department said, 'Whilst the formal structure for employee development has been driven by the HR function, greater emphasis has been placed on the role of the line manager and the individual themselves in adding value to their own roles and influencing career progression.'

This trend accompanied rounds of downsizing that had taken place in most of the companies, with the associated de-layering, shortening of career tracks, and reconfiguration of jobs. In other words, not only were people increasingly expected to self-manage their careers, but career options themselves were severely limited compared with a few years ago. This shift was most marked in Lloyds Bank UK Retail Banking, where the recent cultural change programme explicitly signalled a move away from a paternalistic and authoritarian model (Purcell and Ahlstrand 1994) towards empowerment of the individual and devolution of responsibility from the centre: 'opportunities are limited, a lot is left to the individual' (personnel staff). This was further marked by an end to automatic promotion, a shift to greater work specialization, and the adoption of a sales ethos. The new climate was of personal responsibility. The flatter structure led to redundancies, loss of promotion opportunities, segmented management, and the loss of status for branch managers who saw many of their responsibilities centralized. This is reflected in the relatively high number of respondents who said that they did not have the opportunities for promotion they wanted, both within Lloyds Bank UK Retail Banking and within BT Payphones, which had undergone a similar exercise.

This shift towards self-managed careers would appear to reflect the soft model's emphasis on individual empowerment. However, since in most cases this is accompanied by a curtailing of career opportunities, an alternative interpretation could be that the organizations are adopting a more instrumental approach by employing the rhetoric of soft HRM and empowerment in circumstances that do not permit its use. Similarly, although training may be provided (as in 'soft' HRM), its primary purpose is to improve organizational perform-

Table 2.3. Respondents agreeing/strongly agreeing with the statement: 'I do not have the opportunities I want to be promoted.' (%)

BT Payphones	62
C&W NHS Trust	39
Citibank	33
GP UK	32
HP	33
KJS	47
Lloyds	52
WHS News	35

ance. Individual development is not an explicit goal in its own right, as is suggested by the developmental-humanist stance of the soft model.

CONTROL STRATEGIES

We now turn to the question of *control strategies*. In particular, we are concerned with whether the organizations adopt a strategy of control through commitment (soft model) or control through tight strategic direction (hard model). The soft model suggests that organizations make extensive use of communication with employees as a mechanism to maximize commitment (to the organization) (Legge 1995*b*; Storey 1992).

One of the most striking implications of Table 2.4 is that most of the organizations are effectively communicating their aims to their employees, but that *upward* communication is barely in place, even in those organizations where downward communication is strongest. Interestingly, in only three of the organizations did most employees feel that the strategy was communicated clearly to them. The question of trust was also explored; the soft model suggests that individuals are regarded as worthy of trust and discretion.

Overall, levels of trust (measured in terms of trust in the immediate manager) were quite high, particularly at Glaxo Pharmaceuticals UK and Hewlett Packard, although in Lloyds Bank UK Retail Banking and BT Payphones, both in the throes of major downsizing, they were low relative to the other organizations. At Lloyds Bank UK Retail Banking there was some sensitivity about the relationship between the branches and the company's head office. People clearly felt that the head office was remote and did not listen to them. 'There is great distrust of the bank, a "them and us" feeling,' said one line manager. In BT

Table 2.4. Communication between management and staff (%)

	'I am aware of what management is trying to achieve.' (agree)	'Senior management is well informed about what people at lower levels think and do.' (agree)	'My organization does not communicate its strategy to us clearly as employees.' (disagree)
BT Payphones	67	12	34
C&W NHS Trust	46	14	21
Citibank	64	8	44
GP UK	63	16	54[a]
HP	73	20	53
KJS	68	11	57
Lloyds	59	11	21
WHS News	60	21	21

[a] The question used at GP UK (the pilot study) was reversed, i.e. the statement was positive. The percentage given represents those agreeing with the statement. There is the possibility that this led to a higher score for GP UK.

Table 2.5. Respondents agreeing/strongly agreeing with the statement: 'I do not have a great deal of trust in my manager.' (%)

BT Payphones	53
C&W NHS Trust	37
Citibank	31
GP UK	20
HP	19
KJS	26
Lloyds	49
WHS News	27

Payphones, Employee Communications Plans were drawn up each year, including a two-yearly employee attitude survey. Staff, however, felt they were seen as a resource to be cut, and were sceptical of the value of communications. 'We are inundated with briefings . . . By the time it gets to the shop-floor level, you have got a lot of messages and you lose credibility,' said one line manager. These findings show the extent to which senior management was felt to be out of touch with the views and feelings of employees, in particular in relation to the changes occurring in career patterns and security.

In order to ascertain levels of commitment, we used the Mowday, Steers, and Porter (1978) fifteen-item Organizational Commitment Questionnaire to assess the degree of commitment across our sample, and found a very broad range. (The OCQ was not used in the pilot company, Glaxo Pharmaceuticals UK.) The respondents from Hewlett Packard recorded by far the highest levels of commitment, with a summary indicator of 84 per cent. No other organization scored over 50 per cent. W. H. Smith News was the second highest with 38 per cent, and the lowest was actually a negative score, −1.1 per cent. (Numbers represent the averaged sum of the mean scores for each question, expressed as a percentage.) Using the Mowday, Steers, and Porter (1978) measure, there is little evidence that many companies were achieving high levels of commitment at the time of our surveys. Longitudinal research would show whether initiatives currently being put in place will lead to increased levels of commitment.

In our study, we also looked at the converse area of strategic direction and integration. One factor to emerge from the case studies was that all the companies were unique in the way in which business strategy and human resource factors were, or in most cases were not, explicitly linked together.

These data would suggest that there was limited scope within the organizations for HR to perform an 'architect function' (Tyson and Fell 1986), since its representation at corporate level was so limited. This reflected the findings of Tyson's study (1995*a*), that HR matters may constitute a second- or third-order strategy (Purcell 1989). In only three instances did the HR director play an active role in formulating the overall business strategy, and we do not have data on exactly how that role was fulfilled.

Some interesting differences emerge when we compare these data at the corporate level with findings at the level of the business unit that formed the focus of our research. Glaxo Pharmaceuticals UK and Lloyds Bank UK Retail Banking both had a separate document outlining their people management strategies at the business unit level, although not at corporate level. W. H. Smith News's people management strategy was articulated and contained within the overall strategy document for the unit. None of the organizations reported that there was *no* conscious strategy for managing people within the unit of study, and most reported that the strategy for managing people was an integral part of the business unit strategy.

In none of the firms did human resource considerations take precedence over strategic business considerations. The most sophisticated example of linking business and human resource strategies was found in Kraft Jacobs Suchard, which is a subsidiary of the American conglomerate Philip Morris. Overall strategic direction in terms of core business was determined by the parent firm and, within this framework, financial targets were set by the European subsidiary for the British firm. Working within these parameters, the subsidiary had the latitude to determine its strategy for meeting these targets, which consisted

Table 2.6. Integration of HR factors and strategy at corporate/group level

	BT Payphones	C&W NHS Trust	Citibank	GP UK	HP	KJS	Lloyds	WHS News
HR director member of corporate board	✗	✗	✓	✗	✗	✗	✗	✗
Involvement of HRD in corporate strategy:[a]								
Involved in formulating	✗	—	✓	—	✓	—	✓	✓
Able to advise on people implications once formulated	✓	—	✗	—	✗	—	✗	✗
Informed of strategy and asked to implement it	✗	—	✗	—	✗	—	✗	✗
Corporate value/mission statement included explicit reference to people	✓	✓	✓	✓	✓	✓	✓	✓
Separate document articulating people management strategy	✗	✗	✗	✗	✗	✗	✗	✓
People management strategy integral/implicit part of corporate strategy	✓	✓	✓	✓	✓	✓	✓	✗

[a] Data not available for C&W NHS Trust, GP UK, or KJS.

of four main aims: 'growth through acquisitions, developing the organization, taking out costs, and strengthening core businesses.'

The Human Resource Director at Kraft Jacobs Suchard UK had taken these aims and developed a set of people implications and associated human resource strategies under the headings of hiring, motivating, developing, and maintaining. It was clear that people considerations were very much secondary to business strategic objectives. One senior director at Kraft Jacobs Suchard summed up the position in his firm:

I don't think HR gets factored into the development of business strategies. HR would be involved in our three year planning, in terms of development, succession planning and so on, but it doesn't determine which way the company goes or how the company is going to expand into different cores . . . HR falls out of the business strategy.

There was clear evidence of attempts to make explicit linkages between the various areas of HR intervention to ensure coherence, for instance through various training initiatives, which could be regarded as evidence of their use of strategic control in HRM. Citibank also had strong linkages between strategy and HRM. They, too, had a clearly articulated HR strategy, and the three-year plan incorporated a section on HR implications written by the Human Resource Director, who was involved in strategy formulation. However, in contrast with Kraft Jacobs Suchard, the stress at the bank at a strategic level was on the role of line managers in motivating and developing their staff, and on recruiting, motivating, and retaining key skilled individuals. The performance appraisal of senior directors was linked to their achievement of targets in the area of people management. Whereas Kraft Jacobs Suchard stressed utilizing people to achieve strategic objectives for the organization, Citibank's philosophy was to achieve 'excellence in people management' through 'meritocracy, independent initiative, listening/communicating, and development' (according to internal documentation), founded on respect for the individual. In this sense, Citibank represented the 'soft' model of strategic HRM, although the emphasis on linking people management to business objectives is indicative of the hard model. However, our research found little evidence of any deliberate or realized coherence between HR activities. For instance, one HR officer commented that the firm could be recruiting someone in one department and laying off someone with a similar profile in another.

Hewlett Packard could be described as having a unique 'cultured' soft model of human resource management, in that HR considerations were an intrinsic part of the corporate strategy and management style, rather than being grafted onto it. This created a situation where HRM permeated the culture of the organization, and the whole way in which people operated, becoming 'owned' by everyone, not the HR function itself—'the ownership of managing people and practising the HP Way is a line management-owned function' (senior manager). For instance, the Managing Director articulated the six key processes for the organization as 'customer focus, planning process, order generation, product generation, order fulfilment, people fulfilment'. The emphasis placed in this model on development, fulfilment, and quality is indicative of the soft model. However, a distinction needs to be drawn between the soft model as exemplified in Citibank and as exemplified in Hewlett Packard. Whereas in the bank responsibility for drawing out the HR implications of the business strategy ultimately lay with the HR function (although the management of people itself was carried out in the line), this was not the case in Hewlett Packard, where people considerations were seen as a fundamental component of the business strategy itself. These clearly represent two diverse models of HRM, although both within what might be termed the soft paradigm.

The remaining organizations fitted neither of the models, having what could best be described as 'transitional' models of HRM similar to those indicated by Purcell and Ahlstrand (1994). W. H. Smith News at the time of the research was in transition between a paternalist HR strategy (Purcell and Ahlstrand 1994) and a strategy that emphasized linking HR and business strategies together. The importance of the external environment is well illustrated in this instance, where the firm was experiencing enormous competitive pressures hitherto unknown in its long history. It was these pressures that had prompted a change in overall business strategy towards a focus on productivity and customer service. In this new environment, a paternalist HR function was no longer seen as able to deliver these strategic objectives, and initiatives were being put into effect that sought to improve the quality of performance, accompanied by a major cultural change programme.

Similarly, Lloyds Bank UK Retail Banking was suffering from intensified competition in the wake of changes in the financial services industry and a maturing of the market in the 1990s. In response to these changes, the bank developed a new strategy of focusing on selective market leadership and maximizing shareholder value. This led to a major programme of restructuring and the centralization of many activities. This was accompanied by a move from a centralized paternalistic model where people were promised 'jobs for life', towards an emphasis on performance management, devolution of responsibility to line managers, regional pay and individualized reward schemes, gathered under the umbrella of the 'Personnel Platform', a framework based on job design and grading, competencies, and self-managed careers, which sought to bring coherence to the various HR interventions and activities. Lloyds could therefore be described as moving between a paternalistic model and a variant of the hard model.

Chelsea & Westminster Healthcare Trust was having to define a strategy, mission, and business plan for the first time. Whilst the organization theoretically had a free hand in both strategy and HR matters, in practice, central and professional control continued to be the determining factor in both areas. There was no articulated HR strategy, and no evidence of any coherence among HR activities in different parts of the organization, although an HR strategy was being drawn up at the time of the research. The language of the soft HRM model was in evidence through words such as flexibility, commitment, and quality, but so too was that of the hard model, emphasizing financial control. These sat alongside the traditional public sector human resource management philosophies and practices, leading to a model unique amongst our cases.

We found no evidence that the organizations in our sample were adopting an 'integrative linkage' between their business and HR strategies (Golden and Ramanujam 1985). Most of the firms operated what Golden and Ramanujam term the 'one-way' linkage, where business strategy informs HR strategy, but not vice versa. This was reinforced by the questionnaire responses. Just 14 per cent of respondents overall felt that the HR department in their organization had a clear strategy guiding its activities, although 61 per cent felt the organization had a clear corporate strategy. We take a closer look at the strategic role of the human resource function in Chapter 6. The ways in which line managers support the link between strategy and people is explored in Chapter 7.

Another aspect of strategic control which we measured was the degree of control individuals had over setting their own work targets. Individuals had most control at the Chelsea & Westminster Healthcare Trust, and least control at BT Payphones and Lloyds Bank UK Retail Banking which, as we saw earlier, were those organizations where employees expressed least trust in their managers.

Finally, we examined the concepts of flexibility and adaptability. At Lloyds Bank UK Retail Banking, the rhetoric supported the soft model of HRM. The 'Shaping our Future' communications programme stressed values such as flexibility, specialization, devolution, adaptability, responsibility, and teamwork. The need for flexibility of staff had arisen particularly out of market pressures to open branches for longer hours. One senior manager said in an interview, 'I want my branches to open on Saturday with more flexible staff on short-term

Table 2.7. Control over setting work targets (%)

	Solely responsible for setting own targets	Determine targets together with boss	Boss sets targets but seeks my agreement	Boss solely responsible for setting targets	Not aware of having any specific targets
BT Payphones	4	25	29	37	5
C&W NHS Trust	30	46	7	2	15
Citibank	11	57	22	5	5
GP UK	5	60	26	8	1
HP	6	59	27	3	5
KJS	9	72	10	4	5
Lloyds	4	24	36	27	9
WHS News	11	38	21	14	16

Table 2.8. Organizational flexibility (% agreeing/strongly agreeing)

	'My organization is flexible enough to cope with change.'	'My organization is better placed than any of its competitors to meet the challenges of the 1990s.'
BT Payphones	56	63
C&W NHS Trust	55	38
Citibank	73	59
GP UK	69	66
HP	80	91
KJS	58	47
Lloyds	56	62
WHS News	73	72

contracts. Personnel try to cling to the *status quo.*' However, as Table 2.8 shows, only 56 per cent of questionnaire respondents thought the bank flexible enough to cope with change, one of the lowest scores.

Although we do not have absolute indicators of the degree of flexibility or the relative competitive advantage of the organizations, the questions referred to in Table 2.8 can be taken as proxies for measuring organizational flexibility and performance, albeit through the eyes of employees. For instance, Kraft Jacobs Suchard appeared to adopt most of the tenets of the hard model of HRM with a focus on bottom-line performance in the way people are managed, and yet it scored second lowest of all the organizations in terms of the number of respondents who believed that the company was better placed than its competitors to meet the challenges of the 1990s. Hewlett Packard, which scored quite highly in terms of adopting a soft, developmental, and commitment-oriented approach to its employees, also scored very highly in terms of flexibility and performance. Thus, although the soft model may emphasize individual development and commitment, the underlying principle behind this is still one of bottom-line performance. Chelsea & Westminster Healthcare Trust scored the lowest on both these questions (especially the second), as well as scoring quite low in terms of training, development, and career opportunities. This suggests that it may be close to Miller's (1987) version of non-strategic HRM.

DISCUSSION

The data from our study showed that no single organization adopted either a pure soft or pure hard approach to human resource management. At the rhetorical level, many embraced the tenets of the soft version (training, development, commitment), but the underlying principle was invariably restricted to the improvement of bottom-line performance. The specification of the soft model suggests that soft HRM has the dual aims of improved competitive advantage *and* individual development. This second element appeared to be missing in the organizations we studied. This was most apparent in the case of career development. As we describe in Chapter 4, the onus is increasingly on individuals to manage their careers, and this is expressed by the organizations in terms of empowering individuals to manage themselves. In reality, however, the options for individuals have been severely curtailed by organizational restructuring, and so in many instances this is simply empty rhetoric and perceived as such by employees. Whilst, on the one hand, training was taking place in the organizations, the *aim* of much of this training was not the development of the individual as an end in itself, but ensuring that individuals had the skills necessary to carry out their jobs in such a way as to improve organizational performance. One side effect of this training could be individual development, but it was not an explicit aim.

One conclusion of our study, therefore, is that even if the rhetoric of HRM is 'soft', the reality is almost always 'hard', with the interests of the organization prevailing over those of the individual. It may well be that this focus on the organization is inevitable within the current economic climate, and perhaps, as we move further into a post-recessionary period and firms are growing instead of cutting back, then the interests of individual employees may start to receive more attention.

In all of the organizations, we found a mixture of both hard and soft approaches. The precise ingredients of this mixture were unique to each organization, which implies that factors such as the external and internal environment of the organization, its strategy, culture, and structure, all have a vital role to play in the way in which HRM operates.

There was no evidence of organizations developing or adhering to any particular guiding philosophy in HRM beyond motherhood statements of the 'people are our most important asset' variety. In no case was there a clearly articulated and developed human resource strategy that was translated into a mutually supportive set of human resource initiatives or practices, and then cascaded down through the line. Instead, what we found was a combination of some broad-brush guiding strategy or philosophy, inherited policies and practices which may or may not be integrated in some way, new initiatives, and responses to internal and external pressures.

This brings us back to the tensions and contradictions contained within models of human resource management such as those of Guest and Storey, which contain elements of both hard and soft HRM, with their respective foundations in utilitarian instrumentalism and developmental humanism. We argued earlier that theoretical models of HRM should not contain elements of both, since they are based on divergent views of human nature and strategic control. A more empirically grounded model would, on the basis of our data, suggest that the *rhetoric* of HRM is concerned with hermeneutical man and commitment-based strategic control, whereas the *reality* of HRM experienced by employees within organizations today is based on concepts of modern man and tight strategic direction towards organizational goals. We therefore need to retain this distinction between HRM at the rhetorical level and the reality experienced by individuals in our conceptualizations and models of human resource management if they are to be empirically and theoretically sound. We explore the theme of rhetoric and reality in greater depth in the final chapter of this book.

3

Performance Management in Fast-Changing Environments

PHILIP STILES

Performance management is often claimed to be the area of human resource management which can make the greatest impact on organizational performance (Migliore 1982; Philpott and Sheppard 1992). The use of performance management systems to implement strategy has also been viewed as an important part of the strategy process (Huff and Reger 1987). The topic has received renewed emphasis in recent years, primarily due to increasing competition, which has forced organizations to examine in detail the contribution of various parts of the business (Beatty 1989; Storey and Sisson 1993), and to widespread restructuring initiatives, used to align organizations more closely with the market place, which have involved decentralization to business units and profit centres (Legge 1995b). In such conditions, accountability and measurement become crucial to effective operations.

Performance management has received considerable attention in the human resource management literature, though less so in the strategy field, in spite of calls for increased scrutiny in the area (Simons 1994). The theoretical contributions can be categorized into three broad areas. First, performance management is viewed as a key integrative mechanism, linking individuals' goals and responsibilities to the objectives of the business, and integrating major interventions—appraisal, rewards, training, and development—thereby facilitating strategic fit (Beer *et al.* 1984; Fombrun *et al.* 1984; Storey 1992). Second, performance management has been identified as a means of enhancing organizational control over employees, constructing a consistent statement of managerial expectations, and promoting a unitarist view of the firm (Coates 1994; Latham 1984; Storey and Sisson 1993). Third, performance management is held to be an important driver in determining valuable outputs, such as employee commitment. Identification by employees with the organization in terms of adherence to its values, goals, and desired behaviours is assumed to bring about a strong culture and be conducive to organizational success (Peters and Waterman 1983).

A major problem for performance management is that, as Mahoney and

Deckop (1986) claimed about human resource management in general, it has developed under assumptions of bureaucracy. Such assumptions, including the consistency of job roles and descriptions, the clarity of cause and effect relations concerning the actions employees take and their outcomes, and the centrality of individual performance as opposed to group performance, come under attack when the environment is fast-changing (Mohrman *et al.* 1990; Snell 1992). In this chapter we shall explore how four firms which are operating in 'high-velocity' conditions (Bourgeois and Eisenhardt 1988; Eisenhardt 1989) manage the performance of employees.

THEORETICAL BACKGROUND

High-velocity environments

In an era of increasingly intense competition, global markets, changing technology, and regulatory reform, there has been a good deal of attention given to how firms act in times of fast-changing environmental conditions (Judge and Miller 1991; Schoonhoven and Jelink 1990). But despite the potential importance of this issue for human resource management, little is known about how fast-changing conditions affect the management of performance.

Environmental velocity can be characterized as reflecting both the pace of change in an environment and the predictability of change that occurs (Judge and Miller 1991). In their pioneering study, Bourgeois and Eisenhardt argued that high velocity environments are those in which 'changes in demand, competition and technology are so rapid and discontinuous that information is often inaccurate, unavailable or obsolete' (1988: 816). Velocity is thus similar to environmental dynamism (Dess and Beard 1984) and Bourgeois and Eisenhardt (1988) stated that three industries—microcomputers, banking, and airlines—provided clear examples of high-velocity environments. In this chapter, we follow their definition of high-velocity environments and identify one other industry we believe comes under this heading: pharmaceuticals, an industry which is experiencing fast-changing technology, rapid entry of new competitors, government deregulation, and a large explosion of new companies in emerging technologies, in particular biotechnology.

Performance management as a control mechanism

Performance management is the principal set of practices by which control is manifested in organizations. Control here is defined as any process that is used to align the actions of individuals to the interests of the organization (Snell 1992; Tannenbaum 1968). Under such a characterization, performance management is expected to regulate both motivation and ability (Walsh and Seward 1990). Performance management is usually conceptualized as consisting of three elements: (1) objective setting, (2) formal performance evaluation, and (3) linkage between evaluation outcomes and development and rewards, in order to reinforce desired behaviour (Storey and Sisson 1993). This system is cybernetic, with feedback from both employer and employee driving modifications at each point in the system. Empirical research has tended to be absorbed in the constituent elements of performance management, and studies into performance management viewed as a set of interlocking policies and practices are rare. For this chapter, we intend to adopt a broad systemic view of performance management. Further, most research in this area has focused on formal systems of control, precluding informal modes of regulation. The richness of our data allows us to pick up on this important perspective and present a rounded view of the management of performance.

There are three prominent views as to how performance management may be used to regulate performance, through focusing either on behaviour, or on skills, or on outputs. Monitoring behaviour is largely concerned with articulating operating procedures which are initiated top-down through a centralized bureaucratic framework (Snell 1992). The intent is to monitor employee performance closely, with appraisal used chiefly as an auditing device to correct deviations from set norms (Snell 1992). A less rigid view of controlling behaviour lies in the use of competency frameworks. Competencies can specify behaviours, skills, and knowledge which are deemed desirable for employees to exhibit, and criteria for their attainment are set by the organization, forming an important part of the evaluation process (Boyaztis 1982). Monitoring output is characterized by the use of performance targets which provide some discretion in how employees achieve them. This type of control allows employers to decentralize control and gives relatively objective criteria for evaluation. Employees, while not choosing the targets for required performance, are given discretion in how they achieve them. Since the effects of these three approaches overlap, it is usually the case that firms will employ elements of behavioural, skills, and output controls simultaneously (Jaeger and Baliga 1985; Snell 1992).

If performance management is key to controlling the nature of employee contributions, how is it affected by fast-changing environments? A major dilemma in the management of performance in high-velocity environments is that administrative systems, such as performance management systems, tend to be inflexible and highly resistant to change. Such systems have usually evolved and developed over a number of years, and the degree of documentation and formalization required to implement processes, together with the need to be able to embed the monitoring and evaluation processes so that employees can have a consistent expectation of the effort–reward bargain, makes them difficult to adapt. As Mohrman and his colleagues claim, such requirements 'work against classical bureaucratic notions of control and require performance management practices that acknowledge uncertainty, rapid change, innovation, and professional standards and expertise' (Mohrman *et al.* 1990: 216).

Given the characteristics of high-velocity environments, the demands on performance management systems to assess accurately the contributions of employees are likely to increase substantially. We discuss this below by first looking at the component parts of the performance management system: goal setting, evaluation, rewards, and training and development.

Goal setting

According to goal-setting theory, goals are effective in so far as they indicate a level of performance that is specific, attainable, demanding, and desirable (Latham and Locke 1991; Mabey and Salaman 1995; Mento *et al.* 1987). In high-velocity environments, goal specificity is problematic because the consistency and continuity of the external environment, and in many cases the nature of the work, is unclear. In high-velocity environments we would expect to see goals loosely specified and open to frequent revision. We would also expect there to be greater participation by employees in their goals setting, since managers may not be in the best position to assess the changing demands of a particular employee's work (Latham and Locke 1991).

Appraisal

Performance appraisal has been characterized as having two major aims: auditing employee performance, and identifying opportunities for training and development (Snell and Dean 1992). In firms operating in relatively stable conditions, where goals and job descriptions are consistent, and where there is a good deal of routine to the work of employees, the auditing element of appraisal is much more to the fore (Snell 1992; Snell and Dean 1992). In high-velocity environments, however, where what happened in the past may prove an unreliable guide to what may occur in the future, one would expect appraisal to have a greater emphasis on development, with the aim of encouraging creativity and continuous improvement, rather than monitoring deviations from the norm (Snell 1992; Snell and Dean 1992). Another important part of appraisal concerns the input the appraisee has in the process. Traditionally, performance appraisals have been seen as highly formal, non-participative events (Snell and Dean 1992; Storey and Sisson 1993). In high-velocity environments, we would expect employees to have a large say in their appraisals. The changing demands of work and role, and the emphasis on development needs, would seem to require a strong input from employees, given that the information asymmetry between manager and employee will be greater in fast-changing circumstances. With organizations adopting team-based working and group-oriented output, relying on just the immediate manager's input into the appraisal may reduce the efficiency of the process, as important information may be lost due to inadequate review of the employee's activities. We would expect therefore, in cases where work is increasingly interdependent, that multiple inputs into the performance appraisal would be used. Because tasks become relatively fluid and jobs more difficult to define in high-velocity environments, we would expect less emphasis on formal evaluations and more on informal meetings and greater ongoing appraisal (Gomez-Mejia and Welbourne 1990).

Rewards

In SHRM, the reward process is intended to align employees with organizational strategy by providing incentives for employees to act in the firm's interest and perform well over time. Expectancy theory carries a clear message that employees must feel confident that their effort will affect the rewards they receive. Perceptions of equity are therefore crucial in an employee's decision to remain and produce valuable work. Equity is a multidimensional construct, embracing external equity (the degree to which a firm pays employees the rate they would find in the external labour market), internal equity (the degree to which a firm differentiates pay between employees on the basis of performance in similar jobs), and individual equity (the degree to which employees are rewarded proportionately to their individual performance) (Dean and Snell 1993). Because of the changing demands of performance on employees in high-velocity companies, perceptions of equity in its three forms may become confused, as job roles and job interdependence become more varied and flexible. Since employees would expect that as their job changes, so will their rewards, designing reward systems in high-velocity environments presents a major challenge to organizations. In high-velocity environments, a premium is placed on individuals who are able to operate in ambiguous circumstances and who are able to take advantage of loose job descriptions provided by their employers. Organizations in high-velocity environments are willing to pay proportionally higher salaries to individuals who have such skills. We would expect, therefore, that emphasis on individually equitable rewards as a means of recruiting and retaining highly capable employees would be required (Gomez-Mejia and Welbourne 1990; Snell and Dean 1992).

Rewards can be classified under three broad headings: performance-contingent rewards, which explicitly reward through performance outputs; job-contingent rewards, where pay is contingent on job classification; and person-contingent rewards, in which pay is dependent on the competencies a person has (Dean and Snell 1993). Because both output orientation and job classification may be difficult to measure accurately in high-velocity conditions, the prospect of person-contingent rewards, which may encourage the values of learning, flexibility, and creativity, would seem to be best suited to fast-changing conditions.

Training and development

Training and development are key interventions made in order to address skill deficiencies (Keep 1989), to add value to the stock of human capital (Snell and Dean 1992), and to foster a learning organization (Argyris 1970). What is emphasized in training and development can also underpin the change process by refocusing skills and knowledge within the organization.

A major issue for organizations in high-velocity environments is that they require flexible, creative employees who need training and development to maintain and increase their knowledge base and skill levels in line with changing environmental circumstances. But the nature of training and development, with its rather long 'lead times' together with the time taken for its benefits to filter through, renders problematic the potential of training and development to fit strategically within a high-velocity organization (Mabey and Salaman 1995). We would expect that in high-velocity environments there would be a greater focus on developmental approaches such as building problem-solving skills, coaching, and counselling, rather than an adherence to structured programmes or a menu-driven approach to training and development.

PERFORMANCE MANAGEMENT IN HIGH-VELOCITY ENVIRONMENTS: THE EVIDENCE FROM THE COMPANIES

In this chapter, we examine four companies from three high-velocity environments: Citibank and Lloyds Bank UK Retail Banking from the banking sector, Hewlett Packard from the computer industry, and Glaxo Pharmaceuticals UK from the pharmaceuticals business. This extends previous research by providing empirical data on the design and implementation of performance management systems in fast-changing environments.

The chapter will examine the performance management processes through their constituent parts—goal setting, appraisal, training and development, and rewards—and then examine the nature of the linkages between these interventions. In each section, we shall describe both the practice and the managerial interpretation of that practice, aiming for a rounded understanding of performance management in high-velocity environments.

Nature of the work environments

In this chapter, we are looking at the performance management systems as they apply to *managerial* grades within these organizations. In Hewlett Packard, we examined a group of sales and marketing managers based in the UK operation. These managers were selling in a market place where strong competition and rapid changes in technology made forecasts for product sales inherently difficult. The innovative behaviour of Hewlett Packard also entails that sales managers have to keep up to speed on new products and those of competitors, which requires strong training and development, and there is a clear focus on encouraging creative ways of building customer relationships. Salesmen are part of sales teams and their performance is tied in part to the performance of that team. There is also increasing cross-functional working in groups, as the computer business is a systems business and all parts of the value chain are interdependent. At Glaxo Pharmaceuticals UK, too, sales and marketing professionals were the sample group, again responsible for promoting products and services in a rapidly changing market place, with the NHS changes and the increases in 'me-too' products making demand unstable. Cross-functional teams, comprising members from different therapy groups, HR support, and medical specialisms, are prominent in designing product and service offerings for customers. At Citibank, we studied managers in commercial banking, specifically relationship managers and foreign exchange and capital markets dealers. With the commodification of financial products, increases in liquidity, and widespread availability of information, financial services has a great need for flexibility and creativity on the part of managers in order to secure high-quality revenue. With customer demands for financial products often requiring unique solutions in a very short space of time, teams can come together and then disband very quickly. These teams will broadly comprise a front office staff of relationship managers and a back office staff of product provision and research. At Lloyds Bank UK Retail Banking, we examined the retail bank staff in a geographic region in the UK. Though it was a retail bank under scrutiny, it was affected by the same broad macro changes in the environment as Citibank—increasing competition, technology, and information producing a commodifying effect on products and services. These shifts have resulted in the traditional banking performance criteria such as the ability to lend, and the management of risk, being superseded by an emphasis on sales and marketing—retaining key clients and encouraging cross-selling of products and service. This major shift in mindset has been accompanied by continuous restructuring, which saw the old-style bank branches being 'clustered' into regional centres, with a great deal of discretion taken away from branch managers as products became increasingly centralized. The move to 'unbundle' the bank and judge success on the criterion of shareholder value was another major change, and recently an acquisitive strategy aimed at gaining market share and scale has brought further demands on employees, and the re-evaluation of jobs and the rewriting of expectations between employee and employer has been undertaken.

Goal setting

The four business units studied had all been governed by some sort of 'management by objectives'. But in light of the major external pressures on the firms, difficulties had arisen with the specification of appropriate targets. For example, at Citibank informality is the chief rule of the game. Traders work on projects typically lasting less than a year, and so assessing their performance on the basis of annual targets is difficult. Further, since the traders are responsible almost entirely for generating revenues (and do not manage other employees) the application of soft targets seems inappropriate. At Glaxo Pharmaceuticals UK, one manager saw the performance management process as 'a set of mechanical procedures which do not take account of a rapidly changing environment'.

In Hewlett Packard and Citibank, there has been a long tradition of targets being determined by both boss and employee. This reflects not only the long-standing policy of decentralization within each organization but also the difficulty of imposing performance targets on employees who are facing changing demands and working in fast-changing markets. These conversations are participative. Since work is not routinized, the discussions attempt to cover the diversity of situations the employees would face as far as that is possible to ascertain. In the monthly formal meetings, as well as in informal settings, manager and employee have the opportunity to revise these targets in light of new information about the environment of client behaviour. The revisable nature of the performance targets, together with the degree of influence employees have over their goal setting, means that perceptions of fairness are high in terms of the targets being realistic and achievable. At Glaxo Pharmaceuticals UK and Lloyds Bank UK Retail Banking, the legacy of paternalism entailed that the process of participation in goal setting and the revisability of targets was less well embedded. Indeed, at Lloyds Bank UK Retail Banking, 'managers feel limited control over setting objectives. There is little flex in performance objectives to respond to changing business conditions' (HR internal document).

The overall aim of the objective-setting process is to align performance with business goals. As these organizations are operating in high-velocity environments, strategic goals may change and so communication of the business strategy and changes therein is ongoing. Ernst Brutsche, then head of Global Finance at Citibank, urged managers to 'strengthen our communications system in order to build a common understanding of GF's goals and working practices and to improve each individual's sense of commitment to supporting such objectives'. His preferred means for carrying this out were for managers to hold informal sessions 'at least six times a year' with employees at all levels, and schedule briefing meetings with key officers from other business units to encourage cross-functional working and sharing of information. At Hewlett Packard and Glaxo Pharmaceuticals UK, objectives were explicitly tied to business strategy, at Hewlett Packard through the framework system, at Glaxo Pharmaceuticals UK through the RATIO programme; employee recognition of these linkages was high, reflecting the corporate effort in communication via briefings, workshops and seminars, and newsletters. At Lloyds Bank UK Retail Banking, however, the situation was rather different. A series of internal focus groups set up for the change process found that: 'objectives are rarely agreed and frequently bear no relationship to individuals' jobs or their development needs.'

As part of the change process, Lloyds Bank UK Retail Banking's intention was to 'agree stretching individual goals/objectives/targets, clearly related to achievement of organizational goals over which individuals feel they have genuine influence and which are relevant to their work' (internal document).

Underpinning this initiative, indeed, underpinning the objective-setting process in all the companies, was the introduction of competency frameworks. Relying solely on targets for outcomes was not considered appropriate. At Citibank, competencies were introduced three years ago as part of the Talent Inventory—explicitly to link performance and potential to development. At Lloyds Bank UK Retail Banking, sixteen generic competencies describe 'on the job behaviours' and managers have the discretion to tailor these generic descriptions to local situations. Glaxo Pharmaceuticals UK, as part of the re-engineering programme, introduced competencies as part of the drive towards behavioural change. Interestingly, at Hewlett Packard, there are no competencies so described, but rather 'business fundamentals' on which people are measured, including both hard and soft targets. The underlying philosophy is described by co-founder Dave Packard as follows: 'It has been our policy at HP not to have a tight military-type organization, but rather to have overall objectives which are clearly stated and agreed to, and to give people the freedom to work towards those goals in ways they determine best for their own areas of responsibility' (Packard 1995: 148).

The emphasis on outputs in Hewlett Packard is tempered by the fact that the HP Way provides implicit behavioural norms which serve to constrain deviance from organizational goals. Individual freedom is allowed to flourish, but within a strong belief and value system.

Common to the competency frameworks, and Hewlett Packard's value set, is an emphasis on the values of creativity, teamwork, flexibility, and leadership. Managers felt that these competencies were generic enough to be stretched to suit changing conditions. As one Citibank manager said, 'We feel that in whatever circumstances, we will need people who show certain characteristics. Though the specific details have to be addressed—what counts as evidence—the overall idea is solid.'

The intention in these companies is to have targets which are not crystallized, but are rather left loose and open to amendment. This brittle approach to goal setting is reflected, too, in determining targets for group-oriented output. As these companies moved towards greater focus on team working and cross-functional activity, it was found that, in some cases, teams are formed and disbanded very quickly, working on a particular business solution for a financial product for a client, or the marketing of a particular drug or service. Targets in terms of objectives for these teams would be set usually by the team itself. At Citibank, reward was tied directly to performance as a team, with the team earning a bonus on completion of provision of service to a client, and the bonus being shared between members of the team. The issue of the internal equity of this sharing of the bonus we shall return to in the section on rewards. In the other companies, objectives were a mix of individual and team targets.

Performance evaluation

The use of appraisal as a developmental tool, rather than merely one which audits performance, was a feature of these organizations. The norm was for quarterly formal meetings between manager and employee, culminating in a full annual appraisal. Employee voice in the evaluation was strong, with the exception of Lloyds, where two-way communication has not traditionally been effective. Self-assessment exercises are strongly encouraged, in particular at Hewlett Packard and Glaxo Pharmaceuticals UK (at GP UK, workshops are run on the effective writing of self-assessments), and it is here that targets can be reassessed, and particular developmental needs identified in the light of changing circumstances. Firms in high-velocity environments need employees who are flexible and who have substantial discretion. Employees must be allowed to depart from established routines. In consequence, we found that managers devoted a great deal of time not only to discussing problems and identifying areas for improvement, but also to giving feedback. This occurred not only in formal meetings, but also on an ongoing basis, day-to-day in some cases. This informal process helped to cement new organizational values by correcting and reinforcing behaviours and attitudes. The focus on line managers providing feedback to employees was enshrined in the values statements made by the companies. A problem identified in all the companies, however, was the reluctance by managers to give bad news to employees. For example, at Lloyds Bank UK Retail Banking, 'the appraiser is not sufficiently honest and will always take the short cut. There is also a huge defence mechanism about it. All geese are swans' (senior manager). At Glaxo Pharmaceuticals UK, 'managers want to avoid conflict. Managers do not want to give bad messages to employees' (line manager).

The four organizations had de-linked the appraisal process from the discussion about salary, due to concerns over the appraisal becoming a forum to talk up one's salary: 'we have sought to de-link money rewards from appraisal. The appraisal process is to be a development process' (Lloyds Bank UK Retail Banking HR manager).

Because of the move towards team-based working, and because patterns of work and interaction are changing constantly, immediate managers were not considered to be the sole best judges of how employees were performing. The firms had introduced greater socially based measures of evaluation, including peer assessment and 360-degree appraisal, so that multiple sources of evaluation could give a rounded picture of employee performance.

The use of competency-based frameworks gave some structure to the fast-changing nature of the work setting. They were also felt to have a strong positive effect on communication between manager and employee: 'I think the competencies help to enhance the debate between bosses and staff' (Glaxo Pharmaceuticals UK line manager).

The focus on competencies has also helped to redress the imbalance of quantitative measures of performance at the expense of 'softer' measures. The rules of the game data, however, reveal that there were variations in emphasis between managers over which performance criteria would be given priority. Usually, meeting financial targets and budgetary requirements were high-lighted as the chief goal, with softer values eschewed if the pressure of dead-lines was strong. This is a symptom of the short-termism which all the Leading Edge companies shared. In Glaxo Pharmaceuticals UK, for example, it was revealed by the rules of the game data that there is a 'focus on tangible outputs and there is limited incentive to focus on intangibles—for example, the man-agement of people'.

Networking activity was characteristic of employees, not only to secure ap-pointments to strong projects but also to ensure that persons having an input into an individual's evaluation had good information about them and could see them in their best light. This was particularly apparent in Glaxo Pharmaceuti-cals UK, where the company had dispensed with the traditional appraisal form. Glaxo Pharmaceuticals UK, in common with the other three companies, has experienced problems with the level of bureaucracy the evaluation process generates. Resource constraints in these lean firms means that the time avail-able to review employees formally is limited. Glaxo Pharmaceuticals UK's solu-tion has been to eliminate the appraisal form and to encourage employees to gather a portfolio of evidence to show how they are meeting requirements vis-à-vis their goals and competency development. Details from project lead-ers, clients, customers, and subordinates are collected and used to present a picture of activity and level of performance and achievement.

Rewards

In these organizations, a premium is placed on employees who can demon-strate flexibility and who can operate with substantial discretion. The use of quality systems, in particular continuous improvement, at each of the com-panies makes strong demands on employee skills and requires that employees be creative in finding better ways of working (Snell and Dean 1992). In order to motivate and retain these employees, the reward systems of the companies have been structured to ensure that the distinctions between excellent and average performance are recognized and compensated.

In order to recruit and retain such employees, the organizations have placed considerable focus on external equity. Levels of pay were tied to external com-parisons with competitors using data widely shared through pay surveys. How-ever, though the firms aimed to be in the upper quartile in terms of overall rewards, they were not the highest payers in their respective industries; there were frequent mentions of headhunters approaching managers, offering jobs at competitors with greatly increased salaries. Key staff were retained by payment 'being in the same ballpark as major rivals', but also by such factors as other parts of the company offering career opportunities, training, and the reputation of the firms concerned.

In all the companies, the basic framework of pay was consistent across the business unit, but pay rates differed between employee groups due to the focus on the external market and differences in skill levels. The satisfaction with external equity was high. But it was bought at a price: in some cases concerns over *internal* equity were prominent. A clear example was at Citibank, where bonuses awarded to traders were viewed as internally inequitable by relationship managers, when the bonuses were derived from the outcome of team effort: 'There is a common personnel system but it results in very different pay rates. Traders get six to ten times greater salaries than groups who look after clients . . . therefore an atomized organization results. These businesses are interdependent. Therefore to treat them separately is a strange Achilles' heel' (senior manager).

The issue of separating out individual contributions to team effort was one which the companies have long wrestled with; the solution in all cases was the introduction of 360-degree appraisal. Nevertheless, the linkage of performance to pay—individual equity—was problematic in all four organizations. Because of the complexity of the internal situation, and the degree of interaction between employees through cross-functional team working, employees had difficulty in determining how their performance was factored into pay decisions. At Hewlett Packard, for example, the ranking system was criticized by employees for being opaque and for generating the suspicion that individual performance differences were being flattened into a forced distribution.

The perceived lack of differentiation in the performance evaluation, allied to concerns over pay distribution, also brought problems with internal equity. This was exacerbated by the focus on the external market as a determinant of pay, as in the example of Citibank cited earlier. A further illustration was at Lloyds Bank UK Retail Banking, where the continued use of national pay scales 'doesn't reflect regional differences and makes some people better paid than others' (senior manager). At Glaxo Pharmaceuticals UK, broad banding has been introduced as an attempt to make some progress with internal equity.

Training and development

The performance evaluation process was used primarily as a means of identifying an employee's training and development needs. There was a strong investment in training in the companies and the formal programmes were well received by employees, both in terms of satisfaction and also in terms of supplying the means to do their job well. The reputation of the quality of training in the firms also played a role in recruiting and retaining key staff. This was underlined by the corporate rhetoric: for example, at Hewlett Packard training and development was described as 'our number one priority', while at Citibank training was said to be 'the future of the company'.

Interestingly, however, the provision of formal training programmes was now accorded less priority in times of high-velocity change. The menu-style approach to training reflected a rather static view of employee and organizational needs, one which is now supplemented by a greater emphasis on personal development and learning as staff seek to cope with a rapidly shifting environment. At Lloyds Bank UK Retail Banking there were Open Learning Centres, and at Glaxo Pharmaceuticals UK development centres and creativity workshops were introduced to increase the level of innovation within the organization.

Coaching and counselling were being used significantly in the organizations. In Glaxo Pharmaceuticals UK, a mentor was assigned to each business department team, while at Hewlett Packard, structured counselling activity is now in place. Self-development workshops at Glaxo Pharmaceuticals UK and Hewlett Packard underlined these commitments. The learning process in these organizations was further enhanced by the increasing use of secondments to encourage personal development and organizational integration. At Lloyds Bank UK Retail Banking there was a shift towards these practices: 'we need to develop more on the coaching side. We have had highly structured programmes but coaching as a concept is in its infancy' (HR staff). At Citibank, 'we are pretty good at development. It comes down to an individual's ability and appetite . . . We try to give people support and the right opportunity . . . we encourage them to develop themselves.'

Development is seen as the responsibility of the line, not the HR function. Managers in the four organizations have personal development plans linked to the competency frameworks, and with the focus in each company on enhancing customer service and retaining key clients, there is a trend towards development in-role, rather than encouraging job hopping to gain skills.

DISCUSSION

This study has examined the performance management processes in four organizations operating in high velocity conditions. The objectives of the formal performance management systems in the four organizations, and their design, were largely similar. Despite differences in organizational context and sector, performance management was being used to provide vertical linkage between corporate and business objectives and employee goal setting and evaluation, and to provide horizontal integration—the fit between goals, evaluation, and the outcomes on development and pay. A list of performance management practices common to these firms is given in Tables 3.1–3.4 and is summarized

Table 3.1. Performance management practices: Citibank

	Former PMS elements	New PMS elements
Goal setting	Participative, revenue driven, moderate revocability; individual and team targets	Participative, competency driven—balanced scorecard, high revocability
Performance evaluation	Formal appraisal, bureaucratic—output driven, manager input only; participative; strong informal feedback	Talent inventory—behaviour and output driven; 360-degree assessment; strong informal process remains
Rewards	High external equity; decentralized pay decisions—allows flexibility on local pay; concerns over internal and individual equity	Rewards based on balanced scorecard; concerns remain over internal and individual equity
Training and development	Strong formal programmes; on-the-job training prominent	Formal programmes supplemented by mentoring and coaching; focus on self-development and learning

Note: Data collected 1994.

below. Through inductive reasoning, we have found several factors which appear to facilitate the use of performance management as an instrument of control and motivation. These can be grouped under three headings: structural, managerial, and procedural.

Overview of performance management practices

Goal setting

A major common feature is the intention not to crystallize performance management goals. Goals are set participatively and managers are given a considerable degree of discretion to revise targets in the light of changing environmental conditions. Because performance measures on outputs are no longer appropriate in light of the difficulty of setting realistic goals, they have been supplemented by the introduction of competency frameworks, which attempt to define behavioural goals centred on the strategic aims and

Table 3.2. Performance management practices: Glaxo Pharmaceuticals UK

	Former PMS elements	New PMS elements
Goal setting	Top-down, driven by sales targets; little revisability; no team targets	Participative, competency-based; moderate revisability; individual and team targets
Performance evaluation	Combined both development and pay reviews; manager input; little employee voice, little feedback	Split development and pay review; increased employee voice; 360-degree appraisal; traditional appraisal forms removed in favour of 'portfolio'
Rewards	External equity high; poor differentiation between good and bad performers	External equity remains high; broad banding introduced; individual and team-based rewards
Training and development	Menu-based training; paternalism encouraged view of development as responsibility of the company	Development now seen as primarily responsibility of the individual; creativity workshops, development centres, increased coaching and counselling

Note: Data collected 1993.

values of the organization. Behaviour is not tightly controlled through these competencies; they have enough flex to allow for creativity and innovation, these virtues being central competencies themselves. Further, in all of the organizations there has been increased teamwork activity, and goal setting has reflected this.

Performance evaluation

Given the interdependent nature of many of the jobs, appraisal as a formal process is conducted through multiple perspectives, typically 360 degree, so that the full scope of an employee's work can be judged. Just as important is the reliance on informal feedback processes to maintain monitoring and motivation as employees encounter new situations and problems. The performance review has been split from the pay review in all cases, which has brought greater openness in the appraisal, though the link of performance to pay remains a major concern among employees.

Table 3.3. Performance management practices: Hewlett Packard

	Former PMS elements	New PMS elements
Goal setting	Management by objectives; clear output targets, few behavioural restraints; moderate participation, moderate revisability	MBO remains; individual and team targets set; high participation, increasing revisability; short-term targets dominate
Performance evaluation	Assessed against 'Hoshin' and business fundamentals—hard and soft targets; formal performance evaluations linked to relative ranking system; constant informal appraisal; multiple inputs to evaluations; strong employee voice	Basic approaches remain the same; ranking system reassessed in light of perceived unfairness but remains in place
Rewards	External equity high; internal and individual equity problematic; individual and team rewards	External equity slipping; single status under pressure from continuing internal equity problems
Training and development	Menu-based training; personal development plans	Move to internal consultancy model; function working as 'business partner'; still has mandatory programmes, but more emphasis on consultancy and tailored development plans; coaching and counselling increasing; 'lifelong learning'

Note: Data collected 1994.

Rewards

Rewards have encompassed the introduction of team-based working, but team incentives have not replaced individual incentives, rather they have complemented them. There is a strong focus on external equity as the primary lever for recruiting and retaining staff. From being largely centralized, reward management has been decentralized down to the business unit level and managers have a fair degree of discretion over the distribution of rewards, working within a broad overall framework, which has increased flexibility and accountability.

Table 3.4. Performance management practices: Lloyds Bank UK Retail Banking

	Former PMS elements	New PMS elements
Goal setting	Top-down, revenue driven, no revisability; often unattainable; individual goals only	Increased participation, competency framework introduced; some revisability; individual and team goals
Performance evaluation	Combined both development and pay discussions; little employee voice; manager input only; little informal feedback; no self-appraisal	Split development and pay reviews; increased employee voice; self-appraisal introduced; managers encouraged to give greater feedback
Rewards	High external equity but low internal and individual equity; pay not decentralized— managers with little flexibility to adjust pay to changing market conditions	Introduction of variable matrix to give greater flexibility in pay determination; move to regional pay mooted
Training and development	Emphasis on traditional banking training—traditional menu-based approach	Emphasis on sales and marketing training; more tailored training programmes; personal development plans introduced; increased use of coaching and counselling techniques

Note: Data collected 1994.

However, concerns remain about both internal and individual equity. Glaxo Pharmaceuticals UK has opted for a radical solution—broad banding—but pay remains the problem area in terms of linkage to other performance management interventions.

Training and development

Formal programmes have been supplemented by the increased use of coaching and counselling in order to promote self-development. With the flattening of the organizations, there is less of a focus on development seen as a series of jobs moving up the organization over time; rather, development in-role is viewed as desirable, and secondments and mentoring have helped this process.

Responsibility for development rests with the individual and the line, rather than with HR staff.

Factors which influence the use of performance management

Structural

An important factor concerning the implementation of performance management processes is the degree of change the organization is undergoing and the experience of change the organization has had. At Hewlett Packard, operating in the computer business for twenty-five years has given the firm a long history of change management and a decentralized management style, which has resulted in a flexible performance management system, able to cope with changing circumstances. With this continuity and consistency, the expectations of employees remain relatively stable. The enduring culture, exemplified by the HP Way, also provides continuity in terms of values which in turn reinforce desired behaviours. For the other three firms, adjustment to rapid and constant change is a more recent phenomenon. For Lloyds Bank UK Retail Banking and Citibank, similar external factors have impinged upon their operations. At Lloyds Bank UK Retail Banking, however, a paternalistic, top-down imposed performance process, highly centralized and with no clear linkages between key interventions, together with an appraisal process which emphasized pay at the expense of development and a reward process which failed to address either internal or individual equity, had to be overhauled, bringing with it trauma and pain as the old values of the bank were replaced. At Citibank, the situation was not so stark. A long history of individual responsibility and participative objective setting meant that the large-scale restructuring and additional changes within the organization that took place from the late 1980s onwards formed the basis for a performance management system which only needed retuning rather than overhauling. Glaxo Pharmaceuticals UK, too, underwent a cultural transformation in 1989, but has since gone through numerous changes so that the personnel director now described transformation as a 'core competence'. Again, paternalism has been shed and the devolution of responsibility and commitment to innovation have been largely embedded.

Managerial

The administration of the performance management process is complex. Managers have many demands on their time and so their attention must be rationed (Cyert and March 1963; Simons 1995). For performance management to work, there must be sufficient attention paid to key processes by line managers.

In the firms studied, this attention was manifested not only in carrying out the various formal requirements, but also in undertaking the various informal activities which helped to increase employees' perceptions of fairness and their credibility in the process. Prominent in this regard was ongoing appraisal, coaching and counselling, and mentoring.

However, managers were constrained by the short-termism of the companies, a theme we return to in Chapter 7. This has led in some cases to managers and employees concentrating on narrowly prescribed tasks, making commitment to teamwork problematic. The bureaucracy of the performance management process was also a concern for managers, taking as it did a considerable amount of their time in an already pressured schedule.

Procedural

There was clear corporate rhetoric to the effect that providing feedback on performance was a major managerial goal. Transparency of the performance management system was an intention which, with varying degrees of emphasis, was stated by the firms. This feedback is important in high-velocity environments because not only does it provide more opportunities for managers and employees to discuss performance, so increasing the evidence on which managers can draw for the formal appraisal, but it also allows managers to see whether targets set at the beginning of the year were realistic and attainable, and whether they continue to be so as the year progresses. Regular and frequent feedback can increase perceptions of appraisal fairness and accuracy and reduce bias in performance ratings (Longenecker *et al.* 1987). In these firms, input into the evaluation process was also encouraged, with employees asked to provide their own assessment by conducting self-appraisals. This input, and the ability to discuss the manager's assessment in the review, provided for strong two-way communication in the appraisal process.

The antagonism between creativity and efficiency within organizations (Khandwalla 1973) finds its clearest expression in high-velocity organizations. Because of the uncertainty surrounding environmental conditions, the case companies did not concentrate exclusively on one type of control. Elements of behavioural, output, and skill-based monitoring were implemented together, supporting the findings of Snell (1992), who argued that, with shifting dynamics in the work environment, each control approach serves a different purpose. The major theme of this chapter has been that control becomes problematic when firms experience high-velocity conditions, because it is difficult to set and assess individual contributions to performance. The major conclusion of this chapter is that as organizations operate in increasingly fast-changing environments, their reliance on bureaucratic, formal systems as a basis for human resource management gives way to an emphasis on informal, social mechanisms, which allow for flexibility, revisability, and a greater voice for employees. The interpersonal context within which performance management takes place is therefore crucial for its effectiveness (Nathan *et al.* 1991). Such a shift places a strong emphasis on managerial commitment to the evaluation and development of colleagues and subordinates and demands of employees a tolerance of ambiguity which can be both daunting and challenging.

The Rhetoric and Reality of 'New Careers'

LYNDA GRATTON AND VERONICA HOPE HAILEY

In our discussions with employees and HR teams it quickly became apparent that they were experiencing profound changes in career expectations and career plans. These profound changes were greeted with enthusiasm by some, and with deep anxiety and distrust by others. But whatever the response, one thing was clear: these fundamental changes in careers were touching every member of the organization. In this chapter we explore the rhetoric around these new careers and then compare this rhetoric with the reality of employee and managerial experience. We will argue that whilst these broad changes in careers may be understood at a policy level, the companies are struggling with the challenge of implementing processes and practices which can support a move towards a more individualistic notion of careers.

In all the companies we studied we noted fundamental shifts in structures, cost bases, and labour markets. Many of these shifts have a profound impact on career expectations and paths. We observed four shifts in particular which are fundamental for the careers of employees. First, we observed a shift from vertical functional structures to networks comprising horizontal, cross-functional teams and decentralized business units. For example, at Glaxo Pharmaceuticals UK the creation of cross-functional teams driving projects from research to development, to marketing and sales has destroyed the supremacy of the previously frequently trodden vertical career paths. Second, a shift from multiple layers of management to fewer team-based structures was observed in all the companies. For example, at BT Payphones the downsizing associated with the introduction of team-based structures has increased the pressure on managers and destroyed many of the assistant roles which were previously key development positions and transitional roles. Third, the impact of changes in the cost base has required the reduction of costs through flexible contracts, outsourcing, and the establishment of core and periphery work groups. One outcome of this flexibility has been that none of the organizations we studied were committed to lifetime employment, instead emphasizing flexibility and the employment of particular skills as and when they are needed. Finally, the

Table 4.1. Shifts in the career paradigm

From	To	Impact
Vertical functions	Networks, horizontal working	Destroyed the well-established vertical careers
Multiple management layers	Fewer, team-based structures	Loss of 'assistant' roles
Strong core	Outsourcing, periphery workers	Change in the nature of the employment contract
Technical focus	Customer focus	Focus on customer and interpersonal competencies

profound shift in the competency base of Western economies was reflected in our sample. The effect of globalization in shifting companies from manufacturing to service or knowledge-based economies (Drucker 1993) had resulted in these firms competing on quality, customer focus, and core knowledge bases. For example, at Lloyds Bank UK Retail Banking the new competitive strategy demanded a workforce which had strong interpersonal skills and was capable of operating successfully in cross-functional teams, and a management cadre whose competencies encompassed sophisticated interpersonal skills, project management, and networking—a skill base which was profoundly different from the strong emphasis previously placed on process and technical skill.

THE THEMES OF THE NEW CAREER

Against the background of this profound change in the structural reality of external and internal labour markets, a fresh orthodoxy had developed in these companies around the notion of 'new careers'. The rhetoric of the 'new career' embraced a wide variety of assumptions and conditions underpinning the informal career bargain or implicit contract. Underlying this rhetoric were assumptions about the enabling 'new career' architecture, the perceptions of individual employees, and the role of line management. These three themes are explored in more detail below and are shown in Fig. 4.1.

Theme 1: architectures enabling the 'new career'

The cornerstone of the new career is that individuals may not be guaranteed a job for life, but that the company will offer a contract of 'employability'. The

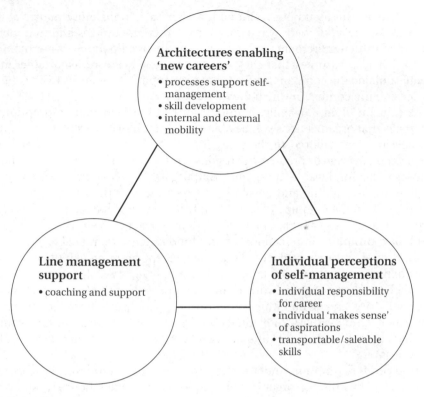

Architectures enabling 'new careers'
• processes support self-management
• skill development
• internal and external mobility

Line management support
• coaching and support

Individual perceptions of self-management
• individual responsibility for career
• individual 'makes sense' of aspirations
• transportable/saleable skills

Fig. 4.1. The new career

realization of this employability contract depends in part on a supporting architecture of processes and policies. These include processes which support self-management, the investment in employees' skill development to enhance their employability outside the company when their skills are no longer required, and the provision of an active internal job market capable of providing information about the organization as an opportunity structure. These initiatives are critical in realigning careers from a vertical to a horizontal pattern, and creating internal job mobility and a series of targeted training experiences to ensure opportunity for employability. Waterman *et al.* (1994) offer practical examples of career resilience programmes which they say should contain two essential ingredients: first, a system that helps employees regularly identify their skills, interests, values, and temperaments, and second, a system that enables employees to 'benchmark their skills on a regular basis'. They also stress the obligation of the company to maintain a dialogue about prospects, to help with exploring job opportunities, and to show a commitment to lifelong learning.

From the perspective of the individual employee, the policy of new careers implies, or assumes, that the focus of career development responsibility will shift to the individual through the transition from paternalism to individualism. This assumes that individuals have a responsibility, and an ability, to 'make sense' of their own aspirations and competencies and to understand the future requirements of organizations and occupations (Waterman *et al.* 1994). It also assumes that they have skills which are transportable and saleable outside the company, and are not so company-specific as to be valueless outside the context in which they were gained.

The concept of employability is underpinned by two further assumptions. The first is that organizations will be able to offer employees access to training and development tailored to their individual needs. This assumes that employees can envisage or predict which skills it is appropriate for them to obtain in order to be employable; it assumes that organizations will give employees equal access to training and development regardless of their long-term perceived worth to the organization; and finally, it assumes that all organizations have the resources available to provide this investment. Again these changes could have profound implications on the fundamental relationship between the individual and the employee. Thus the concept of employability changes the notion of employee worth. In the past an employee's worth may have been considered in terms of hours worked (throughput) or length of service (longevity or seniority); now the emphasis is on actual output. However, under a contract of employability individuals will be valued by their accumulated learning and skill rather than the actual job they perform at any given time (Mayo 1995).

The second assumption underpinning the concept of employability is that mobility, both within the organization and in the external labour market, can occur. The notion of mobility underpins self-management and employability, since without mobility the other two are rendered redundant. An extreme view of mobility is offered by Peters (1992), in which corporations are seen as merely project groups with their members only assuming an interest in any particular organization for as long as this coincides with their own individualistic aims. According to his description of this new form of employment relationship, 'a corporation is simply one way in which we achieve our projects. Stated somewhat differently, persons are only passing through corporations on their way to their respective ends . . . Corporations can be thought of as sets of agreements among members to achieve their projects.'

Theme 2: individual perceptions of self-management

Underpinning the 'new careers' architecture is the notion that individuals, rather than the organization, are expected to take primary responsibility for their career development.

Within the career literature there has been much discussion about the profound change in the psychological contract, from relational contracts to transactional contracts in conceptual terms, and from paternalistic contracts to individualistic relationships (MacNeill 1985; Robinson and Rousseau 1994).

Relational contracts occur where the development of company-specific skills is traded for long-term career development, training and development, and job security. Thus relational contracts are characterized by high degrees of mutual interdependence. In contrast, transactional contracts are characterized by short-term tenures and a narrow emphasis on financial exchange, in terms of both performance output by the employee and the financial reward given in exchange by the employer (Rousseau 1996).

In examining these companies we looked at a number of aspects of the employees' changing perceptions of the self-management of careers. The purely conceptual perspective from the literature suggests that the change from transactional to relational contracts has already occurred in organizations, and that the transition is unproblematic. We wanted in particular to examine whether there are individual or organizational differences. As Guest and Mackenzie (1996) have noted from their research, the personal capability of self-management can take a considerable time to develop amongst employees, depending upon where their starting point is for the transition. At an organizational level it would be oversimplistic to assume that the self-management of careers is relevant to all organizations regardless of their different contexts, products, and market places, or that it is applicable to all groups of employees regardless of their value, level, or contractual arrangements. As Guest and Mackenzie's research suggests, there is scope for a diversity of approaches to careers depending on specific contextual factors. Herriot and Pemberton (1995) hypothesize that, at the individual level, there will be three different groups of workers (core, contractor, and part-timer) which will each have different forms of career management. Therefore this shift along the psychological continuum may be better targeted towards specific types of organizations and groups of employees, and may not be universally applicable. In particular, existing research has suggested that formal career paths are unlikely to be dismantled for fast-track or high-potential employees (Guest and Mackenzie 1996; Herriot 1995).

Implicit within this shift along the continuum of the psychological contract is a simultaneous shift in the form of employee consent and commitment. In the 1980s commentators believed it was possible to elicit 'affective' or 'emotional' commitment from employees to an organization's aims, objectives, and indeed cultural values. This form of commitment, exchanged for the promise of job security, was in return for unquestioned loyalty—a form of relational contract. As a consequence it has been argued that the shift to transactional contracts implies a shift away from emotional or affective loyalty to more of an instrumental or 'calculative' commitment (Salancik 1977; Willmott 1993). This is a form of consent where an employee assesses the likely benefits to be accrued and delivers degrees of commitment based upon that calculation. In some contexts employee consent may be reduced to a form of mere compliance with rules and regulations, and in extreme cases of downsizing a form of alienation from the company's aims and objectives may be experienced (Etzioni 1975; Hope 1993; Penley and Gould 1988).

The shift along the contractual continuum may then result in reduced commitment from employees to the employing organization. This in itself may not be a problem so long as employers are aware that pushing responsibility for careers to their staff may shift either the nature or the degree of effort that employees are willing to exert on behalf of their current employer. This may well have profound implications for business performance. This breaking of the psychological contract can meet with a range of immediate responses, from 'get safe' (where employees feel powerless and therefore 'fulfil instructions to the letter' but take no risks for fear of redundancy) to 'get out', either immediately or when the financial inducement is right, or 'get even', where employees reduce their contribution to the corporation covertly in order to 'even up' the balance for what they see as employers reneging on promises made in the past. As Herriot notes (1995), these reactions are hardly likely to induce greater team working, innovation, or entrepreneurship within organizations. However, it also highlights the simple fact that there will be a range of attitudinal responses (Sparrow 1996).

Theme 3: line management support

The third assumption is that key players in organizations, particularly line managers, will provide active support for the concept of the new career. Line managers are critical players in implementing new initiatives and generating new behaviours and attitudes (Ulrich 1997). However, often short-term business demands prevent them from devoting time to longer-term developmental issues such as career counselling.

It is in this aspect of 'new career' architecture that we would expect to see differences between companies, particularly in the extent to which companies have installed practices and initiatives that support the rhetoric of the new careers. This will be contingent upon their existing competence and capability in HR or personnel management policies and systems in general. For instance, it may be more difficult for companies to engender the self-analysis of personal development needs when their employees are only accustomed to a rudimentary form of appraisal. In comparison, a company which perhaps practises 360-degree appraisal or upward feedback may have an existing architecture that can be adapted more easily to the needs of the new careers.

Likewise, the HR or people management capability of line managers will vary between companies. The rhetoric of new careers places responsibility for career counselling on the shoulders of line managers. They may be willing to take responsibility for this, but they may not have either the time, the information, or the interpersonal skills to complete such a task.

Nicholson has criticized the rhetoric of moving responsibility to line managers. He questions the utility of line managers' 'reliance on initiative and informal knowledge of appropriate career opportunities in other parts of the organization' (1996). He also highlights the potential contribution that information systems could make in 'new organizations'.

THE COMPANY EXPERIENCE

Theme 1: architectures enabling the 'new career'

During the data collection period we surveyed employees regarding the reality of careers in their company, we interviewed a cross-section of people about their career experiences and attitudes, and we spoke to the HR function in each company about their policies for career development and the challenges they faced. In assessing the enabling 'new career' architectures we asked three questions: are there career processes in place which support the notion of employability and the new career, is skill development available, and is there an open internal and external labour market which encourages mobility? In this section we will examine these three topics.

We considered the processes and resources that each company provided to support the concept of the 'new career'. These key supporting processes are presented in Table 4.2, which highlights the 'new career' architecture for each of the eight companies. We expected to find a range of practical initiatives in companies that supported the concepts and rhetoric of the new career, in particular a portfolio of formal initiatives to support employability, access to training and development, and a well-functioning internal and external labour market facilitating job mobility.

In terms of supporting process architecture, Citibank and Hewlett Packard displayed the greatest raft of initiatives to support the 'new career'. These companies had introduced personal development planning, career workshops, lifelong learning programmes, and established relatively open internal job markets. Citibank was also using information systems to facilitate cross-business and cross-national mobility with their Pan-European Notice Board. For the other companies the move from vertical to horizontal, from paternalism to individualism, was proving more difficult. Some had introduced key processes which they believed would act as levers for change. For example, Lloyds Bank UK Retail Banking had introduced Open Learning Centres and had started to use individual development plans. However, these practical initiatives only seemed to have an impact when line managers took responsibility for the career development of their teams and, as we discuss later, this support was not always present.

At the core of the concept of employability is the commitment to training people in skills which are marketable both across and outside the organization. At a policy level the importance of this activity is generally recognized, with many company policy documents referring to the central role played by

Table 4.2. Theme 1: architectures enabling the 'new career'

	Policy	Enabling architecture
BT Payphones	'Move away from traditional approach—want a flexible career plan that offers more than fixed permanent jobs in which promotion is the only route for progression.'	No formal plan, but is touched upon in development plan
C&W NHS Trust	'Careful monitoring of career paths in order to identify areas where inequality of opportunity exists. We will develop a mentoring scheme.'	No direct career management by HR; professional groups responsible for career development
Citibank	'Aims to provide support and assistance to enable staff to take the initiative in managing their own careers.'	Pan-European Notice Board; Euro Training Centre—technical; mentoring scheme
GP UK	'It is intended that both company and individual will take a flexible approach to skills and knowledge development as an integral part of career management.'	Management audit each year describes individuals who are capable of getting to the management grades; Open Learning Centre; 'managers as coaches' training programme; on-the-job training
HP	'People have responsibility for their own career evaluation every year.'	Career development linked to development plan: informal, ad hoc, and self-managed; networking reinforced in internal job posting process; self-development workshops; Lifelong Learning Programme; training for induction and management development

Table 4.2. *Continued*

	Policy	Enabling architecture
KJS	'We believe in helping staff establish and achieve career goals; joint responsibility of manager and employee; career development may mean jobs at a similar level.'	MAP review has career development discussion; GOLD process contains succession planning process; policy of backstopping key roles; European moves supported by process
Lloyds	'Each business unit should have career management processes.'	Open Learning Centres; Corporate Management Resource database; assistant manager development assessment; managerial performance assessment; regional programmes
WHS News	'We aim to ensure a consistently high standard of management development is available when the need arises.'	Formal plan from middle management; below middle management much depends on regional managers; on-the-road packages

Note: Data for this table, and all following tables in this chapter, collected 1993–5.

training. In many of these companies significant investment had been made in training, with the highest training investment in Glaxo Pharmaceuticals UK and Hewlett Packard. As Table 4.3 shows, satisfaction with training, although not universally high, is certainly higher than satisfaction with career management (compare Table 4.4).

As the earlier description of enabling architectures shows, there was a real focus on training initiatives in most companies. The Lifelong Learning Programmes and self-development workshops at Hewlett Packard were very well received; Lloyds Bank UK Retail Banking had introduced Open Learning Centres and was actively using assessment centres to create individual personal development plans at the assistant manager level. In Kraft Jacobs Suchard the training and development department was regarded as one of the successes of the human resource function, and there were also very positive views of training at Glaxo Pharmaceuticals UK and Citibank. Nevertheless, the aspirations of the training processes were not always met by operational reality.

I became a manager two years ago and I did my first development report two years ago, and you're given no guidance whatsoever in how to do this. (line manager, Lloyds Bank UK Retail Banking)

My experience is not very good. When I first came to the company I had two to three hours with the line manager and after that I was left. I am not aware whether personnel knows we are not getting the training. (employee, Kraft Jacobs Suchard)

During the interviews some people expressed the belief that despite the good intentions regarding accessibility to training expressed at senior levels, ultimately accessibility was determined by the line managers' budgets and their choice of how the money was spent.

The focus and budget is given to building job-related skills. But what of creating portable skills which could enhance the employability of individuals outside the immediate work environment? We found that some organizations were more encouraging than others. At Hewlett Packard, for example, many of the people we interviewed acknowledged the need to create portable skills. This involved activities beyond the immediate job brief, resulting in the phenomenon of the 'evening job' where 'you get yourself involved in extramural activities such as task groups' (employee, Hewlett Packard) in order to gain visibility in career terms and broaden one's skill base. Glaxo Pharmaceuticals UK had also instituted project groups and staff were aware that these could be used as vehicles for gaining skills and breadth of experience beyond one's immediate job. The concept of portable skills was also well developed within the professional groups in the NHS trust hospital: 'I think there's a lot of encouragement because we all believe that the people we develop will bring expertise into the organization' (employee, Chelsea & Westminster Healthcare Trust). Furthermore, the risk of losing the organization's investment in training and development was discounted because of the commitment felt to professional development:

Table 4.3. Theme 1: architectures enabling the 'new career' (%)

	BT Payphones	C&W NHS Trust	Citibank	GP UK	HP	KJS	Lloyds	WHS News
Days spent on formal training courses this year:								
1 to 10 days	56	51	55	72	75	57	59	41
11 days and above	14	23	4	19	11	9	11	4
'I agree/strongly agree that I do not have the opportunities I want to be promoted.'	62	39	33	32	33	47	52	35
How satisfied are you with the training you have received?								
Satisfied/very satisfied	66	51	49	75	66	63	67	51
Dissatisfied/very dissatisfied	16	29	21	7	12	17	19	26
Activities that have played a significant/very significant role in career development:								
Secondments/moves abroad	3	3	18	5	9	5	3	4
Secondment to special projects/teams	27	28	22	24	26	17	16	22
Secondments/move to another part of the organization/function	25	17	29	32	26	22	34	24
'This organization does not encourage me to develop new skills.' (disagree/strongly disagree)	31	46	49	71[a]	69	63	37	43

[a] The question used at GP UK (the pilot study) was reversed, i.e. the statement was positive. The percentages given represent those agreeing with the statement. There is the possibility that this led to a higher score for GP UK.

In departmental and speciality terms staff moving hospitals is a disaster, but in personal terms for the candidate it's a great success. At the end of the day I would still put the personal, professional development ahead of the organizational benefit. (medical doctor, Chelsea & Westminster Healthcare Trust)

Mobility underpins self-management and employability. Without mobility the other two are rendered redundant. In this study the primary focus of interest was the provision of internal company mobility, through horizontal development, project work, and cross-country moves rather than through external mobility. We found that although people may have the skills they need, many do not have the opportunity to broaden these skills through wider job experience or mobility. Both the questionnaires and interviews showed that many people were not mobile and felt deeply frustrated by this. The survey data presented in Table 4.3 show that cross-functional and cross-county moves through project work, secondments, or moves abroad played a relatively insignificant role in development.

It became clear that whilst there may be an intention to use mobility to create the 'new career', downsizing, re-engineering, and cost-cutting programmes had all created barriers to internal mobility. This was particularly apparent in BT Payphones and Lloyds Bank UK Retail Banking, where structural changes had profoundly influenced the internal opportunity system. The interview quotes which follow express a common pessimism about lateral job movement.

It's virtually impossible to transfer. (line manager, BT Payphones)

We're losing out an awful lot because we haven't got the ability to exchange people with branches in the same grade. (line manager, Lloyds Bank UK Retail Banking)

There is nowhere to go. Self-motivation is an HP word, but it is difficult to divert into another area even if you are self-motivated. (line manager, Hewlett Packard)

In part these views reflect the reality of organizational life in downsized companies. Job opportunities appear to be limited and middle managers who seem under pressure to perform are loath to lose high-performing staff to other functions. However, these comments also reflect the inadequacy of information systems in creating and maintaining up-to-date and accessible information about job and project opportunities. In addition our interviews revealed that line managers in many of the sample companies seemed unclear of the opportunities beyond their units or the career route that an individual should take.

However, at Citibank, Hewlett Packard, Glaxo Pharmaceuticals UK, and Kraft Jacobs Suchard we saw some processes which had been created to support employability by creating within-company mobility. Citibank had achieved a relatively high level of international mobility through implementing a Pan-European Notice Board which enabled staff to apply for vacancies across the organization. Likewise, Kraft Jacobs Suchard's formal succession planning meetings held in each business unit enabled people to move horizontally. The concept of employability through job breadth is summarized in the following remark:

To get on you need general experience of all aspects of the business. The ones who are getting on are the ones who move backwards and forwards across the business for about five years, before having a meteoric rise through the organization. (operating core employee, Kraft Jacobs Suchard)

Theme 2: individual perceptions of self-management

A sign of the full integration of the concept of self-management is that individuals believe that they, rather than the organization, take primary responsibility for their careers. As the policy statements presented in Table 4.2 show, the rhetoric of self-managed careers was fundamental to the policy of all these companies. The message is clear at a policy level: people are expected to take responsibility for managing their own careers. However, whilst the rhetoric is clear, the reality is far more complex. Across the companies we found clear and profound differences in the attitudes of employees, with line managers and high-potential people most likely to embrace the concept of the 'new career'. From our interviews it became clear that perceptions of self-management were stronger at senior levels, and less well developed at operational levels. The rhetoric of individual responsibility had been accepted by many of the senior managers we interviewed in all eight business units. There was a firm managerial belief that employers' abandonment of responsibility for careers was the way that organizations should and would operate in the future. The strength of the message was such that in some organizations senior managers believed that it was staff who wanted responsibility for their own careers. This quote from a BT Payphones director captures the sentiment:

Our managers and professionals are already beginning to demand a move away from the traditional approach to career development. They want a flexible career plan.

Yet, whilst the rhetoric of self-management was accepted at senior levels, both the questionnaire and interview data revealed a rather different reality in the operating core. As the results presented in Table 4.4 indicate, there was deep dissatisfaction with career management in most of the companies, with a significant proportion of employees expressing dissatisfaction. The interview data told a similar story: for instance, in contrast to his senior manager, a member of the operating core from BT Payphones expressed frustration with his career management opportunities: 'I am waiting for promotion. My manager is responsible for giving me promotion but the process is stuck with Personnel.'

We also observed that in all the companies the rhetoric of the shift from paternalism to individualism had bypassed one core group: the high-potential cadre, those individuals perceived to have leadership potential. Whilst

Table 4.4. Theme 2: individual perceptions of self-management (%)

	BT Payphones	C&W NHS Trust	Citibank	GP UK	HP	KJS	Lloyds	WHS News
How satisfied are you with the way your career is managed?								
Satisfied/very satisfied	21	32	19	21	29	29	27	33
Dissatisfied/very dissatisfied	50	40	40	47	35	34	49	35
How satisfied are you with the development opportunities you have received?								
Satisfied/very satisfied	30	41	46	41	47	39	44	42
Dissatisfied/very dissatisfied	45	35	26	28	25	33	34	33

paternalism may have been dismantled, at the business unit level, as the primary career philosophy for the majority of the employees, for the high-potential cadre a paternalistic career contract remained. The corporate fast-track schemes at BT Payphones, Citibank, and Kraft Jacobs Suchard created career experiences for this core group which were significantly different from those of the majority of employees. The high-potential staff received more senior management interest and there was a strong commitment to manage and protect their careers. None of the companies with high-potential, fast-track schemes had any plans to dismantle these career paths and some, such as Hewlett Packard, were in the process of introducing them.

There were also differences in the ability of the companies to embrace the concepts of the 'new career' and move from rhetoric to reality. It was clear that some organizations were further ahead with this transition to self-management than others. For example, employees at Hewlett Packard and Citibank were generally more satisfied with their career opportunities, though some expressed a view we heard across the companies, that self-management was simply an abrogation of management responsibility:

Management copped out with 'It's your career—you manage it yourself.' They have probably made it too free-format. There is no guidance. (operating core employee, Hewlett Packard)

For Hewlett Packard, despite attempts to provide supporting career development options, the embracement of these new forms of career by individual employees was still limited. The situation in Citibank was particularly interesting. In our view the bank was further down the path of transition towards self-management, a result in part of the complex matrix nature of its structure and the historical emphasis on networking and mobility, which had created a culture suited to individual career responsibility. Yet still people questioned the wisdom of abandoning formal career structures:

I would argue that if you don't do development planning, you can probably make somewhere run well for two to three years, assuming everything else works, but you will then hit a brick wall. (line manager, Citibank)

Yet whilst Hewlett Packard and Citibank had gone some way to supporting the rhetoric of self-managed careers, in other companies, particularly BT Payphones and Lloyds Bank UK Retail Banking, the reality was quite distant from the rhetoric. As Table 4.4 shows, the highest levels of dissatisfaction with career management were found in BT Payphones and Lloyds Bank UK Retail Banking. We would argue that the heritage of these organizations makes shifting staff perceptions a harder task. At BT Payphones, the management was attempting to shift the employees from a civil service legacy of job security and promotion to a culture of individualism. At Lloyds Bank UK Retail Banking people had historically chosen to enter banking because they were attracted by the 'cradle to grave' security that banks appeared to offer at recruitment.

In the introduction to this chapter we discussed the impact on commitment of changes in the employment contract. We argued that the shift to an employability-based, transactional contract could have implications for the commitment of employees and the nature and degree of their effort. We asked a range of questions in the survey to assist us in understanding commitment, including questions concerning levels of loyalty, willingness to put in extra effort, propensity to stay with the organization, and levels of morale and trust. The results are presented in Table 4.5. In those companies which originally had highly paternalistic cultures, the dismantling of the old structures had a profound impact on employees. These interview quotes are representative of some widely held beliefs:

BT has failed to use my potential. If I had progressed, BT would have got more out of me. (operating core employee, BT Payphones)

It's very difficult to keep staff motivated. (manager, Lloyds Bank UK Retail Banking)

In W. H. Smith News there were clear signs of staff shifting to a more calculative form of commitment:

Career management is changing. In the past the company has been a secure employer which means that some people have put up with low wages for the security of the job. But we are no longer a secure employer. The company will have to pay better to retain good experienced people. (line manager, W. H. Smith News)

There were examples of the 'get safe' syndrome ('There were opportunities . . . but what is the use of moving? I am safe here,' said one employee at BT Payphones), but little evidence of the 'get even' or 'get out' reactions, a reflection perhaps of the hostile external labour market. In the corporations which had maintained relatively high levels of commitment we did find references to the 'burn-out' syndrome. This work intensification was a product of downsizing. People were not only working longer hours because there were fewer colleagues with whom to share the workload, but also because as individuals they were reluctant to refuse work in case they were perceived as unhelpful or incapable. This, they feared, could reduce their chances of continued employment, let alone 'employability': 'Some people are stressed, but mustn't show it' (operating core employee, Kraft Jacobs Suchard).

Therefore people were not necessarily uncommitted to their organization, nor highly dissatisfied with their career management, but they were anxious and insecure about their future:

There's a mass of insecurity. (employee, Citibank)

There's a lot of distrust and insecurity. (employee, Lloyds Bank UK Retail Banking)

There's no direction—I find that frustrating. (employee, Lloyds Bank UK Retail Banking)

Theme 3: line management support

It is envisaged in the 'new career' model that responsibility for careers will be devolved, for the majority of people, from a centralized human resource

Table 4.5. Impact on commitment (respondents agreeing or strongly agreeing with these statements, %)

	BT Payphones	C&W NHS Trust	Citibank	GP UK[a]	HP	KJS	Lloyds	WHS News
'I feel very little loyalty to this organization.'	25	15	18	—	14	22	26	17
'I am willing to put in a great deal of effort beyond that normally expected to help this organization succeed.'	76	77	90	—	92	85	75	83
'I would accept almost any type of job assignment in order to keep working for this organization.'	31	7	12	—	26	11	16	27
'It would take very little change to cause me to leave this organization.'	28	24	20	—	14	22	32	24
'Morale is high.'	1	17	22	11	43	20	3	18
'I do not have a great deal of trust in management'	53	37	31	20	19	26	49	27

[a] Some data not collected in GP UK (pilot) study.

function to line managers who engage in 'adult to adult' rather than 'parent to child' discussions about careers. Both the survey and the interview data showed the extent of differences across the companies in management involvement. We asked a number of questions in both the interviews and survey to gauge the extent of line management support and involvement in career planning. In the survey we asked respondents to assess the frequency of career discussions with their boss or personnel representative, and to identify whether having a mentor had played a significant role in their development. We also asked the managers we surveyed to comment on whether they were responsible for carrying out career planning for their subordinates.

Career discussions were most likely to be on the agenda at Kraft Jacobs Suchard and Glaxo Pharmaceuticals UK, and least likely to be on the agenda at Chelsea & Westminster Healthcare Trust and W. H. Smith News. However, as the second question shows, mentoring (presumably by professional colleagues) had played a significant role in developing 28 per cent of the respondents at the trust hospital. Only in Hewlett Packard were significant numbers of managers actively involved in career planning discussions. For the majority of companies less than half the management population carried out career planning activities. It is clear that many line managers had not fully embraced the idea that career management had become a line management responsibility. The interview results supported this:

We are not involved [in career planning]. We work on appraisal, but Personnel looks after that side. (line manager, Lloyds Bank UK Retail Banking)

I don't know what happens . . . it must be very difficult. (line manager, Lloyds Bank UK Retail Banking)

Nobody ever approaches you to talk about it. (line manager, W. H. Smith News)

Some line managers still equated career management with formal career planning, rather than seeing it as part of an ongoing dialogue about general performance and opportunities for development. For instance, a line manager from BT Payphones said, 'I am not really involved in career management. There is little opportunity to help them with their careers because there is so little opportunity for forward advancement.' Other interviewees also noted that their line managers might not have the capacity or information to take a broad view of what was available throughout their organization.

However, our interviews in Hewlett Packard and Citibank revealed a greater awareness of the role of the line manager in encouraging individual responsibility for career progression. Yet managers in these companies also recognized that, in de-layered organizations with larger spans of control, this meant a substantial investment of their time:

The ideas [of line management involvement in career planning] are acceptable but hard to put in place, basically because they involve doing quite a lot of things. You've actually got to talk to people on a regular basis about their careers, probably really seriously once a year, quite seriously twice a year, and at some level once a quarter. There will be twenty-four people out there next year. That's a lot of meetings. Then you've got to do something about what you hear. (line manager, Citibank)

Added to the difficulties created by large spans of control was the impact of individualism on the line managers' relationships with their teams. Particularly at Citibank and Kraft Jacobs Suchard, as line managers increasingly had to take an individualistic line for their own development, this made them less concerned about their staff:

The attitude is, 'this place has a very "change" culture: I'm not going to be here in three years' time, so who cares at all about what happens to them—it's not going to be my problem. I'm far too busy working out what my career development is going to be.' That's the mentality it breeds. (line manager, Citibank)

In summary, the new career deal is based in part on the active support of line managers. Yet from both the interview and survey data the message was clear: many managers felt that they were constrained by the time available to them, their general capabilities in handling people management issues, and the pressures of short-term business targets. Line managers are currently offered few incentives for incorporating people management issues into everyday managerial practice, a theme we return to in Chapter 7 and discuss further in the final chapter.

IMPLICATIONS FOR ESTABLISHING THE 'NEW CAREER'

In general we found that the more integrated and coherent the key career interventions, the lower the resistance to the concept of the 'new career'. Of particular importance here are those processes that are capable of helping people to understand their skill sets and motivations (career plans, personal development workshops, and so on), and those which support the internal job market (job specifications, job posting systems, and the like). With regard to these systems we found in many companies a series of ad hoc piecemeal initiatives, particularly around self-managed learning. Where these had been integrated into a coherent system, as in the case of Hewlett Packard, they had much more impact. With regard to the job market systems, most were in their infancy and, with a few notable exceptions (such as the Citibank system), were not capable of delivering the up-to-date information about job and project vacancies which would be required for a truly flexible job market. We would agree with Nicholson (1996) that the development of these information systems must be a key priority for the future. These information systems would help to reduce the anxiety and uncertainty currently experienced by staff in many organizations due to their lack of knowledge of opportunities.

However, there are some positive results from the research in terms of employability. Training and development received high ratings in terms of levels

Table 4.6. Theme 3: line management support

	BT Payphones	C&W NHS Trust	Citibank	GP UK[a]	HP	KJS	Lloyds	WHS News
Frequency of career discussion with boss or personnel representative:								
Never	24	46	23	16	19	12	19	31
Less than once a year	14	16	25	8	21	9	22	10
Once a year or more	62	38	52	76	58	79	59	59
'Having a mentor has played a significant/very significant role in developing my performance.'	15	28	21	13	27	22	18	25
Managers: which of the following activities do you carry out for your subordinates?—Career planning	56	42	40	—	63	47	34	14

[a] Some data not collected in GP UK (pilot) study.

of satisfaction, although the self-selecting nature of our sample may have skewed the findings in this area. (Companies which perceive themselves to be 'leading edge' in HR, or which are keen to become so, may invest in this area more than others.) Furthermore, we did not ask employees to rate training and development in terms of aiding their employability. Therefore, we cannot discern whether the investment made and the satisfaction felt is because basic provision was simply good, or whether individuals felt that the development opportunities they were given enhanced their potential in the external and internal labour markets.

The other facets of employability—mobility and horizontal development—have been impeded by the downsizing of organizations. Moreover, they can also be impeded by inadequate managerial support systems. In considering the line manager's role in this, our research shows that organizations should be wary of relying on their input to facilitate horizontal movement across organizations, since without supporting information systems they may lack knowledge of where opportunities for their staff lie. Organizations should also recognize that these line managers have their own personal aims and objectives to fulfil, and limited time in which to do so, and that the career development of their staff may not be uppermost their minds. One answer, if senior management is committed to making the notion of 'new careers' a reality, may be for organizations to incorporate an assessment of the career management of staff in a line manager's performance appraisal.

In terms of the self-management of careers, employees are in a transitional stage; they know that the career patterns of the past have gone for good, but are deeply anxious and unclear about what will replace them. This seems to lead employees to 'get safe' rather than to 'get even' or 'get out' in terms of Herriot's (1995) possible responses. There is evidence of a gradual shift to a transactional type of contract (Rousseau 1996) but our research would suggest that organizations are managing this shift with varying degrees of competence. Herriot is right to suggest that transactional contracts work best when there is an equality of negotiating power between the parties concerned. This seemed to be a key source of discontent amongst our interviewees. Not only are employees experiencing grief from the fracturing of the 'parent and child' relational contract, but in moving to a more adult transactional contract, one of the 'adults', the employer, has the upper hand. Employees are experiencing not only an anxiety and a lack of clarity about the future, but also a feeling of powerlessness in the downsized, post-recessionary economic context. We have seen evidence of a short-term stage of shock in which the overall commitment of employees is lessened, and in the longer term it may lead to increased levels of insecurity and stress through burn-out. The concepts of the new career make assumptions about individuals' ability to influence and control their own destiny, and the rhetoric that is heard is the rhetoric of those who have succeeded and are already at the top of organizations.

Our findings support Guest and Mackenzie's (1996) and Nicholson's (1996) contention that the concept of self-management takes time to develop, and is not being applied in a universal fashion in organizations because of the different transitional stages that the organizations are in, in terms of establishing supporting systems. Likewise, it is not being applied universally across all groups of employees. Paradoxically, fast-track employees, seen as core employees, may even be more secure in the context of new careers, and the repercussions of this on the rest of the workforce may only emerge in time.

In conclusion we have found that the downsizing and de-layering of the 1990s has been both a driving force in the emergence of the notion of 'new careers', and also a restraining force in the practical implementation of this concept. Companies appear to have been too fast in embracing the rhetoric of the concept and too slow in providing supporting systems (both managerial and procedural) to turn that rhetoric into a reality. The positive potential leverage for companies wishing to achieve change in this area appears to lie in building on the good rating that the training and development functions achieve to provide customized employability for employees. The notion of the new career does not appear to be applied universally, as fast-track staff across all groups in the companies still seem to enjoy both promised job security and formal career planning. Indeed, in contrast to what the rhetoric might suggest, formal systems are not being abandoned altogether; it is simply that the nature of their mechanisms is changing, with greater emphasis on line manager communication and information systems providing access to opportunities. To stem the gradual erosion of employee commitment, organizations must put these new mechanisms in place as soon as possible.

5

Managing Culture

VERONICA HOPE HAILEY

One of the major UK commentators on human resource management identified the 'management of culture' as one of three features that distinguished
'HRM' from a personnel management approach (Legge 1989). This was perhaps
in part an observation on the growing interest in the 1980s on the part of
practitioners in large-scale cultural change programmes. Much of this
increased interest in the area of organizational culture was fuelled initially by a
few well-publicized examples (Peters and Waterman 1983). Strategic management commentators also started to embrace the softer aspects of strategy by
examining the informal aspects of organizations and constructing models such
as cultural webs (Johnson and Scholes 1986).

The general message of the corporate culture literature was that the culture
of an organization—its values, beliefs, ethos, way of doing things—influences
its performance and that these elements could be actively manipulated by
management. The message also had a prescriptive element, if not always a
practical one (Guest 1992). The organization's culture could be manipulated
(for example through changing managerial style, or the use of communication
mechanisms). The aim was, for example, that through a cultural change process employees would come to believe in the value of being close to the customer, management would come to believe in profitability through people, and
hence both groups would display high levels of 'affective' commitment to their
employing organization (Penley and Gould 1988). The desired end result was
increased profitability.

In response to the burgeoning prescriptive literature a number of critical
studies of cultural change programmes started to highlight both the practical
deficiencies in the way that such programmes were implemented, and the
conceptual contradictions in the very notion of managing or changing organizational culture (Anthony 1994; Hendry and Hope 1994; Hope and Hendry 1995;
Keenoy and Anthony 1992; Willmott 1993).

This chapter describes the different approaches taken by two companies to managing culture. Despite the difference in approach both organizations manage culture relatively successfully in terms of the individual contexts in which the approaches are applied and the specific outcomes that each company wants to achieve. We concentrate on three main themes: a comparative analysis of values or behaviours as a starting point for instituting cultural change; a comparative analysis of top-down or imposed cultural change and incremental and emergent cultural change; a consideration of cultural management as a form of labour control.

This chapter begins by reviewing the current debates under these three headings. Two case studies are then presented, and the chapter concludes with a discussion of the comparisons to be made and the general lessons learnt from the analysis. In particular it draws out the contextual features that are pertinent if companies choose to manage culture, and the different outcomes which that management intervention may seek to achieve.

VALUES VS. BEHAVIOURS

The business case for inculcating shared values through managing culture was based on the idea that ultimately employees could then be given licence to innovate in the confidence that their adherence to corporate values would prevent them from acting against the interests of the company. Thus by prescribing shared values, appropriate behaviour would emerge in such a way that rules and regulations, in the form of bureaucratic corporate policies and procedures, would become unnecessary. In so doing, innovation would flourish through the twinning of freedom and control.

However, the evidence from empirical studies often illustrated the numerous difficulties that this approach encountered. Many 'espoused values' (Schein 1984) were devalued in people's eyes if there was no change in behaviours and ultimately business performance. Thus values such as 'individuality', 'integrity', or 'valuing people' quickly became relegated to motherhood mantras in some companies (Hope 1993). With the emphasis on values there is also a danger that staff will feel manipulated or brainwashed, leading to either cynicism or mimicry (Kunda 1992). The overt management of values can make the culture appear a commodity or product to be 'bought into'—something that exists outside oneself rather than as an integral part of self.

Other commentators argue that instead of focusing on values initially (and hoping that over time behaviours will change), organizations should focus on new behaviours in the first instance. The argument here is that by focusing on behaviours initially, new values will emerge over time. The case for such an approach is that a focus on behaviours is a less intrusive intervention than asking people to change their values. In addition, behaviours are more tangible, and therefore more measurable; they are also more task-related and therefore perceived as a more legitimate area for intervention at work.

IMPOSED VS. EMERGENT CULTURE

Throughout the 1980s the emphasis in the prescriptive literature was on programmatic cultural change implemented in a top-down fashion. These interventions usually involved a comprehensive programme of staff involvement in which groups of staff were encouraged to take 'ownership' of the cultural change and 'cascade' the message down through the organization. Often the new culture was 'sold' to the company staff through a combination of charismatic leadership, symbolic action, and powerful advertising (Beckhard 1992).

Research conducted on cultural change programmes in the 1980s and 1990s highlights the limitations of such implementation (Willmott 1993). First, a project on cultural change in the financial services industry highlighted the fact that senior managers can recognize the need for change at a rational, intellectual level but remain unable to make that change at an emotional level where triggers for new behaviour are most strongly felt (Hope 1993).

Second, an imposed cultural change process may work in the opposite direction to the values it is trying to inculcate. When top-down communication and bureaucratic controls are used as part of that process, the very act of implementation may counteract any motivation on the part of staff to 'innovate' and 'break free' of bureaucratic rules and regulations. To be told you are going to be, for example, 'empowered' and that you should behave in an empowered manner is quite different from feeling empowered. However, the advantage of imposed change is that it can be used to respond to a crisis situation. It can promote clarity about what is expected from staff and provide short-term solutions to crises.

Emergent or bottom-up cultural change in comparison is sometimes slow to mature and unpredictable in its consequences. However, writers such as Beer *et al.* (1990) argue that it is more effective and longer lasting than programmes imposed from the top. Beer *et al.* reported their research in a *Harvard Business Review* article entitled 'Why Change Programmes don't Produce Change'. In addition to critically appraising some of the popular top-down cultural programmes they reported on a process they call 'task alignment'. This process starts within small business units (on the periphery of large organizations) which perceive the need to change working patterns in order to respond to competitive pressure. The starting point is business need and the response is based on changing roles, responsibilities, and relationships. From this experience new attitudes, values, and beliefs are derived which, in turn, gradually become a shared vision of how best to manage and organize. Senior management merely guide rather than sponsor such an approach and are often the last unit of the organization to be changed.

CULTURE AS A FORM OF LABOUR CONTROL

Much of the sociological literature on the subject of corporate culture is concerned with its use as a management tool for maintaining control over employees whilst simultaneously increasing their commitment. Some of the key writers in this area argue that corporate culture can be used as a means of generating normative control over employees as their 'hearts and minds' become legitimate sites for corporate influence (for example, Casey 1995; Keenoy and Anthony 1992; Kunda 1992; Ray 1986; Willmott 1993).

A number of points can be made in relation to arguments about corporate culture as a form of labour control. First, some writers argue that the manipulation of a corporation's culture has emerged as the solution to what is perceived to be a crisis in existing forms of labour management (Ray 1986) or as a response to the demands of the new post-industrial age (Casey 1995). Second, there are inherent contradictions in the idea that the same kinds of values and behaviours, and therefore controls, can be imposed on diverse groups in organizations whether that diversity be based on business divisions, staff groupings, or national cultures (Hofstede 1991; Kunda 1992; Lawrence and Lorsch 1967). Third, the limitations of managed corporate culture are even more convincingly demonstrated by evidence that employees do not act as passive recipients of the cultural change programmes but do react, resist, and reinterpret these changes (Hope 1993; Kunda 1992; Whittington 1992). Earlier comparative research found that intuitively held, unmanaged forms of paternalistic culture were stronger in their control than newer overtly managed or manipulated cultures (Hope 1993). Fourth, it can be argued that recent changes in the world of work have undermined rather than contributed to the case for managing culture. For instance, the so-called 'knowledge workers' (Drucker 1992) who will flourish in the new de-layered, multifunctional, project-based organizations (Peters 1992; Kanter 1989a) may be those least open to cultural management as they will seek greater not lesser autonomy.

Lastly, a limitation of much of the existing research on managing culture as control is the tendency for researchers to concentrate in their data collection on the process of cultural management without examining the existence of other forms of labour control in an organization. These other forms may include output control, personal control, or bureaucratic control (Child 1984). It is important to consider cultural control within the context of these other forms of control in order to avoid the over-elevation of the impact of culture.

MANAGING CULTURE AT GLAXO PHARMACEUTICALS UK

Design and implementation of cultural change

The need for a planned cultural change programme in Glaxo Pharmaceuticals UK was identified within the business strategic planning process in 1988. Recognizing the important contribution that the excellent management of staff could potentially make to the bottom line, the Managing Director gave significant support to the Human Resources Director's initiative to design a set of behaviours that would be critical to business success in the future.

An attitude survey run throughout the company showed some disturbing attitudes and organizational characteristics. They were disturbing in the sense that both the Managing Director and the HR Director recognized that if they were not tackled they would severely hamper the critical success factors that had been established for the business strategy. This strategy was concerned with the changing nature of the customer—the National Health Service in the UK—and the increased competition within the market place.

The survey revealed three key issues. First, there was an attitude of complacency amongst the staff. Staff recognized the changing nature of the market place within which Glaxo Pharmaceuticals UK was operating, but they had faith in, and reliance on, the senior management team's ability to direct the organization in such a way that success, and the consequent rewards which this brought staff, were still assured. In effect, there was insufficient awareness of the responsibility and contribution that was necessary on the part of each member of staff in order to sustain the success of the company. Second, slow decision-making was identified as an organizational characteristic. This was potentially threatening Glaxo Pharmaceuticals UK's ability to respond quickly to the needs of the market place. Third, the existence of strong functional divides within the organization contributed to the slow pace of decision-making. This significantly limited both communication and understanding, and had hindered the development of any sense of shared responsibility for business success.

Focusing initially on behaviours rather than values, a description of the behaviours necessary for the Glaxo Pharmaceuticals UK of the future was drawn up. This was given the acronym RATIO. Broken down this stood for Role clarity, Acceptance of change, Teamwork, Innovation, and Output orientation. In conjunction with consultants from a business school, the senior management team was put through an Outdoor Development course that enabled them as individuals to understand and experiment with these new behaviours. It also enabled them to understand at a personal level the depth of change that was necessary on the part of individuals if the desired change was to be achieved.

The course proved so successful that the experience was repeated for a further 700 staff members within the organization. Staff were invited to revise the behaviours spelt out in the RATIO programme in terms of their own jobs and roles such that each characteristic could be fleshed out. A series of complementary change initiatives was implemented. First a values statement was issued stating the values that should underpin the behaviours that Glaxo Pharmaceuticals UK was trying to achieve through RATIO. The values were identified as follows:

We value:
- our contribution to the health and well-being of the nation;
- our relationship with our partners in the delivery of health care;
- honesty in everything we do;
- the contribution of all individuals and their personal development;
- the learning which comes from listening;
- the effective use of all resources, particularly people's time, energy, and commitment;
- the taking of responsibility for decisions and actions;
- flexibility and responsiveness;
- achievement.

A second initiative was the institution of project groups. These were encouraged in order to break down the functional divides that had been identified by the earlier attitude survey, and promote the emergence of amoebic structures within the organization. A third opportunity to reinforce the change programme was the relocation of Glaxo Pharmaceuticals UK. Members of the senior management team battled to ensure that maximum symbolic use was made of open plan working in order to chip away the functional divides through open and easy communication. A more recent initiative has been to incorporate RATIO within a set of managerial competencies.

Observations

The research team observed that the RATIO programme was extremely well embedded within the organization. All those interviewed knew what it was and, more importantly, could relate it to their work and business success. In addition, many were able to demonstrate how the RATIO programme was supported through the process and content of some of the human resource interventions such as recruitment and selection, as well as training and development. Significantly, it was perceived to be an organizational strategy rather than a human resource strategy. This was described in the interviews as having been devised by the general staff and owned by the whole organization. It was therefore not perceived as imposed programmatic change.

In contrast, the values statement was less well known and staff were seldom able to relate it to specific management interventions. The value of 'partnership' with the British National Health Service was discussed in relation to business strategy, but in general the values statement was less well regarded than the behavioural statements contained within RATIO. In illustration of this one manager said:

To be honest with you, the value side of things I think is very wishy-washy. To give you a classic example, we had a regional managers' meeting which looked at the values. Eight of us round the table went 'What? What's that?' We couldn't even remember seeing the memo that came out. Nobody had explained it to us . . . Everybody knew RATIO and we all felt quite comfortable with that. We were all involved with that. We were all involved in the pulling together of RATIO. It was communicated very well to us. But the values have not been communicated out in the field at all well, I believe. They are just so wishy-washy.

Many staff perceived the values as little more than motherhood statements, and there was particular doubt expressed about the attainment of the value 'honesty' within such a political organization.

The greatest resistance appeared to come from the trading companies, particularly the field staff and regional sales managers. This could be an illustration of the familiar divide between field sales staff and head office staff. Or it could be that different values and behaviours are required for these two sets of working groups. Certainly, if cultural change is concerned with improving business performance, then it seems somewhat counter-productive to have such resistance expressed from staff working at the coalface, namely the sales staff.

A factor that also hampered the implementation of the new culture was the inability of some managers to live out and demonstrate the required behaviours. Whilst this cannot be seen as purposeful resistance as such, nevertheless it was a significant block to the cultural change process. The managers' competencies initiative was viewed as a mechanism for tackling this.

Lastly, a potential misuse of the process was identified through comments on project groups. Whilst it was recognized that their institution had been a useful mechanism for generating a move away from functional divides, staff also complained that often little evaluation was made of outputs from these groups. Others thought that participation in such ventures was made on the basis of informal career planning, the 'way to be seen' in the organization. Commitment to such participation was based on self-interest rather than corporate business success.

Achievements and limitations

In summary RATIO was seen by the research team as well embedded within the organization and perceived as such by the staff. The indicators for this were the thorough understanding of what it meant and the ability to relate the behaviours it encapsulates to tasks, business performance, and some human resource interventions. The message appeared to be successful because it was kept simple and clear, and because it operated at a level of behaviour rather than attempting to inculcate deeper personal values.

The limitations seemed to be more apparent within the sales divisions. There were signs of conflict between the long-term demands of the change programme and more immediate pressures to achieve sales targets, and there were indications that, when under pressure, managers would revert to command and control forms of management. One senior manager commented that too many assumptions had been made by the designers about the level of acceptance and understanding amongst staff at lower levels.

MANAGING CULTURE AT HEWLETT PACKARD

Historical background and recent organizational change

In the beginning of the company's history the founders did not focus on growth *per se*, but focused instead on manufacturing quality products. Choosing not to compete on price, the company concentrated on developing advanced products adapted to customers' needs. In 1957 the company was divisionalized along product lines in an attempt to decrease spans of control and to simulate the ideal aspects of small business units within a global corporation. They planned to give considerable operating freedom to the managers of these business units, but to do so within a set of commercial and management guidelines. These guidelines became encapsulated within a vision statement known as the 'Hewlett Packard Vision', examined in more depth later in this chapter.

Over the last twenty-five years Hewlett Packard has grown at least tenfold. In retrospect, current senior management believe that culturally they had become both complacent and paternalistic, and an implicit policy of no redundancy had become established in the minds of employees. However, by the late 1980s Hewlett Packard faced the same difficulties as its competitors, including increased competition, sluggish markets, decreasing profitability, and a declining stock market valuation. Yet by February of 1994, the group was recording a 41 per cent rise in first-quarter net profits. In 1993 the UK subsidiary increased its turnover by 43 per cent, generating profits of $85 million compared with a break-even position in 1992.

A number of factors appear to have contributed to this turnaround. Apart from market changes, new product launches, and cost-cutting measures, the level of bureaucracy within the company was also attacked. A company that had been started by entrepreneurial engineers, advisers urged that it had become too centralized. In addition, new ideas were being squashed if they appeared too unorthodox. Hewlett Packard's response was to return to a decentralized structure that gave freedom back to the individual business units. This decentralization arguably helped one business division to take off in business terms and capture a significant proportion of a new product market.

In addition to decentralizing, the company also implemented a number of other changes, one of the most controversial being the Voluntary Severance

Programme in which several thousand people were 'released' from the company. To give some idea of the impact of downsizing within Hewlett Packard, one manager commented, 'three or four years ago there were thirty-four managers in this group. Now there are only eight managers with a business three times the size.'

Morale has been dented. Of the people we surveyed, fewer than half agreed that morale was high within the company. However, 92 per cent agreed that still they 'are willing to put in a great deal of effort beyond that normally expected in order to help this organization be successful', while 85 per cent agreed that they 'talk up this organization to my friends as a great place to work'. Also, 89 per cent agreed that they were 'proud to tell others that I am part of this organization'.

How can we account for this continued commitment to and belief in the company? We examine this by presenting two interconnected aspects of management at Hewlett Packard: first, the use of 'the HP Way' values statement, and second the way in which the company employs almost Taylorist methods to monitor individual performance in terms of business performance. These two critical issues of managing performance through business planning and managing people through the HP Way are inextricably connected and account for the success and performance at Hewlett Packard. The central paradox is that within the company there is close, detailed, and exacting attention paid to planning, monitoring, and reviewing business performance. It seems an interesting organizational skill to be able to load such a detailed battery of planning systems onto staff, and at the same time receive feedback which says that staff perceive the company culture to encourage individual freedom and innovation.

People management: the HP Way

The values statement was formalized and institutionalized in 1957 in an attempt to foster individual freedom within a strong belief and value system. So the HP Way focused on a 'belief in our people' which incorporated:

Confidence in and respect for our people as opposed to depending upon extensive rules, procedures and so on; which depends upon people to do their job right (individual freedom) without constant directives. ('The HP Way')

Hewlett Packard is viewed by its staff as having an outstanding organizational culture. The 'Unwritten rules of the Game' interviews conducted with middle managers highlighted the fact that the culture was seen as 'supportive', 'very, very open', with a 'team ethic'.

Over the years the HP Way has taken on the image of the Apostles' Creed: a shared statement of beliefs, but one that can be interpreted in many different ways in a broad, catholic sense. It is almost as though its shared symbolic image is more important than living it as a shared reality. One senior manager called it an 'an assumed culture'. This perhaps is its strength: as a corporate ideology it allows for different interpretations of its words. Thus in Hewlett Packard there is a common language but the meaning of the words differs across divisions.

There is a huge amount of 'white space', 'the bit in the middle', that is not quite clear how it actually works. (senior manager)

It's remarkably confused as to what it is, but it's very strong. (middle manager)

If you ask anyone about the HP Way they will give you a different answer about what they believe it to be. People find it difficult to put their finger on what it is. (non-managerial staff)

There is also an infectious assumption that Hewlett Packard is the 'best' company to work for:

Because it is a paternalistic company and because traditionally HP has been the best company to work for, people assume it is . . . but I would not like to be on a disciplinary procedure in Hewlett Packard. (non-managerial staff)

All of this image-building allows Hewlett Packard to achieve an assumed cultural consistency and at the same time a cultural flexibility. Having said that, within each micro-culture a fit is sought but, importantly, always through informal rather than formal methods of selection or appraisal. It is covert but strongly reinforced through peer pressure:

The difference is the culture. It's very professional and very straight. I love it. I fit the culture and the culture fits me. (employee)

One of our problems is that we're quite clone-like. We hire people in our own mould. (employee)

Yet equally, overly fervent staff do not appear to be welcomed: 'It's a productive environment without too much emotion oiling the wheels. If you're the kind of person who gets charged up by breathing fire and falling out with people then Hewlett Packard is not for you' (employee).

The ability to operate as a team player rather than as an individual is highly valued and reinforced through peer control: the typical personalities were described as 'compromisers, no strong egos'. The importance of selling the customer the 'right product' rather than selling at any cost stresses the long-term nature of the culture. Hewlett Packard are seeking people who wish to become part of the 'family' rather than those who wish to reap high returns over a short period. However, when staff were questioned in interviews about how they came to understand and adopt, in whatever form, the HP Way, many found it difficult to articulate how it was achieved. There was little talk of strong induction training in the values statement.

The flexible and intangible nature of the culture does not only operate at the level of the individual, but also allows for reinterpretation of the HP Way at a meta-level, at a global level, and at a divisional level. For instance, at the meta-level, many people assumed that the HP Way had formally stated a commit-

ment to lifetime employment. This was never actually explicitly
the original HP Way. Therefore when faced with difficult decisions
downsizing in 1992, in the wake of the economic downturn, it was possible
senior management successfully to remind staff of the historical emphasis on
business performance and management by objectives:

The HP Way is respect for the individual, but they have to deliver results. This is not a
holiday camp. We do a lot of things to create a positive environment for our people to
succeed. People forget the 'having to succeed' part and can confuse some of the
downside of not succeeding with an abandonment of the Hewlett Packard Way . . . You
can't grow and make a profit by just being nice to people. (senior manager)

The HP Way is not jobs for life. It's jobs for performers. (middle manager)

Hewlett Packard used to be known as an outstanding employer but we are not so differentiated any more. The HP Way used to set people apart but we have moved. It
has swung away from being people-oriented when the business was fast growing.
(employee)

In the post-recession 1990s, with growth occurring again, the senior management are leading a revival in the 'HP Way' and publicly declare that there has
been too much deviation from the original creed. However, it is unclear to what
extent it is a complete return to the ideals of 1957 and how many of these have
had to be sacrificed *de facto* due to the demands of the market place. For
instance, in the past growth was not seen as an aim in itself; it was seen instead
as an advantageous by-product of a commitment to innovative research and
design and quality production.

The critical issues that the managers identified in helping the HP Way to work
across national boundaries were first, that the national unit manager had to
have the capacity to 'meld' the national culture with the Hewlett Packard corporate culture, but in a sensitive and covert way, and second, that the use of
architecture was extremely important in covertly and symbolically reinforcing
some consistency in approach. Very few managers within the UK unit had
expatriate experience. Thus we were witnessing a very nationalistic unit within
a Californian company.

There also appear to be great differences in culture between the divisions.
Thus the differences between a division of support engineers (with needs for
reliability and security) and a division of sales staff (with needs for instant hits
and fast pace) are acknowledged and worked with:

There are variations in style across business units. (employee)

Sales are quite different in Hewlett Packard as in many organizations. (employee)

So, for instance, in research and development it may be acceptable to wear
jeans and work whatever hours of the day you wish, whereas in sales and
distribution, it is essential to wear suits. This is in contrast to many corporations which insist on adherence to an all-embracing corporate culture.

The final point to note about the operation of the HP Way is that it is perceived as entirely independent of and unconnected to the personnel function.

> ...lly owned by the organization. It is an organiza-
> ... personnel initiative: 'The HR function will never be
> ... However, it is its guardian, its articulator—the real
> ... (senior manager).

...ince at Hewlett Packard

Hewlett ... ...es prescribe values but it also prescribes and measures outcomes in te... of performance required. It is this close attention to monitoring business performance that we now turn to. We consider both formal and informal mechanisms for managing performance at Hewlett Packard under the two headings of HR policies and informal understandings.

HR policies

Reflecting the engineering and systems culture of the company, the planning process can be described precisely from corporate headquarters level down to UK business units and through to the personal objectives of individual members of staff. The company states that the reason for this close attention to detail is paradoxically the promotion of individual freedom, innovation, and entrepreneurial spirit. As one of the original senior managers explained:

> Early in the history of the company, whilst thinking about how a company like this should be managed, I kept getting back to one concept: if we could simply get everybody to agree on what our objectives were and to understand what we were trying to do, then we could turn everybody loose and they would move along in a common direction.

So individuals have their personal objectives defined for them, but how they achieve those objectives in terms of innovative activity or specific behaviour is formally left undefined. How are these objectives then defined? There are three main planning processes conducted at a corporate level: the 'Ten Step Approach', a long-range plan, and an Annual Plan. The Annual Plan is made up of two components: one part identifies areas that need immediate and substantial attention because they are critical for immediate business success—these are called 'breakthrough' areas—while the other part of the Annual Plan focuses on the daily management of the business and the key process measures. In all these planning exercises human resource issues are included alongside commercial factors. So, for instance, one of the Business Fundamentals for 1995 was that all performance evaluations should be received on time. This is not seen as an HR initiative but as a business initiative.

The language used to describe these planning processes reflects the business that Hewlett Packard is in: 'Business Fundamentals management provides the effective management of routine processes, discovers abnormalities or deviations, and prevents their recurrence.'

At an individual level Hewlett Packard also uses a variety of mechanisms to plan, monitor, and assess individual performance: performance evaluation, ranking, and self-development plans. The documentation for all of these processes stresses measures for success. A strong performance ethic is achieved within the company but it is achieved by stressing outputs and making the links between individual performance and corporate performance absolutely transparent. In recent years one of the many planning and monitoring devices to be developed is 'Framework',

a tool which means that an employee's principal duties are clearly defined. Business Fundamentals drive the roles that are carried out. They are linked to the Business Fundamentals of the Business Unit thus ensuring that an individual understands the goals of the unit in which they work and how their performance is measured against the success of their contribution to achieving those Business Fundamentals. (extract from the 'How to use Framework' guide)

One training manager commented: 'if something goes wrong, we tend to blame the system rather than the individual. We're engineers after all.'

How are these various planning processes viewed by staff? Some broad indices are clear from the questionnaire results: 73 per cent agree with the statement 'I know what management are trying to achieve'; 81 per cent agree with the statement 'My organization has a clear corporate strategy'; 80 per cent agree with the statement 'People take responsibility for their own performance'; and 88 per cent agree that the organization will achieve its aims. Fifty-nine per cent of staff state that they determine their targets with their boss whilst a further 27 per cent say that their boss sets the targets but seeks their agreement.

Informal understandings

From the interviews with the middle managers one of the three major themes to emerge was this emphasis on individual performance. These interviews demonstrated that not only is performance measured in a variety of ways, through the business planning and monitoring systems, but it is also aligned in a productive way with the organization's goals. This was illustrated most clearly by the unwritten rule of getting involved in task forces or projects which add value to the overall company. In short, there seemed to be little scope for individuals to further their own interests without contributing in some way to Hewlett Packard:

You need sustained performance; you need success against your scorecard.

I need to keep delivering; I need to make sure that my staff collectively are delivering.

You have a day job and you have what I call an 'evening job' where you get involved in extramural activities such as task groups.

People want to do a good job. If you don't care in Hewlett Packard you won't last.

The whole structure of the way we are measured gets to the heart of the business. (various employees)

What also became apparent from these interviews was that in support of these formal and detailed methods of managing performance was a constant, informal, day-to-day appraisal of performance by line managers such that, as one manager put it, 'nothing comes as a surprise at the performance evaluation'. Of all the organizations in the Leading Edge consortium, Hewlett Packard scores highest for the amount of discussions conducted by line managers with their staff on career management, appraisal, and personal development.

There is no formal mechanism that enforces this informal process of everyday appraisal and discussion other than the implicit rule that you will not get ahead in the company unless you are perceived to be a good people manager. In turn, that implicit rule is monitored through a variety of informal pressures and expectations from peers, superiors, and subordinates that support this understanding. The important point is that the formal and informal processes are entirely complementary in their aim of managing performance.

In summary, the establishment of clear targets and objectives (the 'what') does not necessitate the means of achieving those objectives (the 'how') also being prescribed. This can be contrasted with many bureaucracies where the functions and actions (the 'how') are prescribed. However, neither is Hewlett Packard an 'adhocracy' and the pervasiveness of the planning systems prevents it from becoming a free-for-all. Instead we see in the planning systems a Taylorist, engineers' approach applied to management. Targets and objectives are coordinated globally in such a way that, in the divisions where this matters, entrepreneurial spirit or innovative thought can be allowed to flourish within defined business parameters.

I have to manage costs, have a plan in place, be perceived as a leader, and obviously make quota.

Your objectives are the same as for colleagues: Business Fundamentals, numbers, and being a team player.

DISCUSSION

Values vs. behaviours

Hewlett Packard chooses to make use of its values statement in a less ambitious way than other companies. For instance, affective or emotional commitment is not expected, as illustrated by the comments made by managers about 'too much emotion oiling the wheels'. The actual espoused values allow a diversity of behaviour and an emphasis on individualism to be spawned within the company. As a result of that we found no indications that staff felt brainwashed or manipulated. On the contrary, Hewlett Packard staff indicated the highest levels of commitment in our questionnaire survey.

In contrast, Glaxo Pharmaceuticals UK's initial emphasis on behaviour was better received than its subsequent focus on values. In Glaxo Pharmaceuticals UK it was the values that were greeted with cynicism. How can we account for these different staff reactions? The Glaxo Pharmaceuticals UK intervention is much more short-term that Hewlett Packard's commitment to its values statement over the decades. Glaxo Pharmaceuticals UK were concerned with specifically repositioning their sales divisions within the marketplace. Perhaps behaviours focused on tasks and market-driven competencies appeared more tangible to staff. Behaviours may also be easier to impose than values.

Imposed vs. emergent

Due to changes in the market place, Glaxo Pharmaceuticals UK needed a transformation and did not appear to have the flexibility within existing management systems to change incrementally over time. Therefore the change had to be imposed if it was to achieve its purpose. The behaviours were also imposed on a particular division, the sales division. Glaxo Pharmaceuticals UK did however invest a considerable number of resources in encouraging their staff to take ownership of the imposed transformational change.

Hewlett Packard, in contrast, does not overtly seek to manage or impose its values statements. This adds to the strength of the HP Way. As the 'culture' does not become objectified or fall outside of 'self', individual employees are left to make their own interpretation of the values statement. This seems to engender less resistance than when strikingly similar values statements used by other organizations are pushed onto employees through formally defined selection criteria or other systematic mechanisms. The values are assimilated more by osmosis than management. The strength of the values statement therefore lies not in its inculcation but in its openness to different interpretations. This makes the culture more easily transferred in cross-cultural or cross-functional contexts. Certain contextual features within Hewlett Packard demand this flexibility. The HP Way is a company-wide culture and impacts on all divisions alike. Yet Hewlett Packard's research scientists are unlikely to submit themselves to prescribed behaviours. Even if the company succeeded in constraining their behaviours in this way, the prescription might dampen the very motivation and creativity that the company seeks from them and depends upon for business performance. (The cultural change at Glaxo Pharmaceuticals UK, in contrast, was aimed directly at its sales divisions.) The company also recognizes that it needs to be able to operate across national boundaries as a multinational corporation, not as a global corporation. It therefore seeks to promote a culture that allows different national cultures and the HP Way to mesh together in a complementary manner. Finally, this emergent form of culture also allows different interpretations over time—its very intangible nature allows the culture to be reinvented when necessary. For instance, despite reneging on an implicit understanding amongst employees that Hewlett Packard guaranteed lifelong employment, the management was able to point to the HP Way and reinterpret its essential meaning to suit the demands of the employer in the 1990s. The values therefore emerge in different forms over time, in different national units, and with different occupational groups. In contrast a prescribed behaviour is potentially a much more static concept.

Culture as a form of labour control

The senior managers at Hewlett Packard wish to promote the rhetoric of freedom and innovation within their company. However it is wrong to presume that tight managerial control is not present in such a loose culture. It is simply achieved through another means: output control. The rigorous application of business planning and performance systems ensures that the target of employees' behaviours is tightly prescribed and controlled. How employees achieve that target is not overtly prescribed.

Glaxo Pharmaceuticals UK did prescribe how employees were to achieve their targets and it did meet with some resistance even amongst its sales force:

They're getting back to the stage where they want to control the 'how' as well as the 'what'. Now to me as an individual that's one thing I hate—to be told exactly how to do things. Why are they employing me? With this expertise and experience, why have they put all this training into me in terms of creative innovation? Why have they given me and why have I gone through a range of different jobs in the company in order to acquire a set of skills which they then won't let me use? That's one way to stifle innovation. This is one way to make people react badly to change. (employee)

However, as noted in the previous section, the intention was to achieve some degree of uniformity in behaviour within Glaxo Pharmaceuticals UK's sales divisions. It might not have been achievable had they attempted to spread it across other diverse divisions such as research and development.

Conclusion

Both of these companies managed culture in very different ways, yet both forms of management were successful in terms of the context of each company and the outcomes that they wanted to achieve. This research suggests that the appropriate management of culture lies not in identifying and copying the 'best practice' in this area. Instead, companies should give careful consideration to contextual features such as staff groupings, geographic spread, the number of divisions involved, and the exact outcomes desired from this management intervention. Having identified the significant features within their context, companies can make a choice about how much flexibility is desired, or how much imposition is necessary, depending on what they are trying to achieve.

Contextual Diversity for the Role and Practice of HR

VERONICA HOPE HAILEY

This chapter argues that the normative and prescriptive models of both personnel management and human resource management have been too simplistic
and have failed to address the diverse and complex roles that are required of the
function. These models imply, amongst others, two things: first, that a progression from a bureaucratic form of personnel management to a strategically
integrated human resource management function is desirable for all organizations if they are to manage people effectively; and second, that a best practice
model of people management necessitates a strategic role for the personnel/
HR function.

It seems timely to move the debate on by examining what is happening
in practice across different sectors in terms of people management and the
roles that the HR function may play in order to support these practices. The
first important insight from our research was the diversity both in terms of
HR in practice and the role of the HR function in supporting that practice.
Furthermore there were anomalies in HR practice that existing models could
not sufficiently explain. The second important insight was that an understanding of the influence of both the internal and external context and the stages
of organizational transition is vital for understanding that diversity. This
chapter concentrates on examining inner contextual factors. It does not de-
value the relevance and importance of external influences, but for the purposes
of presenting detailed empirical data we have chosen to emphasize internal
issues.

The conclusions that we draw are first, that the path of development for both
the function and practice of HR may not be linear in nature, as implied by much
of the literature, but cyclical instead, and second, that if one chooses to define
'best practice' in terms of meeting the contextual needs of the organization
rather than matching universalistic or 'HR professional' notions of what the
function should do, then best practice may require the function to operate
at a level other than strategic. Thirdly, we conclude that there need not be a
match in practice between three related aspects of managing people within

organizations: the role of the HR function, the management practice of the HR function, and the people management practice of the organization.

The recognition of this complexity is important. The indiscriminate application of universalistic models, accompanied by insufficient appreciation of differing contexts, can result in the implementation of inappropriate HR strategies and processes and incongruent role posturing by the HR function. The result is that an HR function may fail to deliver a service that meets the needs of its employing organization.

THE DEBATE SO FAR

The body of literature which concentrates on the role of the HR function represents an established debate conducted since the emergence of the function itself at the beginning of this century (Anthony 1986; Armstrong 1984; Legge 1978; Storey 1992; Torrington 1989; Tyson 1987; Watson 1977). For the most part, this debate is situated within the twin schools of thought of 'industrial relations' and 'critical theory'. This work draws out the historical evolutionary path of the function drawing on experience within Western economies, and illustrates how the development of the function is representative of the changing perspectives on the nature of HR's contribution to organizational effectiveness. An evolutionary cycle which summarizes the development of the function's practice is shown in Fig. 6.1. The evolution may be interpreted as internal to an organization or external, as the personnel function itself has developed over the century. To explain more fully: the shift from the welfare role often fulfilled by an underdeveloped function under a paternalistic system occurs when it becomes untenable, for instance, as numbers increase in organizations or as there is a need to systematize interventions such as recruitment and selection in order to achieve consistency in procedure across the organization. The danger in this stage of transitional to personnel management is that line managers hand over responsibility for the face-to-face management of people to a faceless administrative system (Anthony 1986). This classic bureaucratic function may add a collective bargaining or industrial relations role to its portfolio as the next stage. HRM was put forward as the ultimate stage where responsibility for people management would be returned to line managers and integration would be sought between HR and business strategy.

In the 1980s HRM models, situated within the strategic HR body of literature (for example, Beer et al. 1985; Dyer 1985; Fombrun et al. 1984; Guest 1987), prescribed that in order to achieve the implementation of HRM in practice it was necessary for the function itself to take on a strategic and business role more in line with Legge's 'conformist innovator' (1978) or Tyson's 'architect' model (1987). It was anticipated that the need for the roles of 'clerk of works' (a basic administrative function organizing pay and rations for employees, and perhaps acting as a welfare function in addition, often associated with a pater-

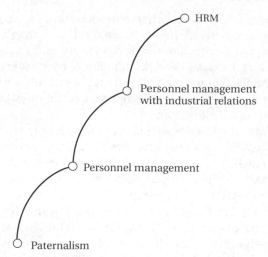

Fig. 6.1. The evolutionary cycle

nalistic style of general management) and 'contracts manager' (a standard personnel management function providing legal, industrial relations, and bureaucratic services) would decline (Tyson 1987). The move for the personnel function to identify itself clearly with the strategic business manager camp was viewed as universally applicable and desirable for all organizational contexts. The function would have to abandon its role as the 'loyal opposition' to its management peers; in other words, it needed to distance itself from both listening to and representing alternative views from different stakeholders within an organization. Thus its pluralistic welfare and industrial relations roots would have to be abandoned in favour of unitarist strategic HRM.

Some normative studies have attempted to introduce an element of contextualism into their analysis of current HR roles and practice. For instance, Tyson (1987) argues that his three roles (clerk of works, contracts manager, and architect) not only reflect different historical stages in the development of the function itself but may also be found at different levels within the same organization. Yet Tyson also implies that the architect is the desired role for the function, and in his more recent research regrets that the shift to decentralization has reduced the strategic role and inflated the role of the contracts manager at the HR divisional level (Tyson 1995*a*). Pauuwe (1995) lists various internal and external features that help to determine the need for a personnel department, not simply its role.

Empirical evidence from the 1980s and 1990s in the UK indicates that many HR functions have yet to achieve the strategic positioning advocated by the prescriptive models. In describing a study of HR's role in change management based on case studies, Storey (1992) also reported four different roles being enacted. These he classified using a two by two matrix, the axes of which are labelled 'strategic/tactical' and 'interventionary/non-interventionary' (see Fig. 6.2). From these axes he derives four main roles: change agent (interventionary and strategic), adviser (non-interventionary and strategic), regulator (interventionary and tactical), and handmaiden (non-interventionary and tactical). Storey argues that it is only the change agent role which is closest to the role envisaged by the HRM models, but reports that few functions within his survey fell into such a classification.

The evidence from the large-scale surveys in the late 1980s and early 1990s also suggests that whilst there were changes in management practice in terms of the management of people, many of these changes were introduced as piecemeal initiatives, implemented as responsive changes rather than as part of any determined strategic shift in pursuit of prescriptive models (Kochen and Dyer 1995; Sisson 1995; Storey 1992). The prompt for this shift has helpfully been labelled as 'thinking pragmatism' (Legge 1995b). The continued absence of boardroom representation for the HR function in 66 per cent of large organizations surveyed in the Workplace and Industrial Relations Surveys (Millward *et al.* 1992) would imply that the HR function's access to strategic planning has yet to be achieved (Sisson 1995). Purcell and Ahlstrand (1994) bring out the dilemma of decentralized business units, operating as quasi-independent businesses with minimal administrative control from the centre, which experience difficulties in adopting a strategically consistent approach to HRM. Given the emphasis in such organizations on diversity and opportunism it becomes increasingly difficult for organizations to impose company-wide standards and norms concerning how people should be managed. Is there, therefore, a need for an overall architect or strategist at the head of the function?

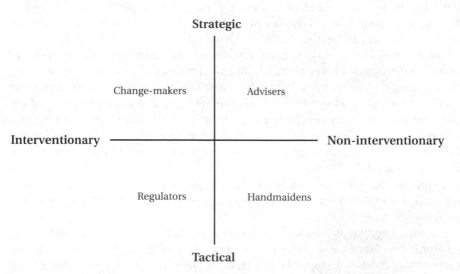

Fig. 6.2. Types of personnel management
Source: Storey (1992)

Thus a pluralism may be recognized at a descriptive level but not applauded at a prescriptive or normative level. Why should this be so? Is it merely that one body of literature prescribes (the rhetoric and unitarism of strategic HR) while another body describes (the pluralistic reality of industrial relations)? Or is it that one is concerned with action (textbooks) and one is concerned with criticism (critical theory)? A number of suggestions can be made. In part it may reflect the fact that management as a science has been dominated by the rationale that there is one best way to manage, and as Legge has argued persuasively in terms of HRM, this belief in universalism has profitably fuelled the business of both university management schools and consultants (1995b).

Arguably, another factor has been the desire by professional bodies within the personnel and human resource management field to promulgate a best practice view for the purpose of maintaining professional qualifications and examinations. Whilst this may have been just possible when the function was primarily positioned as a bureaucratic and administrative service to other functions, it is increasingly untenable as HR practices are subject to strategic choice.

Tyson (1995b) has recently argued that HR as a function is always in transition because the function has to address fundamental people dilemmas for which there is ultimately no resolution. Consequently it is always in a state of change, trying to reinterpret and reconcile societal and individual variables with organizational realities. Therefore, Tyson goes on to argue, the various traditions found in personnel and HR—welfare, industrial relations, manpower planning, and so on—were all attempts to address these unresolvable tensions in different historical times.

An additional explanation for the failure of research to capture the complexity and diversity in practice is that research into HR has often been limited methodologically. Quantitative surveys may be capable of giving an impressively broad picture of what is happening in organizations, but cannot authoritatively explain *why* what is happening is happening (Brewster and Hegewisch 1994; Millward *et al.* 1992). More qualitative research is often based on interviews with one personnel or HR director or develops one case study (Kerfoot and Knights 1992; Ogbonna 1990). Here the danger is overgeneralization, in terms of elevating either one interviewee's interpretation of his or her organization above the views of others, or one organization's experience or history above those of other companies.

The research reported on here attempts to redress the balance. We have come to the conclusion that the current HRM literature is implicitly prescribing for all companies a role for the HR function that may be unrealistic or even dysfunctional. In order for the reader to understand our logic, this chapter presents HRM activities in four of the sample organizations in some detail. The cases clarify the significant variation of current HR practice. In many cases our informants felt that the HR function was operating effectively. We concur with that judgement, based on our analysis, even though what is being done does not easily fit with current models.

An earlier paper (Hope Hailey 1997) presents similar data thematically and comparatively, but therefore necessarily briefly, across all of the organizations in our sample. In this chapter we have chosen to give greater contextual information in order to explore and explain in more depth the diversity that was found in practice. The companies chosen as case studies here were selected from the sample to illustrate the diversity of roles and contextual factors that contribute to that diversity. Hewlett Packard and W. H. Smith News illustrate different stages in the evolutionary cycle (see Fig. 6.1), while Kraft Jacobs Suchard illustrates different product and business strategies, and Citibank different structures and occupational groups. All these companies are sophisticated organizations, yet the HR function in each plays—and should play—a very different role.

HEWLETT PACKARD: STAGES IN THE EVOLUTIONARY CYCLE—HRM OR SHRM

The personnel department in Hewlett Packard is organized into a matrix structure. The Personnel Director for the UK reports both to the Managing Director of the UK and to the Head of Personnel for Europe in Geneva. At the time of the research the UK department was divided into two groupings: policy and operations. The policy grouping was made up of managers heading up units for Compensation and Benefits, Training and Development, UK Pensions, and Personnel Systems. On the operational side there was an overall Personnel Manager for the UK sales region, based at the Bracknell office, who not only reported to the Personnel Director, UK, but also to the Head of Sales, Europe. In addition there were personnel managers providing an operational service on-site to the different business locations in the UK. Communication with the line managers was carried out through the personnel officers, who were assigned to each business unit to act as consultants in the implementation of personnel policies and procedures.

In 1990 the size of the personnel department was scaled down, as there was evidence that line managers saw it as an over-sized function. At that time the number of staff employed in what was perceived as a platform service function was seen as unacceptable in the context of the Voluntary Severance Programme that was running for the first time in the company's history. The redundancies were accompanied by a thrust towards decentralization, the strategic intent being to give freedom back to individual business units.

As we have seen in Chapters 3 and 5, performance is managed at Hewlett Packard through a twin-pronged approach: a tightly monitored business and performance management system, and also the well-known 'HP Way'—a formalized statement of 'the way we work around here'. As we have argued in Chapter 5, Hewlett Packard seems to be able to implement a detailed battery of planning systems ('I need to keep delivering; I need to make sure my staff are delivering; you need sustained performance; you need success'—Leading Edge Forum interviews) and at the same time receive feedback from staff to the effect that they perceive the Hewlett Packard culture as one that encourages individual freedom and innovation. Therefore Hewlett Packard does prescribe beliefs and does prescribe and measure outcomes, but it does not prescribe the behaviours that follow on from those beliefs or that necessarily lead to such outcomes. The end result in terms of human resource management is that working for a people-oriented organization is a key 'motivator' within the unwritten rules of the games (Scott-Morgan 1994).

However, the HP Way is seen as entirely independent of and unconnected to the personnel function. Instead it is perceived as wholly owned by the organization: 'The HR function will never be the owner of the HP Way; however, it is its guardian, its articulator. The real owners are the managers' (senior manager). Therefore the management of people and its strategic significance is an assumption 'taken for granted' and a core value and objective. The personnel department is expected to deliver an operational and administratively excellent platform service that enables managers to achieve their objectives. John Kick, Director of the HR function in the UK, expressed it thus:

The primary role of the HR function is the provision of people-related processes—hiring, firing, moving people around, administering salaries and benefits. All the other things that the function would like to provide are only possible and welcome once the basics are done.

For such a people-oriented company it is surprising to find a number of familiar criticisms levelled at the personnel department. In particular, personnel was viewed from outside the department as not following the company drive for quality, nor was it perceived as understanding what its customers needed in terms of basic service delivery. Therefore a major objective for the function was to achieve a consistent approach to personnel policies across all the business units. This was difficult given the Hewlett Packard structure, because the business unit managers were very strong and, whilst they recognized that people management was a core practice, unless they could see an HR initiative as contributing to business objectives they tended to resist its implementation. However, one personnel officer recently recruited from outside the organization remarked that it was important to remember that 'as a standard HR department their contribution is quite high—but as an HP department it is not high enough'. Or as another line manager put it:

They [HR] are handicapped by the culture. Hewlett Packard provides a culture where most of these human relations issues are not hot. There are no unions; managers do believe they have an obligation to develop their employees and so every manager believes he or she has a role as a personnel manager.

In summary, where line managers do successfully and conscientiously practise good people management, HR may be under-appreciated for its role. There appeared to be a significant difference between senior management's perceptions of its importance and those of lower-level staff. At a senior level HR was recognized as an important and influential function. One business unit manager commented, 'we spend money on two big things: people and facilities, and I can't do that in isolation'. 'People fulfilment' was one of the Managing Director's key business objectives, and other senior managers reported that HR had been part of the strategic debate for a long time. Yet as an operational service HR's influence was perceived as quite low. For instance, 31 per cent of respondents to the questionnaire thought personnel was a waste of resources, only 20 per cent agreed that the HR department played an important part in the success of the organization, and 62 per cent ranked the personnel department as the least influential department in the development of people management skills.

W. H. SMITH NEWS: STAGES IN THE EVOLUTIONARY CYCLE—PATERNALISM TO PERSONNEL MANAGEMENT

W. H. Smith News has 4,300 employees in 72 wholesale houses and over 22,000 retail customers. Above the two main divisions sits a central group structure which sets broad financial and growth targets, with both the Retail and News divisions given large degrees of autonomy with which to achieve them. Each wholesale house has a house manager and each region a regional manager. The houses are run as autonomous businesses with each house manager responsible for meeting tight financial performance targets set by the group. Since the News Division is the cash-rich division within the group, effectiveness in achieving financial targets is vital.

In 1989 the W. H. Smith Group instigated a process of corporate renewal. The need for change in the News Division was particularly strong, as in 1988 the division had lost £40 million of business overnight to the non-unionized rival TNT:

We feared we might lose more business. We had always got contracts on the shake of hand—we had never had to bid for a contract to deliver newspapers before . . . The whole business had to turn on its head. From being a series of individual houses which were autonomously managed, a lot of functions came into the centre, personnel included.

The prevailing style of management was characterized by the Group CEO as 'autocratic, tempered by paternalism. The values of the business were loyalty, security and obedience to orders,' The nature of the work within the News Division also brought strong traditions. The business ran '24 hours a day, 7 days a week, 364 days a year' (only Christmas Day was not worked). The hours are long, deadlines tight, and much of the work, particularly in the warehouse, is physically demanding, all of which has engendered a 'macho' culture. In such a fast-moving business there had been a distinct lack of human resource planning and personnel interventions had been reactive, if indeed there had been any at all. However, the pace and the deadline-driven nature of the business together with clear success criteria, generated a high level of excitement and motivation amongst staff, despite low wages. As one manager said, 'once you are in it becomes a way of life and there is a very strong sense of identity amongst employees'. The company had always prided itself on being a caring company, an expression of the paternalism which ran throughout the division. Nevertheless, alongside the softer aspects of such paternalism were the usual companion characteristics of tremendously powerful positions for the house managers. From the Unwritten Rules of the Game analysis two clear messages emerged: do not challenge the house manager's status or authority, and do not challenge decisions.

Against this backdrop it was decided to instigate a process of cultural change in order to implement a new managerial style of 'directness, openness to ideas, commitment to the success of others, a willingness to accept personal account-ability and the strong development of teamwork and trust. Differing views will be sought' ('Vision' booklet). This was seen as crucial in order to deliver the strategic intent of enhanced customer focus and increased productivity, all of which was perceived to depend on changing the nature and behaviour of employees. This was seen to be a key task for the HR function.

Until that time the personnel department had been an underdeveloped wel-fare function with only three staff, since people management had traditionally been the responsibility of the line managers. However, whereas this would seem to accord with an HRM model, in fact within this paternalistic regime people management was not *consciously* devolved to the line managers as part of a purposefully managed strategy seeking consistency, but rather manage-ment style was determined by the various individualistic personal styles of the powerful house managers.

The development route that was adopted reflected the needs and the context of the business at that time. The house managers were key to the change process, but their strong power base could not be eroded too overtly at first, as they were also key in terms of maintaining the cash cow role that the division provided for the rest of the group. They also held tacit knowledge of 'the way things are done around here'. The absence of any kind of systematic recruit-ment, selection, appraisal, or communication system meant that a textbook transformational change would be difficult without the provision of systems to support it. Equally, for the HR function to demand a strategic role and dictate the changes would have alienated the managers. The division also needed to maintain the cohesion and commitment that had been elicited through the seemingly anachronistic paternalistic culture. In addition the presence of union strongholds in some regions meant that many more obvious and crude initiatives such as performance-related pay were simply not open to the personnel function in the short term.

The route that was adopted, and encouraged from group level, was much more of a Trojan Horse strategy. A female personnel manager was appointed from within the group. She was one of very few women managers within the division and certainly the most senior. She did not demand a place on the executive council initially, but instead set about formalizing personnel systems and offering to take some of the administrative burden from house managers. The department supported extensive training and development activity and in particular was seeking to extend this to non-managerial staff. In addition it defined five objectives for itself: to increase employee involvement; to give support and advice to managers in dealing with problems, such as legislative issues, that could not be dealt with easily at line level; to provide extensive documentation for procedures and policies and to share information through workshops; to keep personnel issues on the strategy agenda for the division; and finally to maintain cordial relations with the group.

The function also introduced a management style survey with the aim of countering what was seen as the strongly deferential culture within the division. The document was sent to all News Division staff by post and allowed them to comment on a series of thirty different characteristics of the performance of their manager. The data were published and shared, on an aggregate basis, amongst all employees. The fact that this information was generated bottom-up gave the personnel function permission and legitimacy for acting upon the insight that it already possessed before the survey was completed.

By providing a more bureaucratic service to the line managers and by seeking to assist rather than confront or overwhelm through more value-led cultural change, the personnel function won many friends and few enemies. Shortly after her arrival the Personnel Manager was invited to join the executive council, and as a result the action plan's outputs always include at least one human resource issue. The function is now recognized as contributing directly to the division's performance, particularly at a senior level:

The personnel function contributes an enormous amount to the bottom line, providing higher standards in recruitment and less mistakes in dismissal. Quite a few people have been made redundant; this was handled with minimum costs and upset. Personnel help with saving money and we have a better-trained workforce.

The research was conducted at the beginning of 1994. By slowly formalizing and systematizing the personnel systems and restructuring the division, the business has now been placed where it may well be capable of dealing with both more radical transformational change and also a more strategically oriented personnel function.

KRAFT JACOBS SUCHARD: PRODUCT AND BUSINESS STRATEGY

Kraft Jacobs Suchard is part of the American-owned Philip Morris corporation. As we described in Chapter 1, our research was conducted at the head office of Kraft Jacobs Suchard in the UK, in Cheltenham, which coordinates the company's central activities including sales, marketing, HR, finance, information systems, distribution, and planning and has over 500 employees. A major organizational restructure was completed in January 1994 creating business-focused units which are supported by platform services including HR. The culture of Kraft Jacobs Suchard UK is based on the concept of continuous improvement, providing clear objectives and strategies and supporting a strong results-oriented approach to the business. A 'process-oriented' management style has developed as a result which means a strong adherence to policies and procedures, tight reporting requirements, and a focus on the business planning process. Clear financial targets, detailing growth figures in turnover and profit, are agreed by Kraft Jacobs Suchard in Zurich, the European headquarters, and each country devises its own broad strategy to fulfil them. The severity of the targets together with the strong emphasis on driving costs out of the business has brought a culture which stresses short-term payback. With the emphasis on results and strong performance measures, and with the company operating in a very competitive market, there is little welfare activity. The needs of the business come first and treatment of individuals could be characterized as 'tough love' (Legge 1989), an approach which does not tolerate employees' weaknesses but aims rather to secure employee development and good performance. In the Kraft Jacobs Suchard UK headquarters there is no union representation.

The HR Director's presence on the board of the UK division provides a clear integrative linkage between the strategy-making process and the management of human resources, on both a formal and an informal basis. The interaction may best be described as 'facilitative', however, with one senior manager saying:

I don't think that HR gets factored into the development of business strategies. HR would be involved in our three-year planning in terms of development, succession planning, and so on, but it doesn't determine which way the company goes or how the company is going to expand into different cores . . . HR falls out of the business strategy.

The HR function in the UK operates within a framework of US policy and initiatives. The majority of senior managers viewed the HR department as crucial in aligning people to the business strategies and ensuring the delivery of objectives. In addition to the formal process, the members of the HR staff are also part of the management team of each business unit, and so HR perceives itself to be 'operating very much alongside the business strategy because you are working alongside the people who are developing the business strategy'.

A clear example of HR's role downstream from business strategy can be seen in the company's acquisition strategy process. Kraft Jacobs Suchard UK as an organization is a function of a number of high-profile acquisitions. This strategy has strong implications for HRM and the importance afforded this strategy has consequently given the HR function a strong profile. HR is not directly involved in the acquisition 'in terms of the economics of putting the thing together'; it is once the acquisition has been settled upon and agreed by the

Philip Morris board that the HR Director becomes intimately involved with the acquisition team.

Our determination is that we will need only so many people, our determination is that there will be a cost of terminating people, can we move them, and so on. HR is very involved in this. (HR Director)

In addition, as one would expect in a fast-moving consumer goods business, the HR function runs a very tight performance management system in order to support its commitment to continuous improvement. It also places great emphasis on management development. (Kraft Jacobs Suchard does little direct recruitment into sales, preferring to poach young sales reps who have been inducted and trained by other companies.) The role of the HR department, both in effecting strategic linkage and in maintaining the continuous improvement culture, has strong support from most senior managers.

CITIBANK: STRUCTURE AND OCCUPATIONAL GROUPS

Global Finance Europe, the corporate banking arm of Citibank in Europe, employed at the time of the research a total of 3,470 people, 1,790 of whom were based in the UK. These people were supported by an HR staff of 60 across Europe, 28 in the UK, and by a training centre employing 12 people.

Global Finance Europe was structured as a matrix with ten functional 'activity centres', such as Financial Institutions, Derivatives, and Capital Markets, each acting as an autonomous business unit headed by an Activity Centre Manager. In addition each country had its own management structure responsible for overseeing all operations in that country. Whilst an individual might have been located within one activity centre, they might also have worked closely with people from another centre, in which case they would have a dotted line reporting relationship to them in addition to that to their immediate boss and country manager. Consequently many people working for the bank had multiple reporting lines. A recent emphasis on team working had also meant that departments now worked closely together on many projects.

Given decentralization and an emphasis on opportunism it can become difficult to impose country-wide standards and norms. The situation is exacerbated at Citibank because the staff are autonomous, quasi-professional knowledge workers who handle products with a highly variable lifespan. Products, departments, and teams can be disbanded overnight. This is a necessary by-product of a strategy that first emphasizes closeness to the customer and responsiveness to needs, and secondly is subject to the constraints and restrictions of a highly regulated external environment. The knowledge workers have specialized expertise and experience and therefore highly individualized requirements of HR.

Therefore the HR function organized itself as a matrix. The senior HR

Director for Global Finance Europe had seven country HR managers reporting in to her. In addition five product HR managers and their teams were attached to the activity centres providing generalist support on a Europe-wide basis. Thus the personnel officers reported both to their country heads and to their product managers. In addition there was the centralized HR support that provided administrative back-up in areas such as payroll to front-line HR staff.

The HR generalists each enjoyed a close relationship with their activity centre manager and were important members of the senior management teams. The interface worked extremely well at senior levels and all the activity centre managers interviewed spoke highly of the contribution of individual HR professionals and the importance of people management to their business. One key role played by HR was to 'make the matrix talk'. However, our research found that at manager level and below there was a lack of understanding of the role of HR, particularly since, following a downsizing exercise which included HR, there was no time for HR to play a 'tea and sympathy' role.

Linkages between business strategy and HR were quite strong and there was an open door policy allowing the HR Director to attend directors' meetings if she wished. The Managing Director also actively supported HR. However, developing an overall HR strategy to guide all HR activities in such a diverse and fast-moving organization is difficult. As a consequence:

There is no HR department as a whole . . . we face out towards different businesses that are not that closely linked . . . We don't behave as a department on a weekly basis, we interact as we need to . . . But I don't think you could look at us and say we are a department . . . that puts us very close to the business units.

The responsive and flexible nature of the service provided by the function also meant that the overall impact and contribution of the HR department as a whole was somewhat fragmented, resulting in individual contributions by HR officers being highly valued by line managers, but the function being under-valued. Yet the department was meeting the needs of the business strategy.

DISCUSSION

The evidence from our general findings and from the four case studies presented above points to a diversity of roles enacted by the HR or personnel function. A number of interesting observations can be made from this study which deserve further exploration at a future stage.

First, it is possible for an organization to be managing its people in a strategic manner but for the HR function to be fulfilling a role other than that of 'architect' (Tyson 1987) or strategist in the way that the HRM models envisage. This gives rise to a further potential stage or practice within the evolutionary path which we call *Integrated HRM*. The organizational conditions that would support such a stage are described below (see Fig. 6.3).

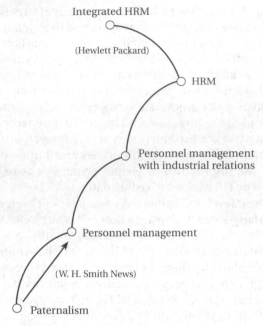

Fig. 6.3. The evolutionary cycle

In 'Integrated HRM' people management as a source of competitive advantage is integrated within mainstream management thought such that the presence of a powerful and lobbying HR director and function may be less important. It is less important because line and senior managers are capable of incorporating HR processes into their thought processes in an informed way, and as such do not require prompting or influencing by HR specialists. These managers still need specialist advice in terms of implementation options, but this can be provided either by the HR function acting as an internal consultant, or by external consultants who may be brought in on a flexible basis when necessary. People management as a strategic lever becomes an assumption taken for granted within management cognition. However, the HR function may be required in practice to fulfil any of the functions set out in the evolutionary path depending on the needs of the business and the context in which it finds itself. In that sense the path becomes much more of a cycle than a linear progression.

Hewlett Packard provides such an example of this practice within our sample. The HR function at divisional level within Hewlett Packard is expected to provide a good platform service more akin to excellent personnel management than to HRM, and to act as an internal consultant to general managers when required. However, HR is not seen as being in the driving seat of people management within Hewlett Packard. It may be that this reflects the divisional role and that an examination of the group role at Hewlett Packard would reveal some differences. If so, this would bear out Tyson's reflection (1995*a*) that the shift at divisional level is towards the 'contracts manager' role.

Our second observation is that where an organization is placed in terms of *transition* is important. An organization cannot jump through the stages too quickly, nor can it always omit a stage (the exception probably being the stage of personnel management with industrial relations, collective bargaining in the formalized sense not being present in all organizations). For W. H. Smith News to move forward from the paternalistic phase it was necessary for them to go through a bureaucratizing phase in order to formalize and systematize personnel interventions. To do this they needed to take responsibility away from line managers for a period of time before personnel processes were in a sufficiently manageable condition for responsibility to be returned to line management. The contextual factors of the business (in particular its position as cash cow, the power positions of the barons, and the unionization in parts) prevented it from moving too fast towards a powerful HR function which could have alienated and destroyed motivation, and with it business performance. In contrast, Lloyds Bank UK Retail Banking arguably moved too fast with the implementation of their performance management systems and their attempt to shift the personnel function into a more strategic position (see Chapter 3). They failed to allow sufficient time and give sufficient support for branch managers to make the transition from their autonomous paternalism to being as much managed as managers. The consequence was that the 'managers jumped into the trenches with the troops' and the personnel function was widely discredited. Yet in model terms the Lloyds Bank UK Retail Banking personnel function would have fitted far more of the HRM criteria than the function in W. H. Smith News.

The third point we would like to make is that there are many significant *contextual features* that affect the practice of HR. The contextual features that we found led to different practices appear to include:

1. Stages in transition: as noted above for W. H. Smith News and Hewlett Packard (and Lloyds Bank UK Retail Banking amongst the other companies in our sample), this can limit the speed and route of development of the HR function.
2. The nature of staff employed: in Citibank (and the Chelsea & Westminster Healthcare Trust amongst the other companies in our sample), the staff employed—knowledge workers and professionals—and the product and fast pace of the business means that HR can achieve strategic integration with the business in a covert form, but could never be accepted as a true architect of the business as the staff would not accept such obvious direct control over their activities. Their need for personal autonomy is too high.
3. Business strategy and product: Kraft Jacobs Suchard, operating in a fast-moving consumer goods business, can maintain an HR function which

takes a more controlling position, because of both the kind of staff employed (sales representatives) and the needs of the business (its short-term targets and its acquisitions).

4. Structure: for those businesses operating with decentralized, autonomous business units, such as Citibank and Kraft Jacobs Suchard (and the Chelsea & Westminster Healthcare Trust amongst the other companies in our sample), a more advisory role (Storey 1992; see Fig. 6.2) may be appropriate.

The significance of these contextual variables supports the work of Pauuwe (1995).

CONCLUSION

The research conducted so far suggests that a greater appreciation of contextual variables needs to be achieved. Depending on such variables, different forms of organizational people management practice, HR functional practice, and different roles for the HR function itself may coexist. This suggests that the development of function and practice may be more cyclical than linear, the development being more dependent on contextual needs than practitioner sophistication.

More importantly, this research refutes the argument that the role the HR function enacts within an organization determines or reflects the sophistication of people management practice practised at a broader organizational level and its ability to meet the strategic needs of the business (compare Purcell 1995). The picture painted within this chapter is much more complex than that. More research is currently being conducted with the same sample organizations as part of a longitudinal study. We hope to assess the impact of contextual variables on HR and people management practice more exactly within this second stage. In broader terms, the data collected so far would suggest that both practitioners and academics alike should move away from either promulgating or testing for the existence of universalistic models of HRM. Instead attention should shift towards gaining a greater understanding of the reasons for the diversity of practice that exists in reality.

HRM Policies and Management Practices

PATRICK McGOVERN

THE ROLE OF LINE MANAGERS IN HUMAN RESOURCE MANAGEMENT

One of the characteristic features of the human resource management literature is the pivotal role which has been given to line managers as a delivery point for a variety of employment policies that are intended to raise the performance of the workforce. Guest's (1987) initial reconstruction of the core tenets of HRM within the British context identified the role of line managers as one of the central components of HRM. He stated that the attitudes of line managers, along with their behaviour and practices, were crucial if the importance of human resources was to be genuinely recognized and integrated into the organization. Consequently, line managers should 'accept their responsibility to practise human resource management although they may use specialist resources to assist in policy development, problem solving, training and the like' (Guest 1987: 512).

Legge (1989), in her review of US and UK models of HRM, concluded that HRM is 'vested in line management as business managers responsible for coordinating and directing *all* resources in the business unit in pursuit of bottom line profits' (1989: 28). She argues that this approach differs from the classic personnel management model in which the line's role simply reflected the view that all managers were responsible in a general sense for personnel management since they all managed people. It also meant, according to Legge, that most specialist personnel work still had to be implemented within various line management departments by a dedicated function. Managers under HRM, by contrast, handled such responsibilities themselves which meant that the human resource dimension was an integral part of business strategy rather than something which flowed from it. In short, the overall argument is that if human resources are really so critical then HRM is too important to be left to personnel specialists (Storey 1995). In the British context, this has traditionally been depicted as a *devolution* of certain personnel activities to line managers after a voluntary reallocation of responsibilities by the personnel specialists, possibly as part of a strategic review of their work (Storey 1992). Again, there is considerable ambiguity over how an organization, or its personnel function, would devolve its activities in practice.

While the message that line management has an important role to play in HRM is reasonably clear, some questions may be raised about the assumptions behind it. There is also considerable ambiguity over what this actually means in practice. First, the distinction between the role of line managers under personnel management and under HRM may be somewhat thin. While there may be some basis for such a distinction when comparing stereotypes of personnel management and HRM at an abstract level (Guest 1987), there is little empirical evidence to support the existence of these stereotypes within organizations. For instance, one of the characteristic features of the role of front-line supervisors has always been the direct control which they exerted over the output of the 'human resources' under their command. This included the hiring, performance monitoring, and firing of employees (Child and Partridge 1982; R. Edwards 1979). Second, the idea that line managers should internalize the importance of human resources and behave accordingly suggests that they should also engage in good *people management* practices (which would include interpersonal skills, team-building skills, and so on) along with implementing personnel policies. However, this distinction between human resource and people management practices has never been made explicit. Third, there are no indications of what the role of the supervisor should be under HRM. Lowe (1992) has tentatively suggested that the predominant management style might be that of a coach, enabler, or facilitator; the preferred method of labour control would be that of personal control; there would be high levels of status and authority, and high pay differentials, compared to that of the nearest subordinate; and finally career opportunities would be quite open. While these features describe an ideal type, they may be much more difficult to achieve in practice.

While there is of course a vast literature on managers' jobs and managerial behaviour (see, for example, Mintzberg 1973; Nicholson and West 1988; Scase and Goffee 1989; R. Stewart 1989; Watson 1994) there is still a remarkable lack of empirical material on the role of line managers within HRM in comparison with other HRM areas such as the link with business strategy (for a review, see Truss and Gratton 1994). An exception here is Paul Edwards's (1987) innovative survey of factory managers which examined how they managed their subordinates and how they themselves were managed. But, as Storey (1992) comments, Edwards's survey-based analysis of managers' roles in labour relations provides limited information on the actual practices of line managers.

The research which has examined line managers under HRM to date has produced rather mixed results in relation to the process of devolution and the knowledge and ability of line managers. Storey's (1992) research indicates that line managers were becoming far more important in determining how human resources would be used across a sample of manufacturing and public sector organizations. They had clearly become more important as a delivery mechanism for human resource policies. However, these changes did not arise from a formal redivision of human resource responsibilities between human resource specialists and the line. They had, instead, been brought about by changes in manufacturing processes, in labour management generally, and by the assertiveness of the line managers themselves. Many of these saw an attempted switch from the 'traditional supervisor' to the 'first line manager', who was expected to embody a new management style which included involving, developing, and communicating with employees. It is also worth noting here that Clark (1993) has found that technical change has also led to increased line manager involvement in employee relations issues.

Also, in relation to devolution, Bevan and Hayday (1994) found that line managers were not adequately consulted about the devolution of responsibilities and were, as a result, unclear about their roles. In any case, they were reluctant to take on personnel responsibilities, because they felt that they were really the work of the personnel function. This, in turn, meant that many human resource departments were reluctant to devolve responsibilities to the line.

The results with regard to the knowledge and ability of line managers to take on these responsibilities are rather bleak. The case studies conducted by Kirkpatrick *et al.* (1992) and by Lowe (1992) found that devolution to line management was severely constrained by the short-term pressures of the business and by the low educational and technical skill base of the supervisors. This made it more difficult for them to focus on the developmental or 'soft' approach to labour utilization. Similarly, recent research by Hyman and Cunningham (1995) indicates that there has been a lack of training and competence amongst line managers and supervisors in key areas, though this was something which they were aware of. Attempts to devolve 'hard' (where the emphasis is on cost control) and 'soft' practices to the line were also undermined by limited resources, particularly for training, and the equation of performance with cost-cutting in an effort to satisfy short-term financial control criteria (see Chapter 2).

This chapter seeks to develop and extend these initial findings by focusing on two related issues concerning the viability of HRM in practice. The first of these concerns the existing state of line management practice. Here we provide evidence on the practice of performance appraisal as a prelude to our discussion of the factors which enable and constrain line involvement. Performance appraisal was selected as an example of management practice for a number of reasons. First, it represents an example *par excellence* of the direct involvement of managers with their staff. Second, it is an area which combines both the 'soft' and 'hard' (Legge 1989) elements of HRM since it requires certain professional interpersonal skills on the part of managers and is concerned with the monitoring and control of employee performance. Third, it frequently feeds into other policies such as remuneration, training, and career development. Finally, it is important to note that our selection of performance appraisal is not based on the assumption that it is a practice whose design and delivery has recently been devolved to line managers (not least because performance appraisals have always been conducted by line managers). Our aim instead is to explore the prospects for the further devolution of the design and delivery of such policies to the line given the existing state of human resource practices amongst line managers.

The second general set of issues concerns the configuration of incentives and constraints which shape the level of line management involvement in areas such as performance appraisal. Here we are concerned with the implementation of human resource policies, specifically the consistency and quality of practice across different managers.

The next section of this chapter describes the findings on the degree of management involvement and on the factors which influence the involvement of line managers. In the concluding part of the chapter we draw out some of the implications of this research for the theory and practice of HRM.

PERFORMANCE APPRAISAL

Before we present our findings on performance appraisal in detail, we would first like to provide a brief overview of the general distribution of human resource responsibilities between the human resource department and line managers in the case study organizations. (A more detailed account is given in Chapter 6.)

The distribution of human resource responsibilities

During the course of the research we examined the distribution of responsibility for human resource policies and practices. In general, line managers were directly involved in the selection, appraisal, and development of their subordinates in all of the case study organizations. Such areas were clearly viewed as being the responsibility of the line. The general view, from both line managers and human resource specialists, was that line managers should 'own' these activities because it was they who worked directly with their staff on a daily basis and also because it was they who were ultimately responsible for the performance of their departments or areas. In these cases, the human resource function acted in an advisory capacity whilst monitoring recruitment and appraisal procedures, and the like.

In sum, the dominant model was of line managers being directly involved in HR activities supported by a specialist human resource function. To paraphrase Legge's (1989) description of personnel management, cited earlier, human resource management was still the work of specialists as well as of all those who were involved in the management of people at work.

Performance appraisal

Two key findings emerged during our research on human resource policies. First, the involvement of the line does not necessarily mean that policies are implemented consistently by all line managers within the organization. Second, even where they are carried out, the quality of practice is frequently not of the kind which we might assume from the spirit of the prescriptive models reviewed by Legge (1989). (These models have been strangely silent on managerial practice.) In short, the results indicate significant variation both across and within organizations.

Each of the organizations involved in this research claimed to have formal performance appraisals for all categories of employee, with one exception. In W. H. Smith News, the trade unions which represented the shop-floor workers had resisted management's attempts to introduce this policy (see below). Officially, according to company handbooks, all of the organizations had annual performance appraisals or evaluations, some of which included quarterly updates (Kraft Jacobs Suchard, Hewlett Packard, and Citibank). However, the results of our survey present a different picture (see Table 7.1) which suggests a discrepancy between rhetoric and reality. (An appraisal was defined in the questionnaire as 'a time set in advance in which you spend over 30 minutes discussing your performance'. Since we had established from interviews that employees were fully aware of the existence of appraisals and evaluations we

Table 7.1. 'How frequently is your performance at work appraised?' (all respondents, %)

	Never	Once a year or less	Twice a year or more	Every month or more
BT Payphones	2	41	20	37
C&W NHS Trust	42	42	12	4
Citibank	1	86	13	0
GP UK	0	40	60	0
HP	1	58	29	12
KJS	0	34	56	10
Lloyds	1	7	82	10
WHS News	22	21	55	2

Note: Data for all tables in this chapter collected 1993–5.

saw no need to distinguish them further from, for example, discipline or promotion interviews.)

The responses indicate considerable variation between the organizations.
Few employees appear to have appraisals every quarter. The closest was Lloyds
Bank UK Retail Banking, in which 82 per cent of respondents said they had their
performance appraised more often than twice a year. Citibank also came close
to having a standard annual practice with 86 per cent reporting that they had
appraisals once per year. But what is of most interest here is the variation in
practice within each organization. Apart from these organizations, fewer than
half (58 per cent) of the responses from any of the organizations fall within a
particular frequency pattern. Clearly there is much variation between different
departments and managers.

It's different in different departments. In my area, it seems to be an afterthought. In
Marketing, it is used more like a tool for development and to move the business forward,
a more integral part of the process. (line manager, Kraft Jacobs Suchard)

It's not official, it goes on, it's just never structured. One is appraised on a daily basis by
our colleagues and we do get a certain amount of feedback from that. (clinical manager,
Chelsea & Westminster Healthcare Trust)

In addition to the variation in the frequency of practice, we also found that
there were significant differences with regard to the actual conduct of the
appraisals. Here there appeared to be a rather wide working definition of what
constituted an appraisal:

I set very precise targets which I assess at the end of the year. I assess development needs
halfway through the year. I do appraise staff on a day-to-day basis but I have a training
background so I do not know how typical this is. In terms of my own performance, I have
been appraised on the staircase and in the car park. It really pisses me off. (line manager,
W. H. Smith News)

Appraisals are done every year, but people aren't always open in an appraisal. The
appraiser isn't always open and the appraisee isn't always open . . . You can sweep it
under the carpet for a while, and just hope everything's fine, or the person being appraised thinks, 'If I mention this, I'm going to be suppressed, repressed,' or whatever.
(manager, Citibank)

For my first appraisal, it was pre-written. I was told that if I wanted to change anything,
I could get it re-typed. But I know of others who had disagreed with their appraisals and
who had asked for them to be amended and nothing had been done. Because of this, I
had a very negative attitude towards appraisals. But my last two have conformed to the
rules and have renewed my faith. (employee, Hewlett Packard)

Such variations in practice were clearly not systematic in the sense that they
reflected a conscious policy to have different types of appraisal for different
types or groups of employees. It was therefore not surprising to find that these
variations inevitably led to a sense of dissatisfaction about the fairness of the
ratings assigned to individual employees. Evidence of this emerged in numer-

ous interviews within organizations where the credibility of the system was
called into question (notably in Lloyds Bank UK Retail Banking and W. H. Smith
News). In these organizations the performance appraisal process had some
problems which the personnel function was in the process of addressing. In
both cases, these problems undermined the credibility of the performance
review systems. In W. H. Smith News, managers stated that the manager with
whom they had their reviews (the 'house' manager) was too removed from their
daily work in comparison with other managers within the distribution house.
Furthermore, there was a feeling that grades were assigned before the review
meetings in order to meet with what could be afforded as performance-related
pay. In Lloyds Bank UK Retail Banking, managers felt that their objectives were
imposed uniformly across different regional areas without sufficient discussion
of local variations and pressures. This led to a feeling that managers were
'failing in their jobs'.

The objectives are just imposed. There is no room for negotiation. The targets are not
achievable, which isn't exactly motivating. (manager, Lloyds Bank UK Retail Banking)

   Problems such as these have already been identified in the extensive literature on performance appraisal and appraisal interviews. This body of work
reveals that the process has always contained difficulties for appraisers and
appraisees, including a lack of training amongst those appraising (see, for
example, Fletcher and Williams 1985; Randell 1989). What is worth noting here
is that managers actually find it difficult to use a system whose credibility is
lacking. Some managers admitted to 'going through the motions'. In other
words, they felt less inclined to conduct the reviews, and when they did it was
merely a paper exercise. Given the subjective nature of appraisals, in particular
the tendency for appraisals to *construct* the truth rather than discover it (Grint
1993; see also Townley 1989), it is quite likely that appraisal systems do not
have the credibility or legitimacy we might expect from what is frequently
presented as a *tool* or *technique*. What is interesting here is the finding that
the lack of credibility of such techniques *amongst managers* can inhibit their
implementation.

SOME CONSTRAINTS ON MANAGERS' HUMAN
RESOURCE PRACTICES

One of the most striking findings from this research was that line managers'
human resource practices were influenced, and frequently limited, by certain
constraints within the organization. We have identified four such constraints
from our interviews. These relate to the institutional reinforcement of human
resource practices, the policies and traditions of trade unions and professional
associations, managerial short-termism, and de-layering. The last two are

Table 7.2. Constraints on HRM practice

	Performance objectives	Trade union/ professional	Short-termism	De-layering/ downsizing
BT Payphones	✔	✔	✔	✔
C&W NHS Trust	✗	✔	✔	✔
Citibank	✔	✗	✔	✔
GP UK	✔	✗	✔	✗
HP	✔	✗	✔	✔
KJS	✔	✗	✔	✔
Lloyds	✔	✔	✔	✔
WHS News	✗	✔	✔	✔

similar in that both curtail the amount of time which managers have available for people management. We have distinguished between them because managerial short-termism consists of a process in which business priorities are consciously decided. It should be noted here that our use of the phrase 'managerial short-termism' is not intended purely as a criticism of these organizations but as a description of a particular kind of pressure with which managers have to work.

The fourth constraint, de-layering, may accentuate these other tendencies in managers' jobs because of increased workloads, although the effect is more indirect. Finally, it is also important to note that management practice was not constrained by all four in every organization, nor to the same degree by each one in all of the organizations (see Table 7.2).

Why do managers bother? Institutional and personal incentives

If the organizations are committed to having their line managers involved in human resource practices, it might be assumed that this role would be formally institutionalized and reinforced through the organization's policies. This, in turn, should be reflected in managers' views as to why they take on such responsibility. We looked for evidence of the formal institutionalization of line managers' roles in two areas. The first area was that of individual managers' performance objectives (or job descriptions). Was their role in human resource activities formally stated within their own objectives? The second area concerned the training of managers. If line managers are to act as a fulcrum for personnel policies, then organizations might be expected to provide managers with the appropriate training to handle these responsibilities.

Table 7.3. 'How important a factor is it in your performance appraisal that you success-fully implement personnel policies?' (line managers only, %)

	Important/very important	Neither important nor unimportant	Not very important/not at all important
BT Payphones	43	26	31
C&W NHS Trust	46	30	24
Citibank	28	24	48
HP	45	24	31
KJS	46	26	28
Lloyds	44	20	36
WHS News	52	28	20

Note: No data available from GP UK pilot study.

Performance measures

There were some differences between the firms on the incorporation of human resource issues into performance objectives. Five of the eight organizations had human resource activities formally stated within managers' performance objectives. However, fewer than half of all managers who were surveyed con-sidered successful implementation of personnel polices to be an 'important' or 'very important' factor in their own performance appraisals (see Table 7.3).

Table 7.3 suggests that many managers do not feel strong institutional pres-sure, in the form of their own performance appraisals, to give serious con-sideration to those aspects of their job which encompass human resource management. It should, however, be appreciated here that the relative lack of importance attached to HR activities has to be balanced against other job priorities such as achieving targets in the area of profit, sales, and so on.

Training

In addition to specific appraisal objectives, it might also be assumed that the training of managers in human resource activities reflects a strong emphasis on human resource practice amongst line managers. Interestingly, 'training and development' emerged as the greatest influence on the development of people management skills for many of the respondents within all of the organizations (see Table 7.4).

The emphasis on training in human resource activities, however, was mixed. All of the organizations ran training courses in appraisal and in some other areas. However, the problem was not so much with the existence of the training as what was subsequently done with it.

Table 7.4. 'Which of the following have the greatest influence on the development of your people management skills in your organization?' (line managers only, %)

Ranked no. 1	BT Payphones	C&W NHS Trust	Citibank	HP	KJS	Lloyds	WHS News
Training and development	57	46	39	40	44	56	63
Personnel department	3	3	0	2	5	1	0
Peers	8	30	10	15	8	4	5
Subordinates	10	8	11	12	16	9	5
Boss	17	8	35	24	25	25	24
Other	5	5	5	7	2	5	3

Note: No data available from GP UK pilot study.

A major block is the people management skills of our line managers. It's to do with software and hardware. You can put the courses out there and the development plans and processes, etc., and that can all be incredibly practical. But unless you get the software right—the way they do it—it will fail. A lot of managers still feel that managing people is what personnel does. (personnel manager, Lloyds Bank UK Retail Banking)

In other words, while the institutional recognition of the role of line managers is a necessary condition in placing personnel activities firmly amongst line managers, it is not sufficient without the goodwill of the managers involved.

Institutional and personal influences

What, then, explains the involvement of line managers? We have tried to answer this question by developing a questionnaire survey item which asks managers to rank a range of factors that motivate them to become involved in personnel activities (see Table 7.5).

'Personal motivation' emerged as the largest category of 'first ranked' response for virtually all of the organizations. This accounted for almost half of the respondents in the four British private sector organizations. 'Business targets' also emerged as a significant source of motivation in all but one of the organizations. Other items such as 'company philosophy' and 'vision and personnel policy' seemed to have limited impact. One tempting interpretation of these results would be to argue that the personal motivation of managers was of much greater importance in explaining the involvement of line managers than formal institutional incentives and pressures. However, it was also clear that managers' business targets were influential. In any case, the personal motivation of managers may have been influenced by their organizational environment.

In sum, it would appear that line management involvement is problematic because it requires both institutional reinforcement and personal motivation. While many of the organizations attempted to make involvement a formal requirement in the work of their managers, they encountered problems in developing the required expertise and commitment among their managers.

HRM, trade unions, and professional organizations

The (in)compatibility of HRM and trade unions has been one of the distinctive themes of the debate over HRM in Britain (Guest 1987; 1989; 1995; Millward 1994; Storey 1992). Typically, the argument is that the adoption of a 'full-blown' model of HRM is likely to undermine the existence of trade unions because of its underlying philosophy of unitarism and individualism. This, however, underestimates the barriers to the implementation of HRM policies and practices in settings where employees belong to trade unions or professional associations. It is interesting to note here that many of the American companies

Table 7.5. 'Please rank the following in order of what motivates you to be involved in personnel activities in your organization.' (line managers only, %)

Ranked no. 1	BT Payphones	C&W NHS Trust	Citibank	HP	KJS	Lloyds	WHS News
Personal motivation	31	26	23	27	37	48	47
Business targets	21	15	23	23	15	22	5
Personnel poicy	14	19	5	7	9	10	6
Company philosophy/vision	11	11	6	18	4	3	4
To advance my career	4	4	9	5	7	5	18
Boss's expectations	6	7	9	2	15	6	5
My appraisal/rewards	5	0	8	2	11	3	13
Peer group expectations	6	11	1	3	0	1	2
Other	2	7	16	13	2	2	0

Note: No data available from GP UK pilot study.

that are used as exemplars of HRM—Hewlett Packard, for instance—are non-union companies (see Guest 1989). Consequently, there has been little consideration of the possibility that trade unions may actually inhibit the introduction of certain HRM practices for their own good reasons. This is all the more surprising when you consider that it has already been established that trade union policies generally represent an area of uncertainty for managerial strategies (Streeck 1987). In other words, much of the literature is concerned with the possibility that HRM may undermine the role of trade unions in the workplace rather than vice versa. Similarly, there has been no discussion of the extent to which HRM can be introduced into organizations which are strongly influenced by the professions. In this research we encountered examples of each of these cases.

Only one quarter of W. H. Smith News employees—the managerial grades—are appraised and are therefore eligible for performance-related pay. The remainder are not appraised. These employees obtain their annual wage increase through nationally negotiated agreements. Middle managers negotiate some of their pay increase through national negotiations between the company and their staff association. There are also some local agreements which the company has been trying to bring into line with the national terms. At the time of this research, management was considering introducing performance appraisals for all levels of staff. Should the appraisal system be introduced it would not be linked to pay. Management feared that any plan to link individual performance to pay would be perceived as an attempt to break with the annual national agreements and could lead to serious industrial relations problems. Approximately one third of the workforce belong to the General Print Makers Union and while relations with the unions are reasonable they are still 'hotbeds of activity', particularly in London where 'anything within the M25 is effectively a closed shop'. Thus, the value of the appraisal for management would be the introduction of a new method of communication between managers and employees, one which effectively forced indivi·lual managers to have 'one-to-ones' with their subordinates.

This case illustrates the difficulty which management faces when introducing practices which would give front-line managers greater control over the effort–reward bargain. Should they eventually introduce appraisals for non-managerial staff, their managers will still not be able to pay for performance. This also reflects Storey's (1987; 1992) finding that HRM practices were 'bolted on' to the pre-existing and ongoing industrial relations structures and practices with some of the newer practices only covering white-collar staff (career and succession planning were good examples of this in our cases).

The second example is drawn from our research into a professional organization—an NHS hospital trust. This also indicates that the introduction of management best practice, in HRM or in other areas, is difficult and in some cases impractical. Some of the problems attached to the ongoing changes in the management of NHS trusts have been discussed elsewhere (Bach 1994). Here, we shall again restrict ourselves to the reasons for the limited use of appraisals within the Chelsea & Westminster Healthcare Trust (see Table 7.1). While the actual performance criteria are often a source of conflict with management in organizations where there are engineers or chemists (Raelin 1985), hospitals are more complicated in that they have a large number of different professions working alongside each other. For instance, should the appraisal be conducted by the organization in the form of a manager or by the profession in the form of a colleague? Is it necessary to have different types of appraisal and different criteria for each of the different professions—consultants, doctors, nurses, physiotherapists, occupational therapists, radiographers, and so on? In order to resolve this problem the personnel department had allowed the various directorates and professional groups to conduct their own appraisals using a version of the standard appraisal document offered by the personnel department. Most areas had some form of performance review in place. The nurses and midwives had the best-established system, while others, such as Pharmacy, Acute Paediatrics, HIV/GUM, and Physiotherapy, had adapted the system to meet their own needs. Other areas either tailored the system that was used by other groups or conducted informal appraisals.

However, the result was inconsistent. As one director stated, 'appraisal is very patchy'. Some areas used appraisals regularly while others never had any at all. Some of this inconsistency could be attributed to the problems which this newly formed trust faced in trying to get the professions to take on more managerial responsibilities in order to overcome the management versus medic syndrome which had arisen as part of the NHS reforms. The response from the professions was that these duties simply added to their existing workloads. When faced with time constraints they placed their professional duties before administrative tasks which in any case, did not feature in their professional training.

The dynamics of managerial short-termism

Much has been written about 'popular' short-termism—the tendency for UK and US companies to have a relatively low record of investment as a result of the financial system (for a review, see Marsh 1990)—while 'managerial' short-termism has only recently received detailed attention in the UK (Demirag et al. 1994). Marsh, in his review (1990: 52–60), suggests that managerial short-termism need not necessarily be triggered by the influence of financial markets, though it may be accentuated by them. It is usually the result of such things as the way managers are rewarded, the time horizons within their jobs, the performance measurement and management accounting systems within the organization, the internal capital budgeting and project appraisal systems, and, in transnational corporations, the relationship between the head office and the subsidiaries. The latter source is likely to be most evident where a 'financial control' strategy exists (Goold and Campbell 1987).

In this research we found that short-term pressures of a managerial origin had two distinct effects on the practice of human resource management in private sector organizations. First, managers understood both formally, via performance objectives, and informally, through the demands of their superiors, that their main priority was the 'hard stuff', 'the numbers', for example monthly sales targets, while the softer people management issues were of less significance. This was a direct reflection of the short-term philosophy of business which characterized some of these firms. Second, managers had (as a result) little incentive to invest time in policies such as career development, which did not have a short-term pay-off.

Before elaborating on these points, we would like to indicate the extent to which this philosophy governed our case study organizations. Apart from Chelsea & Westminster Healthcare Trust, all of the other seven organizations were driven by these pressures to varying degrees. However, a number of organizations did stand out. Two of the firms, Lloyds Bank UK Retail Banking and Kraft Jacobs Suchard, emphasized short-term performance. It was not surprising to find in Lloyds Bank UK Retail Banking that this tendency towards short-termism was influenced by the stock markets. One manager stated a widely held view as follows: 'If you cannot achieve income then cut the budget. We are managed for tomorrow and not for the next century. It's the City' (manager, Lloyds Bank UK Retail Banking). Another manager stated that the Chief Executive's commitment to share value meant that the bank was run in a manner comparable to a 'chemical business without R. & D.'

The fast-moving consumer goods company Kraft Jacobs Suchard was a subsidiary of a major transnational with a reputation for managing its various businesses around the world according to tight financial control criteria. As one of the managers explained: 'We're very focused on money. It's incredibly short-term pragmatism to meet targets as opposed to medium or long-term' (manager, Kraft Jacobs Suchard). The origin of this approach lay in the strong financial control systems imposed on the UK subsidiary by the European head office and, in turn, by the US headquarters. The explicit emphasis was on meeting profit growth targets.

Cost management was a priority in each of the other organizations. W. H. Smith News, for instance, was considered to be a 'cash cow', managed with strict budgetary controls which brought in large revenues. Budget control came close to being the defining feature of management in BT Payphones and in Chelsea & Westminster Healthcare Trust.

The impact of this approach was evident in managers' jobs. In the semi-structured 'Unwritten Rules of the Game' interviews (see Chapter 1), we asked managers to identify what they understood to be their key measures, or the key items for impressing their superiors, and what the associated unwritten rules were for surviving or getting ahead within the organization. We thus ended up with a list of unwritten rules which described what managers saw as their key priorities within their jobs. These always reflected what managers were actually measured on. As one manager stated, 'what gets measured gets done'. The following is a list giving the single most important priority from each organization:

> BT Payphones: 'Focus on the key targets—serviceability and costs—for your monthly one-to-ones.'
> Chelsea & Westminster Healthcare Trust: 'Monitor your budget carefully.'
> Citibank: 'Making deals is what really matters.'
> Glaxo Pharmaceuticals UK: 'Focus on tangible outputs.'
> Hewlett Packard: 'Revenue/quota performance is what really counts.'
> Kraft Jacobs Suchard: 'Focus on the numbers, profit and/or volume.'
> Lloyds Bank UK Retail Banking: 'Focus on the financial services income; keep within budgets and headcount.'
> W. H. Smith News: 'The numbers are what really matters.'

People management, either in the form of carrying out human resource policies or in general, did not emerge in the list of unwritten rules or measurement priorities within any of the organizations. The reason for this was described by one manager as follows:

My boss's planning document is all headcount and costs, there's nothing on people management, recruitment. I know what I have to do to survive here, and that's meet the expense and the budget that are set outside my control. I'm told a number and have to manage within that. There is no commentary on people. We've had a lot of problems as a result. There's no trust or empowerment: you really are in a company that's managed by a bottom line. (line manager, Citibank)

The second area where short-termism had a negative impact was on human resource policies designed to develop employees. There were two aspects to this. First, managers had little incentive to invest time in lengthy discussions with their subordinates because it would have limited impact on the manager's immediate goals. While such activity might be of benefit to both the organization and to the individual it was not something which managers in any of the organizations considered to be a priority (see Table 7.6).

In only two of the organizations (Hewlett Packard, 77 per cent; BT Payphones, 61 per cent) did approximately two-thirds or more managers report that they carry out the activity or help with policy-making and carry out the activity. Within the next three highest organizations on this ranking, approximately half (Kraft Jacobs Suchard, 57 per cent; Chelsea & Westminster Healthcare Trust, 56 per cent; Citibank, 46 per cent) do one of these. This still means that almost half of the managers who responded have no direct involvement with their subordinates on this matter.

The second finding to emerge here was that line managers find it highly frustrating when no action is taken by the human resource function after they have submitted appraisals or helped an individual to prepare a career development plan.

There is an annual appraisal. In three months you need to do a Performance Development Review. It works in terms of the documentation. Where it doesn't work is the

Table 7.6. 'Which of the following personnel activities do you carry out for your subordinates as part of your job?'—career planning (line managers only, %)

	No involvement	Carry out the activity	Help with policy-making and carry out the activity	Help with policy-making
BT Payphones	28	56	5	11
C&W NHS Trust	19	42	14	25
Citibank	36	40	6	18
HP	13	63	14	10
KJS	18	47	10	25
Lloyds	44	34	4	18
WHS News	64	14	3	19

Note: No data available from GP UK pilot study.

outcome, because it is all very well saying that someone needs to do this to develop if there is no opportunity for him to do it. This is the biggest show-stopper we have. (line manager, BT Payphones)

In this instance, managerial short-termism is influenced to some extent by the inactivity of the human resource department but more generally by the lack of promotional opportunities in a downsizing environment. The overall result is that managers have limited incentive to spend much of their time on human resource activities because their return on the effort invested is not quantifiable in the short term.

The impact of organizational restructuring on management practice

The argument here is that organizational restructuring, especially where there have been redundancies at the managerial level, can lead to larger workloads for the managers who remain with the organization. This, in combination with the pressures associated with short-termism, constrains managerial involvement in the softer human resource activities such as appraisals, career development, and the like. The result is that managers are less inclined to find time for activities which will not produce an immediate return. Our evidence on this point is drawn primarily from issues which emerged from interviews with managers within some of these organizations. We believe that this finding is important because it contradicts many of the widely accepted beliefs amongst management about the benefits of de-layering. Second, it raises an important research question about the possibilities for the high-commitment model of employment in the context of industrial adjustment.

All but two of the organizations we studied had undergone a significant programme of restructuring. These were the result of strategic decisions to privatize, de-layer, introduce matrix management, or to acquire and merge with other organizations. All of these changes led to job losses. The actual percentage ranged from 15 to 50 per cent of the workforce. Unlike earlier phases of job shedding in British industry, this phase was unusual in that the 'de-layering' approach was targeted at professional and managerial staff.

The managers who remained with these organizations found themselves with a wider span of control, with the result that they now had much larger numbers of staff reporting to them than previously. This placed considerable pressure on the time which line managers could allow for people management activities in general. To illustrate this point we shall return to some of the cultural issues at Hewlett Packard we explored in Chapter 5. Hewlett Packard managers were the most conscious of these issues, not least because it was the only organization in which managers' performance was assessed in this area.

Like others in the computer business, Hewlett Packard faced increased competition, sluggish markets, decreasing profitability, and declining stock market value in the late 1980s. Hewlett Packard took what were, in the context of this organization, drastic decisions to tackle these problems. Of these the most dramatic was the introduction of a Voluntary Severance Programme with several thousand employees being 'released' from the organization worldwide. Since it was the first time that the company had incurred job losses, many employees had to revise their expectations of a 'job for life'. The Voluntary Severance Programme was used to facilitate the introduction of a 'flatter organization'—to remove layers of managers between the chief executive and shop-floor employees. For example, one manager stated that three years previously there had been thirty-four managers in his group. This had been reduced to a total of eight managers whilst the business had grown to three times its original size. The impact on managers' jobs was also dramatic. They still had to achieve at least their previous level of performance while taking on more managerial responsibilities, but without the support which they previously had. As one manager explained, 'There is by definition little immediate support in a flat structure.' In short, de-layering had led to an intensification of effort.

One result of these changes was that managers were now finding it more difficult to find time for people management issues. There were two aspects to this. First of all they had less time to respond to day-to-day people management issues: 'I now have nowhere near enough time to deal with people management issues, though we are expected to have an open door' (manager, Hewlett Packard). Second, managers were reluctant to invest time in training up junior staff because of the opportunity costs of forgoing other activities. One manager expressed the view of her colleagues in this way:

I and my colleagues don't really like to take on junior people. We can't really afford to train them . . . The opportunity for that has reduced substantially because higher business expectations are taking more of your time. (manager, Hewlett Packard)

These quotes clearly reveal the hidden costs of de-layering organizations (see also *The Economist*, 3 Sept. 1994; *Wall Street Journal*, 7 June 1994). This case also suggests that when organizations are 'flattened', the softer elements of managerial roles are among the first to be squeezed out of the day-to-day activities. It also means that career management and the management of career expectations becomes a problem area (McGovern *et al.* 1998). More generally, it also has the effect of undermining attempts to develop the 'soft model' of human resource management.

CONCLUSIONS

This chapter has examined the involvement of managers in human resource activities in order to establish the prospects for the devolvement of such activities to the line in the manner prescribed by prevailing models of HRM. We found that managers were responsible for the implementation of a variety of human resource policies. However, the limitations of line manager practice and the constraints on line managers provide a rather different picture from the scenarios sketched by the prescriptive models of HRM. We found that in the case of performance appraisal, management implementation was uneven within organizations and that the actual quality of the practice was also subject to significant variations. We also identified four constraints on management practice. The first concerns the lack of incentives for line managers to become involved in human resource activities. We found that there are limited institutional pressures, for instance in the form of performance objectives or in training, to reinforce the importance of carrying out human resource activities. In these circumstances, the involvement of managers in such activities is often a matter of personal rather than institutional motivation. Second, trade unions and professional associations may adopt positions which effectively block or alter the shape of management policies and practices. Third, the short-term nature of managerial activity leads to a tendency to put a greater priority on the achievement of the numbers *per se* rather than the achievement of numbers through people. This finding is similar to, and extends, those of Kirkpatrick *et al.* (1992) and Lowe (1992). Finally, the downsizing and de-layering which most of these organizations have experienced places tremendous pressure on the time which managers can allow for people matters generally.

What then are the prospects for devolving human resource activities to the line? Of the constraints which we have identified, the first may be the only one that management can control in the short term. Management influence over the others is less certain, even in the long term. We would therefore argue that the prospects for full-blown devolvement to the line are not promising given the current priorities of these businesses. Attempts to devolve HR to the line in any grand sense can only be regarded as quixotic. This is not surprising when judged in the context of many of the criticisms that have been made of the prescriptive approach to management. Sisson (1989) in his review of these criticisms argues that they fail even within the terms of the prescriptive approach, which is to help management to manage. Typically, there is no discussion of what actually happens in practice, or in the presence of trade unions and legal constraints. Similarly with differences in organizational structures. All of these, as Sisson rightly states, have a profound impact on management practice in general and on personnel practice in particular.

So what are practitioners to do? One option would be to proceed by establishing, or reinforcing, institutional measures which would encourage managers to place greater priority on their human resource activities (that is, to tackle the first constraint identified here). This could, for example, be achieved by incorporating such activities into managers' performance-related pay and by more extensive use of HR audits. It would also require additional training and probably sharper monitoring of the process by the human resource function. However, such measures are arguably contrary to the spirit of the prescriptive models of HRM; they would continue to give a central role to the human resource function in the implementation of various policies, although in this instance the role would be that of policing managers' human resource processes. Thus, devolution to the line may be possible but only if accompanied by increased monitoring on the part of the HR specialists.

Moreover such a scenario also runs contrary to the spirit of 'developmental humanism' which underlies many of the HRM models (for a discussion, see Hendry and Pettigrew 1990). This typically depicts managers as being empowered to take responsibility for their own HR requirements in order to unleash the hitherto untapped potential of their staff. Rather than being empowered, managers would become caught up in an increasingly bureaucratic web of human resource policies and procedures in which they not only implement policies but also have their own implementation of such policies monitored, evaluated, and rewarded.

More generally, it can also be argued that the 'developmental humanism' which underlies many of the HRM models naïvely underestimates the extent to which short-term pragmatism is embedded within capitalist enterprises (for a critique from a different angle, see Kamoche 1994). In such circumstances, managers find it difficult to follow blindly the apparently logical assumption that the systematic selection, development, and long-term retention of employees can contribute to mutual gains for the employer and the employee. Those who wish to promote such an idea need to address some of the wider problems in contemporary business such as management training, managerial short-termism, and the tendency to treat employees as *resources* rather than as *humans* if they want their message to have a genuine impact on managerial practice.

Transformation at the Leading Edge

PHILIP STILES

In 1984, British Telecom, one of the largest companies in the UK, had a workforce of 250,000; ten years later, that figure was down to 150,000 employees, with a stated target of 100,000 before the end of the century. In addition, BT has undertaken major organizational restructuring and introduced a new vision and new values to decentralize power and increase the responsibility of lower level managers. At Glaxo Pharmaceuticals UK, Lloyds Bank UK Retail Banking, and W. H. Smith News, major cultural change programmes instigated in the early 1990s were aimed at breaking down the tradition of paternalism and narrow functional working, and freeing up managerial initiative to deliver greater customer service. At Citibank, a comprehensive turnaround of the commercial bank from its 'near-death experience' of 1991 to become a 'global relationship bank' just three years later has brought fresh strategic orientation and dismantled old ways of working. Add to these examples Hewlett Packard's restructuring in 1991, Kraft Jacobs Suchard's reorganization into business units and its acquisition of Terry's in 1993, as well as the NHS reforms and the winning of trust status for the Chelsea and Westminster hospital, and it is clear that a major element of the Leading Edge story concerns the management of change.

Major structural and cultural effects have occurred as organizations have attempted to move from one image of themselves to another in a bid to maintain and enhance their competitive capabilities. In this chapter, we shall describe how the companies have managed the transition process, particularly in terms of their use of human resource management to facilitate change. We shall examine the causes of change, the key levers the organizations have used to manage the process, and the effect the change initiatives have had on employees. We shall argue that the methods adopted by organizations have been broadly similar and follow a similar pattern. But there are a number of intangible factors within the organizations which contrive to constrain the implementation of the change process: these are the nature of organizational identity, the embedding of the performance management systems, and the involvement of middle managers.

Within the literature on organizational change, there has been a good deal of research on the complex interaction between contexts, strategies, structures, and cultures involved in the change process (Doz and Thanheiser 1993; Pettigrew 1985; Whipp *et al.* 1989). In cases of major change, usually prompted by dramatic shifts in environmental conditions, there are sharp changes in organizational strategy and the formal structure of the organization (Bartunek and Rinquest 1989). These are accompanied by the breakdown of the established order in the workplace and a radical shift in employees' interpretative schemes concerning the nature of the organization (Bartunek 1984; Fiol 1991; Weick 1979). In pursuing fit between the environmental context and the organization's strategy and structure, a substantial amount of interpretative activity on the part of managers ensues, together with a change in their cognitive structures. The change process, therefore, far from being solely a rational, straightforward process, involves the shifting viewpoints of managers, which can be highly significant and instrumental.

In this chapter, we shall examine the change process from two perspectives. First, we shall consider the nature of the change process and the human resource management activities used to support that change; and second, we shall draw out how these initiatives have been received by employees—how they have been *interpreted*.

FACING THE CHALLENGE OF CHANGE

With the exception of the Chelsea & Westminster Healthcare Trust, which has been in existence as a business only since April 1994, the Leading Edge companies all have long histories, are all in the top five in their sector with long-established products and services, and all have strongly established norms and accepted forms of behaviour which give them their unique organizational identities. In this sense, the organizations are mature, and to this extent they face the significant challenge of renewal.

This challenge has arisen because of the changing nature of the external environment and the consequent shift in the basis of competitive advantage. As we saw in Chapter 1, forces such as deregulation, rapid technological innovation, increased competition, and greater access to information have increased the turbulence of business conditions and have tended to commodify the products and services which used to be the foundations of the leading companies' competitive edge. For the companies in this study, these external forces have included the following:

BT Payphones: privatization; deregulation; new entrants; new telephone technology.

Chelsea & Westminster Healthcare Trust: restructuring and reformation of NHS; drive for trust status.

Citibank: removal of national regulatory barriers; global financial market; new technology; increasing liquidity in market.

Glaxo Pharmaceuticals UK: NHS reforms; changes in customer base; expiry of patents; emergence of biotechnology industry.

Hewlett Packard: emergence of clone manufacturers; declining markets.

Kraft Jacobs Suchard: increased size and diversity of the business; falling in step with European structure.

Lloyds Bank UK Retail Banking: deregulation; new technology; increasing competition.

W. H. Smith News: impact of lost News International contract; Monopolies and Mergers Commission report implications; increased competition.

Though it was the business unit which formed the level of analysis for our research, nevertheless the change pressures identified above ensured that it was the organization *as a whole*, rather than just a subset of the organization, which would be affected by the changes in the external environment. Within each company the gap between the strategy, structure, and culture of the organization as it stood and the configuration required to adapt to the new business circumstances meant that a large-scale planned change programme was necessary.

Though each change process was unique and was tailored to the demands of its particular organizational context, a number of common responses were made to the challenge of change forces, which we shall now describe. After we have described these dimensions of change, which, following the work of Doz and Thanheiser (1996), comprise the reframing of the strategic and structural contexts and the alignment of the emotional and rational, we shall turn to their effects on employees, which provide a rich source of variance for the acceptance of the change initiatives.

The difficulties facing organizations attempting to push through change initiatives are considerable. The classic model of change intervention is provided by Lewin, who argues for three stages of change: unfreeze, movement, and refreeze (1973). Although we shall not rely on this model in this chapter, for illustrative purposes we have set out in Tables 8.1–8.8 some of the major changes within the companies using this framework.

REORIENTING THE STRATEGIC CONTEXT: FOCUS ON CUSTOMER SERVICE

All of the organizations reacted to the threat of the external pressures by reviewing their strategic focus and examining the nature of their relationship with customers. The reappraisal of the strategic logic of the firm enabled a fresh identification of those businesses considered to be core and those which were

Table 8.1. Major changes within the companies: BT Payphones (1994)

Level	Unfreezing	Movement	Refreezing
Individual	Downsizing of workforce; new vision and values	Retraining; 'involving everyone' programme; balanced scorecard	Training portfolio; empowerment; reward for teamwork
Strategy and structure	From regions to SBUs; decentralization; from product to customer focus	Service value analysis; Breakout project to examine new strategic ideas	Integrated performance management system; trading unit status
Climate	Paternalism to individual responsibility	Emphasis on new values; focus on CARE survey; move to open communications	Vision and values indices included in evaluations

Table 8.2. Major changes within the companies: Chelsea & Westminster Healthcare Trust (1995)

Level	Unfreezing	Movement	Refreezing
Individual	Clinicians to participate in 'business model'	Heads of directorates are clinicians	Reward systems linked to bottom-line outputs in directorates
Strategy and structure	Move to trust status—a self-governing business; five directorates introduced	Organic strategy of increasing catchment population; possible merger with other trusts	—
Climate	Traditionally departmental based; high care for patients; introduction of general management seen as a 'threat'	Easing to tension between management and clinicians over time; loyalty is to the directorate at the expense of the Trust as a whole	—

Table 8.3. Major changes within the companies: Citibank (1994)

Level	Unfreezing	Movement	Refreezing
Individual	Redundancies; de-emphasize revenue focus	Balanced scorecard; global training provision; Talent Inventory	Variable pay linked to scorecard concept; formalization of appraisal and career management processes
Strategy and structure	Global bank, built on key customer focus; new matrix structure	Lead bank initiative	Restoring of credit rating; resumption of payment of dividend
Climate	Wall Street culture and strong internal competition discouraged	Greater emphasis on teamwork; intolerance of 'arrogance'	Task force to address issue of pay inequity

not. In Lloyds Bank UK Retail Banking, for example, the focus on delivering shareholder value saw the disposal of underperforming businesses. At Citibank, the new strategic intent to 'become the number one international bank' brought the elimination of geography from the structure, and the signal to employees that responsibility to customers did not end at national boundaries. The widening of Glaxo Pharmaceuticals UK's strategy to be *more* than the end of the value chain for Glaxo R & D opened up many possibilities for sales growth, such as licensing deals with competitors' products.

The major reorientation was to focus explicitly on customers to a much greater extent. As Beatty and Ulrich argue: 'competitive advantage comes from understanding and meeting customer needs in unique ways' (1993: 63). Many of these changes were profound and significantly altered the basis on which the companies competed. In W. H. Smith News, managers were focused on providing quality service to publishers. When the rules of the game for the industry changed through the Monopolies and Mergers Commission report on news distribution, almost overnight *retailers* became the most important part of the competitive equation: managerial attitudes towards retailers had to change rapidly in order to preserve market share. For Glaxo Pharmaceuticals UK, the NHS reforms entailed that instead of relying on bulk purchases of drugs by the NHS, individual doctors became responsible for their own budgets and

Table 8.4. Major changes within the companies: Glaxo Pharmaceuticals UK (1993)

Level	Unfreezing	Movement	Refreezing
Individual	Functionally based; little experience of empowerment; revenue driven; compliant managers	Drive for cross-functionality—task forces, project teams; new behaviours and competencies identified	Decision-making devolved to local teams; performance now measured against competencies
Strategy and structure	Functional silos; hierarchical; focused on individual drugs	Re-engineering, decentralization to regional businesses; customer focus programme	Adoption of 'disease management' concept; greater segmentation of target markets; strong structural logic reflecting new shape of NHS
Climate	Bureaucratic, paternalist; problems of internal communication	Internal barriers broken down as a result of restructuring; encouragement of two-way communication	Fewer directives; more experimentation; greater tolerance of ambiguity

purchasing, which meant a huge shift in Glaxo Pharmaceuticals UK's approach to satisfying customers.

Such changes required large shifts in the mindsets of employees. The transition process was largely driven from the top and cascaded down through workshops, team briefings, and, in some cases, experiments on a small scale with new ideas in service delivery. For example, at Glaxo Pharmaceuticals UK, there were trials under way in certain areas of the country on the provision of care services for patients as well as drugs, in line with the perceived need to undertake 'disease management', and in some cases, the provision of aftercare services without the sale of drugs at all, representing a huge shift from the product-led strategy of five years previously. In BT Payphones, task forces were used to identify areas of performance improvement and to introduce the concept of cross-functional working.

The move towards greater customer service was accompanied in most cases by the introduction of new statements of vision and values, and by the

Table 8.5. Major changes within the companies: Hewlett Packard (1994)

Level	Unfreezing	Movement	Refreezing
Individual	Downsizing; move to flexible working	Restatement of HP Way, but concern over 'work-life' balance	Job security for high performers; new stress initiative
Strategy and structure	Drift towards centralization; cost-cutting on PCs; focus on client-server systems	Return of the founders; cut number of committees; greater segmentation of customers	Return to decentralized decision-making; operating expenses cut; internal merger of computer products and computer systems divisions
Climate	Creeping bureaucracy; strong people orientation	Trying to get 'organized chaos'; encouragement of risk-taking	People orientation remains strong

Table 8.6. Major changes within the companies: Kraft Jacobs Suchard (1994)

Level	Unfreezing	Movement	Refreezing
Individual	Reduce 'process' mentality and increase innovative behaviour through new values	Breakthrough project 'to free up everyday thinking'	Innovation recognized in performance evaluations
Strategy and structure	Refocus on four core businesses; from functions to SBUs; acquisition activity	Strategy linked to quality approach; harmonization of terms and conditions for acquired firms	Continued search for acquisition targets as market suffers from overcapacity
Climate	Strong process culture; short-termism	Cross-functional teams introduced; attempts to shift 'blame' culture	Less hierarchy; increased flexible work practices; greater empowerment

Table 8.7. Major changes within the companies: Lloyds Bank UK Retail Banking (1994)

Level	Unfreezing	Movement	Refreezing
Individual	Entitlement mindset; traditional focus on generalist banking skills; downsizing	Encouragement of more specialist skills; focus on self-development	New policy framework; greater developmental focus; rewards for sales and marketing excellence
Strategy and structure	Introduction of shareholder value; selective market dominance; cost reduction	Unbundling of the bank along portfolio lines; processes centralized	Acquisitions and divestments to increase shareholder value; segmented management in the branch network
Climate	Bureaucratic, command and control style; 'inward-looking'	Attempts to increase two-way communications; some devolution of responsibility	'Shaping our Future' programme; outward-looking— emphasizing customer service

Table 8.8. Major changes within the companies: W. H. Smith News (1994)

Level	Unfreezing	Movement	Refreezing
Individual	Blue-collar, unionized; strong loyalty to firm; trade-off between low pay and job security	Reframing employment, end of 'jobs for life'; job security for high performance; appraisal to be extended to all employees	Promotion for innovative and entrepreneurial employees; new competencies introduced
Strategy and structure	Offering focused on publishers; structured into four regional areas with individual warehouses taking all titles	MMC report refocused offering on retailers; continuous improvement introduced	Hub and spoke structure (some warehouses merged) to increase efficiency
Climate	Paternalism, authoritarianism, command and control style	Culture change programme to end cult of seniority and deference	New vision and values initiative

implementation of quality programmes. At Kraft Jacobs Suchard and W. H. Smith News, continuous improvement schemes have been introduced; Hewlett Packard has adopted Total Quality Management practices, while at BT Payphones, management has signed up for the European Quality Award programme. The benefit of the quality initiatives has been to measure customer satisfaction in a systematic way and provide tangible benchmarks for improvement. The linking of the new vision and values (which are typically concerned with customer satisfaction) with employee evaluation processes has also brought about an alignment between the organizational strategy and human resources.

REORIENTING THE STRUCTURAL CONTEXT: DOWNSIZING AND DECENTRALIZATION

The organizations have all undertaken significant restructuring to gain greater focus and to align the architecture of the company with the new strategic aims. Initiatives such as downsizing, de-layering, restructuring, and re-engineering are transformational; they typically address the whole organization, including strategy, and they help to develop a completely new organizational configuration (Jick 1993). A key strategic objective of many organizations is to reduce structural and process complexity, to rethink how they provide value to their customers, and to create an organization of people who are more responsive to change.

For the companies studied, there had generally been a move away from functional structures towards focused business units. In BT Payphones, the old district structure has given way to five core business units. In Citibank, the country structure, which was viewed as hampering the process of delivering quality service to customers, has been progressively changed to a pan-European structure and now a 'global relationship bank', where revenue is 'not known for Germany or France, but we can tell you how much we earn from, say, Exxon, worldwide'. In Glaxo Pharmaceuticals UK and Kraft Jacobs Suchard, the former functionally based operations have been supplanted by business units in core markets. In each case, the reporting lines have been shortened in a bid to increase speed of response of managers to customers. In each case, too, there have been redundancies.

In some cases, the downsizing was dramatic. BT is the best-publicized case, but at Citibank, too, 14,000 jobs have been cut worldwide since 1991, and at Lloyds Bank UK Retail Banking, following the cutback in the branch network, they now employ 25 per cent fewer people than in 1990. Even at Hewlett Packard, 2,400 people were released in 1993 alone.

The focus of the restructuring has been to align better with the customer base. In Glaxo Pharmaceuticals UK, the organizational structure in the Pharmaceuticals business now mirrors the structure of the NHS, while at Citibank, the elimination of geography from the structure of the commercial bank has reflected the nature of the multinational companies which form the key clientele for the bank.

Restructuring has also aimed at decentralizing the organization and giving power to lower-level managers, who are closer to the customer, in order to increase the speed of response and enable the tailoring of products and services to local needs. At Hewlett Packard, for example, the centralization of the computer business had led to a stifling bureaucracy and prolonged delays in sign-off for decisions. The return of the founders, Bill Hewlett and Dave Packard, restored the company to what it had originally been: a highly decentralized company with strongly empowered line managers. At Glaxo Pharmaceuticals UK, sales managers now are 'like chief executives, with responsibility for £10 million businesses. It is scary for some, liberating for others' (personnel director). A further consequence of restructuring was to enable more detailed measurement of individual businesses. Splitting into business units made performance more transparent and helped the resource allocation process within the firm as a whole.

ALIGNING THE EMOTIONAL WITH THE RATIONAL: THE ROLE OF HUMAN RESOURCE MANAGEMENT

To use a metaphor from Ulrich and Lake (1990), what we have discussed so far in terms of change concerns the hardware of the organization—the introduction of new strategies and structures, and new systems such as quality programmes. However, for change to occur, new software—adjusting and aligning new employee behaviour—must also be put in place. This section deals with the nature of the human resource levers organizations pull in their attempt to effect change.

As Johnson and Scholes state, 'it is unrealistic to suppose that strategic change can be implemented if the current beliefs and assumptions and ways of doing things remain the same . . . Recipe change is essentially to do with cognitive change—changing the way in which members of the organization make sense of their organizational world and its environment' (1986: 307).

Though the cause of failure of organizational change programmes is often laid at the door of poor implementation processes, we have seen in our research that a major factor in aligning employee behaviour to the new values and image of the organization concerns the way the organization manages the sense-making activity of employees.

Changing the mindset of employees is a difficult and often lengthy process. In the organizations we studied, a number of processes have been used which have attempted to solve the problems of aligning employees with entrenched attitudes and behaviours to a new set of organizational goals. In this chapter, we shall examine three: breaking down existing structures and creating new ways of working, readjusting the performance management system and focusing on new behaviours, and using procedural justice by bringing middle managers on board.

CREATING NEW WAYS OF WORKING

The companies attempted to generate behavioural change through the breaking up of existing structures to encourage cross-functional working and to drive down responsibility to those employees actually facing customers. Changes in the organizational work setting strongly influence individual behaviour and, in turn, organizational outcomes (Robertson *et al.* 1993). New ways of working are developed through real-time learning, with the company introducing task forces, project teams, and experiments with process innovations. Glaxo Pharmaceuticals UK is a company which illustrates this approach. The change to a regionally structured, customer-focused organization in the Pharmaceuticals UK business saw the established hierarchy (dominated by the marketing function) broken up and numerous project and task teams set up in an attempt to anticipate and influence the strategy of the firm's major customer, the NHS. The radical concept of the firm moving away from providing only products (in the form of drugs) to provide also services (such as aftercare and diagnosis), forming a complete disease management offering, was being trialled in selected areas of the organization in a form of controlled experiment. The intention is to break down internal barriers caused by rigid functional silos and replace them with horizontal working in order to transfer knowledge and encourage entrepreneurial behaviour. The redesign of job roles, flattening hierarchies, and shortening reporting lines have been introduced to a greater or lesser degree in all the organizations.

FOCUSING ON NEW BEHAVIOURS

We saw fundamental changes in what people were assessed against. One of the functions of the performance management process, in addition to being seen as the 'objective' measure of individual performance, is to communicate organizational norms or 'culture' and to reinforce the change process. As we saw in Chapter 3, performance management, with its aim of linking individuals' goals and responsibilities to the objectives of the business and integrating key interventions—appraisal, rewards, and training and development—can be seen as a core strategic process, facilitating strategic alignment. In all the organizations, new competency frameworks have been introduced which reflect the new values and strategic focus. These competencies have centred around leadership and leadership development, as well as explicit emphasis on teamwork and customer satisfaction. In Citibank, a major organizational initiative called the Talent Inventory, based on nine competencies and linked closely to the appraisal and reward process, was introduced in 1994 to add formality to development and career management. At BT Payphones, the 'living the values' initiative also rewards employees for adherence to the new organizational value system.

The interpretation by employees of required changes to behaviour was coloured by a number of factors. First, obviously enough, was the degree of change from existing behaviours:

What we wanted was for the regional sales manager to move from being a supervisor, administrator, a postbox and sometimes a shop steward, to become the managing director of a £10–12 million franchise or business . . . There are very real clashes as people move towards the new behaviours. I think we don't realize how deep authority and level concepts are. (HR staff, Glaxo Pharmaceuticals UK)

The further the new behaviours were from the old ones, the more anxiety was produced, and in some cases this could act to resist the change process: 'To be effective as a branch manager, you have to act as a buffer between "the Bank" and the branch staff' (line manager, Lloyds Bank UK Retail Banking). For clinicians at the NHS Trust, concerns over taking on additional managerial responsibilities were common: 'What I enjoy is treating patients. I don't want to fight for resources' (clinician, Chelsea & Westminster Healthcare Trust).

A second issue concerned the degree to which jobs and reporting lines would change, and the extent to which there was a clear picture of how the new role would in fact look:

At the bottom it is total distrust. People are apathetic. They are very angry and argumentative. It is, 'Where am I going to end up tomorrow?' (manager, BT Payphones)

The restructuring into a global relationship bank has produced a highly complex matrix. It's very difficult to grasp and a lot of the pain of change has been around people not knowing what their jobs will be in the new organization and who they will be working for. (HR staff, Citibank)

A third factor concerned the transparency of the new system. We believe that one of the central planks of successful change is the transparency of the processes in human resource management. At Hewlett Packard and Kraft Jacobs Suchard, the processes are simple to understand (for example, Hewlett Packard's Hoshin diagram fits on a single sheet of paper) and employees are very familiar with their objectives, how they fit into the strategic objectives of the firm, and how they will be measured and rewarded. Managers are measured on how well they undertake these processes (they are fully devolved to the line and are not part of the HR function's remit) and managers have received extensive training in the key performance management activities. Not only this but, as we saw in Chapter 3, there was considerable evidence that the managers in Hewlett Packard and Kraft Jacobs Suchard undertook a greater deal of informal performance management activity, notably providing frequent one-to-ones, high levels of feedback, and coaching and counselling activity. Such commitment demonstrates that for managers, the performance management process was ingrained, thought to be useful, and did not detract from focusing on the short-term figures which Hewlett Packard and Kraft Jacobs Suchard demanded.

In such organizations, recognition of strategic objectives, clarity of work goals, satisfaction with appraisal and rewards, and the receiving of appropriate training and development were all scored highly in the employee surveys. In these organizations, the performance management system has been established for many years and is capable of being fine-tuned according to circumstances. Team working has had a long history in these firms, and it is characteristic that a large degree of slack has been driven out of these organizations, making the gaining of company-wide support for the business goals critical. Communication of changes, even if the changes are not finalized, reduced the spread of rumour and lessened fear and anxiety. The few layers between senior managers and customer-facing employees encouraged strong feedback processes.

In the organizations making large changes in terms of identity, the embedding of new performance management processes was difficult to achieve as managers stuck to the old values which had served them well in the past. At Lloyds Bank UK Retail Banking, cluster managers acted as buffers between top management and non-managerial staff to protect their staff from the effect of the changes and to maintain morale. At Citibank and BT Payphones, the introduction of the balanced scorecard, to reduce the emphasis on revenue generation and increase customer satisfaction and teamwork, generated resistance as the status of managers remained rooted in their ability to bring in revenues. At Kraft Jacobs Suchard, a new stated value was employee commitment to innovation, but the short-term nature of the performance targets sent down from Philip Morris, the parent company, entailed that there was little room for error on meeting targets and led to a blame culture which discouraged experiment.

BRINGING MIDDLE MANAGERS ON BOARD

Because we are concerned in this chapter with *planned* organizational change, it is no surprise that these change initiatives were primarily top-down in character. Nevertheless, attempts to bring middle managers into the process were made in the majority of the companies. Vision statements emphasized the role of line managers in taking responsibility for decision making at local levels, and for their encompassing responsibility for developing subordinates and providing support through feedback and coaching. Middle managers typically formed the cross-functional teams which aimed to improve the status quo. At Glaxo Pharmaceuticals UK, managers from all divisions within the pharmaceutical business met to design the optimal organizational structure following the takeover of Wellcome, while at BT Payphones managers were seconded to the 'Breakout' team, comprising managers from the whole of BT, to identify strategic opportunities for the organization overall.

We also found some evidence to support Quinn's (1989) finding that senior managers use informal networks of managers at all levels not only for feedback on the implementation of proposals, but also to gather data on dissatisfaction with the status quo, and use such information to reinforce the change initiative. At Glaxo Pharmaceuticals UK, persistent feedback from sales and marketing staff on the inability of the structure to deliver good customer service signalled the need for a radical shift in product delivery. Such information was at first resisted, and then integrated into the management team's thinking.

The interpretations of managers concerning involvement in the change process were affected by the identification of a clear trigger for change. Either this was prompted by a key external trigger, which galvanized middle management concern, or the change coincided with (and indeed was influenced by) bottom-up calls for change in order to maintain market position.

Up to 1991, there was a culture and an ambition in the organization for size. In 1991, we had a near-death experience and then we got focused on the five-point plan. We got the organization aligned around certain goals that we've never known before . . . most people see the logic of it and it makes sense. (senior manager, Citibank)

In the case of Hewlett Packard, it was line managers who led calls for change in 1990 over the degree of bureaucracy which was stifling attempts to get sign-off on important customer decisions. For firms where the external trigger was less well perceived within the organization, there was less impetus for change: 'We are always trying to move ahead of the market . . . Sometimes it would help if people could really see the *need* for change' (HR staff, Glaxo Pharmaceuticals UK).

There was also a calculative aspect to managerial interpretations. Some middle managers were winners and some losers in the shake-up in the organizations. Some had more power given to them, some had power taken away. Reaction to the change process was influenced by how managers weighed up this prospect.

Consultants were more powerful than they are now. They now feel that things don't stop with them. There is another layer of authority that they have to deal with. There is more insecurity among the consultant staff. (non-clinical manager, Chelsea & Westminster Healthcare Trust)

I don't know where I am going. A few years ago you could plan, but the changes have been rapid and comprehensive. (manager, Lloyds Bank UK Retail Banking)

Those managers who had their status and power enhanced were those, naturally enough, who were seen to be open and amenable to the change process. These managers were used in the manner of change champions, whose persistent reinforcement of the change message and undermining of the old consensus were key to driving change throughout the organization. The empowerment of middle managers by the refocusing and restructuring of the organization was a key theme in all the organizations, and was an important part of the corporate rhetoric.

In companies experienced in the strategic change process, there was a clear history of middle management involvement in the refocusing activity. At Hewlett Packard, the environment is high velocity, and in the computer business constant adaptation is essential. In order to achieve this, employees must be self-reliant and able to view change in a positive manner. Employees at this stage *assume* that change is the norm, and the frame of reference they have for the company does not distend too much precisely because it is constantly evolving. The key to enabling employees to remain in a constantly changing environment, yet maintain their sense of involvement and belonging, concerns the nature of organizational identity. At Hewlett Packard, change takes place against a background of cultural stability expressed through the longevity of the HP Way. The values of the organization are enduring and this provides a constant fixed point for employees as they are subjected to change. No matter how large the change, the fabric of the identity of the organization is never stretched too far and torn.

It made sense to me. It meant I would have to work harder and have more responsibility, but I was still working with the same team and I still had the same deliverables. (manager, Hewlett Packard)

Compared to the previous [internal] merger, this was a piece of cake. We only had to merge 150 people and because it was basically a takeover situation, we were sure that the Glaxo identity and focus would be largely the same. (manager, Glaxo Pharmaceuticals UK, on the merger with Wellcome)

On the other hand, managers in companies for which change represented an abrupt shift of an unprecedented nature found the change much more distressing. At Lloyds Bank UK Retail Banking, for example, one manager said, 'It is rather like destroying a much loved building. They have taken down the old values and put nothing in their place.'

EXPLAINING VARIABLE REACTION TO CHANGE: THE ROLE OF ORGANIZATIONAL IDENTITY

Earlier in this chapter we described research which suggested that how employees make sense of the organization is a key variable in explaining their degree of acceptance of strategic change. The argument was that the greater the identification of employees with the old sets of beliefs and values systems, the more difficult it would be to effect change away from these and towards a new vision or structure. The picture which emerges from our data supports this view. In terms of consistency, it was evident that in Hewlett Packard and Glaxo Pharmaceuticals UK the changes, though far-reaching, were viewed as incremental and part of what constituted the normal operating procedure of the firm. Both firms were viewed as operating in dynamic markets, and had implemented a series of changes over recent years which had given them competency in handling the change process. Despite the changes, both organizations maintained their strategic vision, so that the shared view of the firm held by employees was not changed dramatically (see Weick 1979). The events that triggered the changes were well signalled to employees; in Hewlett Packard's case, falling stock prices and the personal intervention of the two founders precipitated the anticipation of change. At Glaxo Pharmaceuticals UK, recognition of the fragmentation of the market, the expiry of the Zantac patent, and the restructuring of their major customer, the NHS, together with increasing merger activity in the industry as a whole, gave a clear indication that major change would be undertaken. Before the events occurred, rumours abounded in each firm, typically expressing anxiety and speculating about the shape of the new organization. These early frames of reference were then confirmed by the beginning of the event itself. Both companies had elaborate communications procedures through which to spread the change information. As a prelude to change, task forces were set up and a number of small experiments in new ways of working were introduced which helped to sow the seeds of the change initiative and break up traditional power balances within and across departments. Throughout the process, employees saw parallels with previous change initiatives, in Hewlett Packard the reorganization in 1971, in Glaxo Pharmaceuticals UK the internal merger between Glaxo Laboratories and Allen and Hanbury's—changes which fell within their cognitive paradigm and showed that this current activity was not something dramatically new. This undoubtedly helped in those areas where the new reality of the organization sat side by side with the remnants of the old. At this stage there is generally confusion about the new behaviours required and the new signals coming from management, but in Hewlett Packard and Glaxo Pharmaceuticals UK there was a clear understanding of where the changes would position the company and what the new roles and responsibilities of employees would look like.

The companies which experienced difficulty in the change process were largely those firms which had been in markets largely isolated from strong competition and which had developed internal cultures dominated by paternalism, rigid hierarchies, and strong centralist command and control styles. In many ways, these cultures had been a boon, providing stable employment and a vertical career ladder, encouraging a strong relational psychological contract (Rousseau 1996). However, the strength of their organizational identities was such that, when the time for change arrived, the leap to a new form of organization proved very hard for employees to make in cognitive terms. Disbelief at the changes and nostalgia for old ways of working were typical reactions. For many, it was their first experience of change. Added to this, for many employees, the organization had not given any idea of what the new work setting would look like, nor what this would entail for job roles and responsibilities.

CONCLUSION

In this chapter, we have reviewed the nature of planned change programmes which have sought to refocus and restructure the organizations in order to maintain their competitive edge. The change processes have involved a number of common elements, what Doz and Thanheiser (1993) call the 'boring regularities'. These include, first of all, an increase in the strength of external factors influencing organizational transitions and, second, the nature of the response to these. This response has, by and large, featured downsizing, de-layering, re-engineering, the introduction of quality programmes, and the splitting up of businesses within organizations to increase accountability and transparency.

In terms of the human resource levers the organizations were using to align behaviours with the new goals and values, changes in the work setting were accompanied by attempts to empower lower-level managers and increase their involvement in decision-making processes. Changes in job roles were supported by the refocusing of the performance management systems and linked to them, in particular to the introduction of competence frameworks intended to give tangible benchmarks to support the new climate.

Much of this activity, therefore, shows common themes, problems, and solutions. What we have found, however, is that in the intangible factors of the change process there is a wide variance concerning employee interpretation of change issues and the degree to which employees accept or resist change.

We have identified three areas which have influenced the organization's capacity to manage change: the organizational identity, the embedding of the performance management system, and the involvement of middle managers. The difficulties which some of the companies had in managing the strategic change process resulted in part because the need for change was relatively new; for them, the changes represented a corporate upheaval unlike anything they had experienced before. Now that this has been undertaken, it is expected that these upheavals will be followed by ongoing learning and renewal, and a developing competence in the process of managing change.

9

People Processes as a Source of Competitive Advantage

LYNDA GRATTON

A key challenge facing organizations in the late 1990s is to continue to deliver sustained competitive advantage in the short term whilst at the same time preparing for longer-term success. Although the prime sources of competitive advantage in the past decades may have been access to financial resources or the use of technology, these are now viewed as necessary, but not sufficient. For many companies the sources of sustained competitive advantage lie not only in access to finance or capital, but within the organization, in people and processes capable of delivering the customer delight or rapid innovation which will place them ahead of competitors (Barney 1991; Lundy 1994; Wright *et al.* 1994).

What is the precise role of people and processes in the delivery of sustained competitive advantage? This is a question which has been central to our research agenda here. Clearly people processes are an important element of the complex systems architecture which describes an organization. We are increasingly of the opinion that these processes are a critical element, particularly in embedding the capacity to transform a company.

A key aspect of the Leading Edge research has been to use the case-based methodology to build a map showing how the link between strategy and individual performance is played out. In building this map we have considered the following three key propositions.

- Transformation capability depends in part on the ability to create and embed processes which link business strategy to the behaviour and performance of individuals and teams. These clusters of processes link vertically (to create alignment with short-term business needs), horizontally (to create cohesion), and temporally (to transform to meet future business needs).
- These clusters of processes can be described and observed in many organizations.
- The strength of linkage between people processes and business strategy can vary across both processes and businesses.

In some of the companies in our sample the linkage between business strategy and people processes is strong: as business strategies change over time, so the processes are capable of subtle realignment and adaptation. In such a company the transformation and embedding of these processes could be a key aspect of sustained competitive advantage. In other companies the linkage is weak; there is limited ability to realign and adapt key people processes as the strategy changes, with the processes remaining inflexible and incapable of ongoing transformation, instead reinforcing behaviours which may once have been appropriate but which are no longer so.

It is clear that within any company there are individuals or groups who add positive value by having skills or motivations which are unique, or skills, knowledge, or networks of contacts which cannot be imitated by competitors or replaced by another resource by a competing company (Barney 1991). Yet whilst these people or groups are crucial, their skills and motivations are, in part, the result of a whole portfolio of people policies, procedures, and processes which serve to train, develop, and retain. These policies and processes are not of themselves capable of creating sustained competitive advantage since they could potentially be imitated or replaced. However, they do play an important role in developing sustained competitive advantage through the development of the human capital pool. In effect, the systematic leverage of people policies and processes can bring competitive advantage. 'HR practices moderate the relationship between the human capital pool and the firm effectiveness, such that the pool is effective only when combined with the right practices that capitalize on the advantage through eliciting employee behaviour' (Wright *et al.* 1994: 320). Taken to its conclusion, strong linkage between business strategy and human resource processes and policies is likely to lead to greater competitiveness and organizational effectiveness.

Even the most casual observation of life in many companies will pinpoint the crucial impact of a lack of integration or linkage between business strategy and people processes. How often do corporate plans and mission statements remain simply that—senior executive rhetoric which has little meaning to those people tasked with delivering customer delight or bringing complex products rapidly to the market place? Corporate mission statements may extol customer delight or product innovation, but when the communication fanfare is over and the customer-focus workshops have been completed, what is left? A group of people trying to make sense of the paradoxes and mixed messages with which they are faced: people who try to understand the underlying message of customer delight when no attempt is made to provide them with the skills necessary to deliver this delight; people who are extolled to think long-term but are rewarded and promoted for delivering short-term financial targets; people who see those who try hardest to understand customer needs penalized for the time they take to do so. Faced with this plethora of contradictory messages the employees, in their quest for 'sense-making' (Scott-Morgan 1994), look at which behaviours are rewarded, which skills are promoted, and who is developed. It is the messages from reward, appraisal, and training processes, not simply the corporate rhetoric, which form the basis of sense-making and which give the steer on how to behave. If these people policies and processes lack linkage and fail to reinforce business strategy, then the performance of the business will suffer.

PROPOSITIONS OF THE PEOPLE PROCESS MAP

The map we developed over the course of the research is based on three propositions: that the delivery of business strategy is most successful when linkage occurs on three dimensions; that at the core of the linkage are a set of key clusters of processes; and that the linkage between business strategy and these people processes can vary from weak to strong.

Proposition one: dimensions of linkage

Vertical linkage

The map has at its core the vertical linkage between the strategy or business objectives of the company, individual behaviour, and ultimate performance. This vertical integration where leverage or linkage is gained through procedures, policies, and processes is widely acknowledged to be a crucial part of any strategic approach to the management of people (Dyer 1984; Mahoney and Deckop 1986; Schuler and Jackson 1987; Tichy *et al.* 1982; Truss and Gratton 1994). It ensures the presence of an explicit complementary relationship between internal people policies and processes and the external product market or larger business strategy, and creates and supports the individual behaviours and competencies which have the potential to be a source of competitive advantage (Wright *et al.* 1994). Linkage ensures a focus on what Jackson *et al.* (1989) have described as 'needed employee behaviour', that behaviour which is central to the delivery of the business strategy.

Horizontal linkage

Horizontal linkage between the processes also has a major role to play by ensuring key people processes have cohesion and coherence. Underlying this concept is the proposition (Guest 1987) that cohesion is likely to create synergistic benefits and the company's strategic plans are more likely to be successfully implemented. If, for example, the business objective is to create customer delight then this should be central to the performance management processes. The objective-setting process should focus on the customer, customer satisfaction measures should be collected and fed back, customer training should be provided, and those people who deliver high levels of customer service should be rewarded for doing so. When this occurs horizontal integration has been achieved, and as a consequence customer service as a corporate objective is more likely to be delivered.

Temporal linkage

In this map the temporal perspective is seen as crucial. Processes to deliver short-term performance are crucial to a company, but they must be balanced with the ability to create success in the longer term. This notion of two axes of time is central to our model. An emphasis on transformation and the management of change (Hendry and Pettigrew 1986) acknowledges that at the heart of the delivery of long-term competitive advantage there must be a vision for the future and a focus on concerns which are broader, more long-term oriented, and less problem-centred than typical short-term concerns (Mahoney and Deckop 1986). A key issue for delivering long-term success is the need to create an iterative learning loop between current capabilities and future aspirations. Without this iteration and learning, people strategies remain static and tactical. A central concept of this map is that of the time frame between the present and the longer-term planning cycle. This time dimension is believed to be so crucial that the phrase 'temporal linkage' has been coined. A long-term vision is a particularly crucial aspect of people strategies because the time cycles for people resources are considerably longer than those for financial or technological resources. Consider the following points:

- It takes ten to fifteen years to select and develop an international senior executive cadre.
- It takes a minimum of three years to pilot and implement a reward system refocused on supporting a new set of competencies.
- It takes at least five years to reshape the technological skill base of employees.

In sum, for some of the most crucial people issues the temporal perspective is not months but years, and could even be decades. So the planning cycle for people resources must be capable of creating a foundation for skills and behaviours that reach far beyond the two-year cycle favoured for many business strategies. This distinction between delivering short-term business goals and the creation of longer-term capability is especially important since it has been forcibly argued by a number of commentators (Hamel and Prahalad 1989) that too many Western companies emphasize the short term to the detriment of longer-term success.

Proposition two: the core people policies and processes

At the core of the map are three clusters of people processes, policies, and procedures which serve to link strategy with individual and group performance. The notion of a process is used here in the broadest sense, encompassing broad value-driven approaches to both formal and informal activities: both policies which are formal, explicit statements of principles guiding particular areas of people management, and informal activities practised by specialists and line managers in their management of people strategies (Schuler and Jackson 1987). In this model the word 'process' is intended to embrace philosophies, policies, and practices. However, the emphasis is on practices and embedded processes, those which take place in a systematic rather than an ad hoc manner, and which have a procedural reality rather than being simply philosophical rhetoric.

Proposition three: the strength of the linkage

The first proposition of the People Process Map suggests that the link between business strategy and people processes can be expressed vertically, horizontally, and temporally. The third proposition refers to the strength of the linkage, and proposes that this linkage can be described as a continuum ranging from strong to weak linkage. The strong and weak linkage is described for each of the eleven people processes in Tables 9.1, 9.2, and 9.3. Strong linkage exists when the process is so strongly linked to the business strategy that, as the strategy changes, so the process is capable of adjustment and refinement to accommodate these changes. For weakly linked processes the process is so ad hoc and informal that changes in the business strategy cannot be reflected.

There have been previous attempts to describe the concept of linkage and these have either focused on single processes (for examples of strategy development, see Quinn Mills 1985; Tyson and Fell 1986), or simply described the strongest level of linkage without describing the weakest (for example Ulrich and Lake 1990; Walker 1980). In this model the linkage across all the processes is described at five potential levels of strength. These descriptions are developed from the literature and from an in-depth analysis of the case companies. They use as a base methodology the behavioural descriptors developed most effectively in competency descriptors. Whilst these descriptors are a useful starting point they serve mainly as a basis for further research and discussion.

THE PEOPLE PROCESS MAP: A DESCRIPTION

We have reviewed the three key propositions from which the model was created. This section presents a description of the model. The strongest level of linkage is described in detail in each of the sections, whilst a summary of strong and weak linkage is presented in Tables 9.1, 9.2, and 9.3.

The short-term cycle

At the core of the ability to deliver short-term goals is a group of processes which were described in some detail in Chapter 3. These serve to link annual business objectives to the performance of individuals through objective setting, performance appraisal and measurement, rewarding, and targeted technical and short-term training. Although each of the first three processes is described separately, in reality the setting, appraising, and rewarding of performance form a coherent and integrated cycle of activities.

Objective setting

An essential aspect of performance management is the process which cascades business objectives into the objectives and responsibilities of individuals and teams. This is increasingly important as the trend towards decentralization gives managers and employees more authority and responsibility for the delivery of business objectives, a trend which is based on the assumption that pushing down accountability yields the advantages of reduced costs and increased efficiency (Purcell 1995). This aspect of management involvement and communication is a critical element of the objective-setting processes, which are strongest when linked to business strategy.

Strong linkage:
- The business objectives of the overall strategic plan are clearly articulated to the individual and are transformed into clear objectives which are discussed and agreed on an annual or biannual basis.
- Processes exist which ensure that individual objectives are realigned to take account of annual changes in the business strategy.
- The quality of the objective-setting process is monitored and changes are made to ensure that it remains effective.

Performance metrics

Measurement and appraisal of performance becomes vital in those organizations in which responsibility is placed on individuals and teams. This measurement serves as the basis of management control (Child 1974) and as the means by which the contribution of the business unit to the organization can be recognized. Moreover, the potential feedback from understanding the performance of teams and units can be a central aspect in leveraging organizational learning (Argyris 1977).

The emphasis in metrics has historically been on financial measures such as profitability or return on assets. However, for those companies striving to create strong linkage with business strategy, the emphasis has to be on metrics associated with all aspects of business strategy, not simply financial targets. So to achieve the strongest level of linkage, the processes have to be capable of measuring a wide range of outcomes, including those requiring 'softer' measures such as customer satisfaction (Ulrich and Lake 1990), innovation, or team-building competencies. This combination of the 'hard' and the 'soft' is a central aspect of those performance metrics and appraisal processes which are strongly linked to business strategy.

Strong linkage:

- The aims of the business strategy are reflected in a series of performance measures which address each of the business imperatives. These measures cover Key Result Areas (KRAs) such as financial performance, customer satisfaction, team motivation and development.
- The metrics are reliable and valid. For example, team motivation is measured through systematic team feedback and team development by the completion of development plans.
- An individual's performance against these KRAs is systematically and frequently measured, using well-established and valid measures.
- Information from the KRAs is provided as feedback to the individual in a systematic and timely manner by line managers who are committed and skilled.

Rewards

Reward processes can be one of the greatest sources of leverage available to a company in its quest to increase organizational performance and effectiveness, yet remain one of the most underutilized and potentially complex tools for driving organizational performance. The importance and complexity of linking reward strategies to business goals in a systematic manner has been a recurrent theme in the research in this field, as has the importance and difficulty of linking rewards to the longer-term view (Hambrick and Snow 1989). In describing the strongest level of linkage the emphasis has been placed on Lawler's (1990) description of reward processes which are capable of reinforcing the behaviours crucial to business strategy (such as long-term versus short-term, customer focus versus financial results).

Strong linkage:

- Team and/or performance outcomes are accurately measured and directly related to the achievement of business goals. A proportion of the individual or team remuneration package reflects business goal-oriented outputs. This proportion is sufficiently great to have a significant impact.
- The relationship between the achievement of business goals and pay is

clear to individuals, as is the basis on which they receive performance-related pay or bonuses.

Short-term training

A key aspect of the delivery of short-term business goals is the ability rapidly to develop skills and competencies. This can be crucial as sectoral technological changes can demand whole new sets of skills. The emphasis is on understanding the skills and competencies required, analysing individual and team training needs, and delivering the training (Butler *et al.* 1991).

Strong linkage:
- The key technical and managerial competencies, skills, and techniques required to deliver the business objectives have been systematically analysed and shared with managers.
- A range of on-line and off-line development programmes and experiences have been designed to deliver these core technical and managerial competencies, skills, and techniques. All the core technical and managerial competencies, skills, and techniques are addressed by the training, which is of a high quality.
- Evaluation processes are in place to ensure that the training remains of high quality and focused on business needs.
- Individual and group training needs are accurately diagnosed and individual training plans created. Delivery of training takes place around these plans in a systematic and timely manner.

The long-term cycle

Whilst the processes required to deliver short-term business goals are relatively well understood and widely discussed by scholars and practitioners, those elements which link to the longer term are rather more opaque, more complex, and made up of clusters of processes. With a number of notable exceptions (for example Walker 1980), the focus in the human resource literature has been on the short term. For a longer-term perspective one has to consider the change management and strategy literature.

The long-term perspective can provide a vision of the future which creates a frame against which human resource processes can be flexed and adapted (Gratton 1994). It creates the context for executive and workforce development, and focuses attention on the real issues rather than on a succession of fire-fighting initiatives (Purcell and Sisson 1983). In essence the longer-term perspective can mean the difference between brief competitive advantage and sustained competitive advantage.

The longer-term perspective is described here as the ability of the organization to continue to create success in a rapidly changing environment—to embed within itself the capability to transform. At the core of this cycle is the ability to create a vision of the leadership, workforce, and organization of the business.

Leadership development

This section describes the cluster of processes and routines capable of developing future leaders by understanding what is required for the future and identifying those people with leadership potential. At its centre is the creation of development tracks capable of delivering significant work experience and targeting development. The processes which support the development of high-potential cadres are well understood and have been documented in many companies (Rosenbaum 1979). They cover a broad range of activities which include training, coaching, self-improvement, and the provision of significant job experiences.

Strong linkage:
- A detailed and systematic competency profile and a needs analysis of the requirements for future managerial talent is undertaken. These profiles form the basis of the identification and succession planning for high-potential people.
- Succession processes exist which provide a pool of talented people from which future managers can be drawn. There are a range of systematic processes in place which ensure that adequate provision has been made to replace the current senior management cadre.

Workforce development

The contribution of senior executives and the management team to the sustained competitive success of the organization is well understood (Barney 1991). However, there is an increasing awareness that whilst leadership capabilities have a key role to play, so too do the motivation and skills of people in key roles, or those who have tacit knowledge (Nonaka 1988) of organizational procedures or customers which it would be difficult for a competitor to imitate. As Wright et al. (1994) have argued, sustained competitive advantage is likely to come from the larger pool of human capital that is the entire organization. This wider group can play a key role because it is directly involved in the production of the product or service, and is also less mobile.

The cluster of processes which transform the current skills of the workforce to meet future needs has two elements. The first is the forecasting of the future skill needs (Walker 1980), the basis of which is those processes concerned with preparing for long-term business success. The second element is those career planning processes which support the longer-term development of the workforce. Whilst this commitment to the longer-term development and retention of people with key skills may be vital to a company, the policies and processes which support this commitment are fraught with difficulties. No Western company can now support a policy of lifetime employment; to do so would run counter to the skill flexibility and cost effectiveness which may be central to long-term success. Companies face a real paradox here, as dismantling the processes associated with long-term careers creates flexibility, but breaks the psychological contract (Robinson and Rousseau 1994) which may be crucial to retaining key skills. However, those with the strongest linkage with business strategy will have created a portfolio of career development processes which provide broad support to the development of the workforce.

Strong linkage:

- There is analysis and debate about the work experiences most appropriate to developing the skills, abilities, and motivations of the future workforce.
- These imperatives are translated into a portfolio of policies and career planning procedures which ensure that people have an opportunity to participate in a series of work experiences and programmes which prepare them for future challenges.
- These policies and procedures refer not only to job experiences, but also to wider aspects, including teamwork, mentoring, and coaching.
- Individuals are aware of these career imperatives and actively try, in partnership with the company, to ensure they are a part of their work experience.

Organizational development

The focus on individuals' skills, motivation, and commitment is central to the transformation of the organization. At a macro level there is a set of processes which support the transformation of the organization. These processes link the understanding of the longer term with current capabilities: they include understanding the current state of the system, planning for change, transitional management, and understanding the desired outcomes (Ulrich and Lake 1990). This requires a capacity to implement strategic plans, yet be adaptive and responsive in the face of unanticipated pressures at all levels of the organization (Guest 1987). This capability must be supported by project management and change agent skills amongst a significant number of managers, models of change, and an understanding of the patterns of change over time (Pettigrew and Whipp 1991).

Strong linkage:

- There are clear examples within the organization of successful transformation. This has involved the successful communication of the need for change, a clear statement of what needs to be done, and the plementation of processes and policies which allow this successful transformation.

- As a consequence, there is transformational capability within the organization, through cascaded communication processes, incremental change processes, or skills in change management.

Feedback and redirectional elements

The short-term cycle of processes (objective setting, metrics, rewards, and short-term training) and the long-term cycle of processes (leadership, workforce, and organization) are complex sets of processes which are central to the success of the company. However, without being part of a feedback loop between aspirations and capability they remain static and unadaptable. To create a dynamic model other complex sets of elements must occur:

- the scanning of current capability and future long-term people trends;
- an analysis of the gap between capability and business needs;
- the creation of a people strategy which influences the design and delivery of the people processes.

This cycle of activity operates in both a short-term perspective (that is, within the next six months) and a longer-term perspective (that is, in the next two years and ahead). These two time perspectives are shown in the long-term and short-term cycle of the model.

Scanning people trends

The feedback and redirectional elements are essentially a set of inward focused processes designed to understand the people implications of the short-term and long-term business strategies. Strong linkage is associated with evidence of systematic scanning. The range of these scanning processes is well understood and includes trend analysis and the environmental scanning of demographic, sociocultural, political, and legal trends (Butler *et al.* 1991). These scanning processes allow the management group to 'identify the issues which rise to attention', and by so doing identify also those issues likely to be sources of 'pain' or 'gain' (Walker 1980).

Strong linkage:
- There is frequent and systematic scanning of short-term and long-term people trends (for example demographic, aspirational, contractual, and skill-based). These trends are discussed and documents and plans produced which describe the future key people issues and how these can be addressed.
- These documents, and supporting conversations, play a central role in the process of long-term strategy creation.

Table 9.1. The short-term cycle

	Objective setting	Performance metrics	Rewards	Short-term training
Strong linkage	Articulation of strategic plans; close link to objectives; annual realignment; quality monitored	KRAs address all key business imperatives; reliable and valid measures; systematic measurement; systematic feedback	Rewards directly related to achievement of business goals; proportions significant enough to have impact; relationship clear	Key skills required to deliver business strategy analysed; all core skills addressed; accurate diagnosis and delivery
	Articulation of strategic plan; some linkage to objectives; no explicit monitoring	KRAs address many business imperatives; reliable and valid measures; systematic feedback	Rewards directly related to achievement of business goals; proportion not significant enough to have impact; relationship clear	Some anlaysis of skills required; range of training not updated to reflect strategy; ad hoc diagnosis
	Some articulation of strategic plan; no clear linkage with objectives; annual objective setting for all	KRAs measure some business imperatives; unreliable measures; some feedback	Some attempts to relate to business goal; link not explicit; relationship unclear	No systematic analysis of skills required; training reflects limited diagnosis—'sheep dip'
	No articulation of strategic plans; no link with objectives; some employees set annual objectives	Some attempt to understand behaviour or output; no link with business plan; some discussion	Some attempt to measure performance; not linked to rewards	No systematic anlaysis of skills; limited, generic training; no diagnosis of individual needs
Weak linkage	No articulation of strategic plan; no link with objectives;infrequent, vague, ad hoc discussions	No KRAs; unreliable measures; infrequent, vague, ad hoc discussions	Not linked to rewards; no opportunity to flex pay	No systematic anlaysis of skills; very few training programmes; majority do not receive training

Table 9.2. The long-term cycle

	Leadership development	Workforce development	Organizational development
Strong linkage	Detailed understanding of management capabilities required for long-term strategy; high-potential people identified on the basis of this understanding; range of systematic processes in place to provide necessary development	Detailed understanding of key capabilities required of long-term strategy and necessary development and training experiences; portfolio of development processes in place to prepare for future; individuals aware of career imperatives	Past history of successful transformational change; clear communication and implementation processes; current capability in change management
	Some understanding of future capabilities; incorporated into identification; some processes in place to provide necessary development	Some understanding of future capabilities and development experiences; one or two initiatives directed at future needs; career imperatives communicated to employees	Some examples of successful transformational change; processes in place; current capability in change management
	Identification on basis of current capability needs; some process to fill key roles	Primary focus in current capability; some communication of future and broad directives discussed; no clear long-term policies or practices	Mixed transformational change—some failures; current capability relatively limited and disconnected
	Identification on basis of current capability needs; many roles filled in an ad hoc way; succession plans for some key roles	Focus on current capabilities; no communication of broad future policies; career initiatives focus on present	No examples of successful transformational change; no skills base or experience
Weak linkage	Senior roles filled in ad hoc manner; no forward planning	No career initiatives; development ad hoc, following paths established over time	No examples of successful transformation; examples of uncoordinated, ad hoc, and tactical response; no skill base or experiences

Gap Analysis

This cluster refers to those processes which bridge the gap between the vision for the future and the current capabilities. The major emphasis is on the diagnosis and understanding of current capability and the feedback loop established between this and the needs of the longer term. Gap Analysis is at the heart of this dynamic model of human resource strategy. By understanding the alignment between future needs and current capabilities, the strategy for human resources can emerge (Gratton 1994). Understanding alignment requires the diagnosis of current capabilities and analysis of the link to the future. Such an understanding of current capabilities might include, for example, ratings of employee performance and accurate diagnosis of current levels of education, skill sets, and motivations. The importance of diagnosing current capability is well understood and is seen as the crucial element in an organization's ability to learn (Senge 1990). As Ulrich and Lake (1990) have argued, 'understanding the state of the system' provides a crucial link to the transformational processes by creating a feedback loop of current capability.

Analysis of the gap between current capabilities and future needs forms the basis of a feedback loop which is a central aspect of emergent strategy (Mintzberg 1994) and the strategic planning process. It creates the possibility of moving beyond a narrow, technical focus and a concern with forecasting work to a concern for establishing linkages between people planning and organization strategy and business planning (Mahoney and Deckop 1986). The iterative, feedback nature of these diagnostic processes is shown in the model by the arrows which connect current capabilities (the short-term cycle) and future visions (the long-term cycle) (see Fig. 9.1). The emphasis is on the way in which these diagnostic processes create a bridge or link between future strategy and current capabilities by emphasizing the ability of individuals and groups to respond to future needs. However, it has been argued that these processes have a broader role to play, as a means of identifying current core competencies (Hamel and Prahalad 1990). The classical strategic planning model begins with competitor positioning and market analysis, and from this develops a competitive strategy to which human resource considerations are aligned. It has been argued, by Purcell (1995) amongst others, that since the external environment is in so much flux a better starting point for defining the business strategy might be current capability. This definition of capability includes the identification of those core competencies which arise from people. Purcell argues that this may be a more durable basis for strategy than a definition based on needs (such as markets). As a consequence he believes that the most pressing human resource issue is not to link strategy with human resources, but to identify current unique (human) capabilities.

Strong linkage:
- The current capabilities, competencies, skill sets, aspirations, and motivations of the workforce are accurately measured (for example

Table 9.3. Feedback and redirectional elements

	Scanning people trends	Gap analysis	Creating a people strategy
Strong linkage	Frequent systematic scanning of broad range of short-term and long-term HR trends; findings shared; plays central role in creation of strategy	Current workforce capabilities accurately measured; systematically provided to managers; alignment with future needs understood	Scenarios/plans created; broad people implications articulated; alignment with current capability understood
	Some ad hoc information collected; findings frequently discussed; some influence on management thinking	Some data on workforce capabilities; systematically provided to managers; alignment with needs understood	Some opportunity for systematic discussions of future; some people implications articulated; broad understanding of alignment
	Some ad hoc information collected; findings occasionally discussed; remains largely within the function—limited influence	Some data on workforce capabilities; ad hoc, impressionistic information collected and shared	No systematic process, ad hoc task force; focus on current problems; essentially tactical
	Informal information collected; infrequent discussions; very limited impact on strategy	No data on workforce capabilities; ad hoc, impressionistic information collected and shared	No systematic process; some managers plan for short term; focus on numbers and skills
Weak linkage	No collection of information; no policy meetings; focus on short-term tactics, no impact on strategy	No reliable data on workforce capabilities; ad hoc, impressionistic information kept within HR team	No systematic process; focus on delivering current objectives

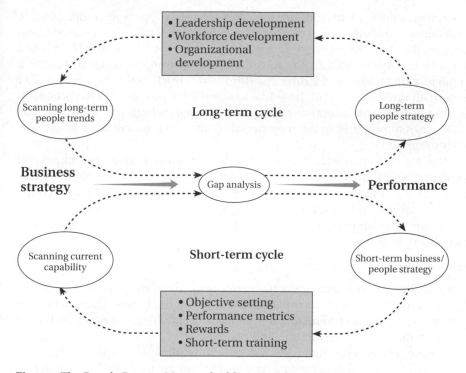

Fig. 9.1. The People Process Map: embedding transformational change

through systematic surveys of aspirations and motivation, and analyses of
appraisal and training needs).
- These diagnostic data are collected, recorded, and systematically provided
  to business managers.
- There is a clear awareness of the alignment between the needs of the future
  scenarios and the current capabilities. This gap is acknowledged and results in a series of action plans which form the basis of the transformational
  process.

Creating a people strategy

As far back as the 1960s it has been well understood by organizations such
as Shell (De Geus 1988) that the ability to respond quickly to changing needs
and to build long-term organizational capability depends in part on the
ability of managers to visualize and create mental pictures of the future, to
move from a fire-fighting mode to one where they have the potential to think
in the longer term. Yet whilst this concern with the longer term has been
widely acknowledged as 'a good thing', the actual cluster of practices and

processes which might support this perspective is less well understood. A number of processes and routines have been described to facilitate and support the ability of the organization to experience the future, and by so doing reshape its view of itself in the future. Amongst these are scenario planning models, simulations, and games (Gratton 1994; Ulrich and Lake 1990; Walker 1980). Our understanding of the actual usage of these future-oriented processes is limited. With the exception of a number of well-publicized cases (De Geus 1988), current practices in the majority of companies have not been systematically examined.

As a consequence it is rather difficult to predict exactly the cluster of processes and practices supporting the long-term reshaping of the organization. Strong linkage would be suggested by the evidence of embedded (rather than one-off) routines and processes in which managers spend time visualizing the future of their organization, and attempting to understand its people implications.

Strong linkage:

- Cross-functional management teams work through a process in which they discuss the various potential scenarios of the future. These scenarios are described according to a number of key variables, some of which refer to people, culture, structure, and process.
- These discussions create an understanding of some of the key determinants for future success and how these can be measured and mapped against current capabilities.
- There is also an understanding of the alignment and gap between the needs of the future scenarios and the current capabilities.

KEY QUESTIONS

The People Process Map represents our own view of some parts of the complex architecture of large, transformational organizations. It has as a central concept the notion of temporal linkage, and a realization that the real challenge many companies face is to create processes which are sufficiently permanent to bring cohesion and continuity, but sufficiently flexible to adapt to changing business circumstances and the resultant strategies. This tight yet loose combination is expressed in the second key notion, that of linkage: that there should be an attempt to link the people processes into the strategy in such a way that as the strategy changes, so the process is capable of similar changes. These strong linkages are expressed in many ways, by objectives which articulate the current business strategy, by performance metrics capable of capturing the real elements which are central to success, by remunerative processes which consistently reward those people who have delivered business-related performance, and by career processes capable of developing leaders who will take the organization forward; in other words, by a complex group of processes which are tightly linked to strategy.

There are two questions which we have explored in more detail in this chapter:

- Given the many people processes which characterize the architecture of an organization, exactly where are organizations placing the emphasis and leveraging their resources?
- Do organizations differ in their ability to create people processes capable of delivering short-term business performance and longer-term capability? What elements characterize those companies more capable of creating strong people processes?

This close examination of strategic linkage has provided a clear signal of how companies in the mid-1990s are responding to the competitive market place in which they operate. It allows a fuller exploration of a contentious subject, the potential relationship between people processes and company performance. The extent of the impact of excellence in people processes on company performance is still unresolved. Some have argued that strongly linked people processes make for strong corporate business performance, whilst others have argued that this linkage is particularly difficult to achieve and can only be expected in firms with specific characteristics, for example those which have 'mutual commitment' and the strong support of multiple stakeholders (Kochen and Dyer 1993), or those which are in growth industries with a predominantly white-collar workforce, or are traditionally non-unionist with a strong corporate image (Noon 1992). So complex is this linkage to achieve that others (such as Guest 1989) have argued that high levels of linkage are unlikely to exist outside a few American and Japanese firms. By examining the strength of linkage across seven companies we hope to test these propositions and add further to our understanding of the concept. A brief overview of the linkage for all the processes is presented below and in the following section we highlight those with the strongest and weakest linkages.

The short-term cycle:
- objective setting: strong linkage. Clear objectives set in most organizations;
- performance metrics: medium linkage. Strong metrics around financial performance, but much weaker metrics around 'softer' people elements;
- rewards: strong linkage, particularly in the American multinationals, but weaker linkage around team pay and upwards feedback;
- short-term training: strong linkage. All had significantly invested in training to meet immediate skill needs.

The long-term cycle:
- leadership development: strong linkage, with well-established leadership development and high-potential cadres;
- workforce development: weak linkage, with a focus on the present rather

than the future. Career planning and the psychological contract is problematic in many companies;

- organizational development: medium linkage. Some have a clear view of OD, while others lack both a clear view and sufficient capability.

Feedback and redirectional elements:

- scanning current capability: medium linkage. Some use of surveys and skills audits, but scanning tends to lack cohesion and integration, and is rarely sufficiently well communicated to line managers;
- scanning long-term people trends: weak linkage. Isolated use of long-term visioning, with limited feedback to managers, giving a broad directional element rather than clear articulation;
- creating a short-term people strategy: medium linkage. There is an articulated HR strategy plan and influential HR people in most organizations, but the link between the espoused and the enacted can be weak;
- creating a long-term people strategy: weak linkage. The vision rarely looks more than two or three years ahead. Generally the process is not embedded, and has limited impact on management decisions.

TRENDS ACROSS THE COMPANIES: STRONGLY LINKED PROCESSES

One of the overarching themes shared by many of the companies was the changing context in which they operate and the implications of this for business strategy. As we saw in Chapter 8, all had reshaped, and continue to reshape, the ways in which they compete in the market place. At Citibank the strategic challenge was to support the concept of the target market. In Glaxo Pharmaceuticals UK it was to develop a partnership in health care; in Hewlett Packard, to create the will and capability to bring product cycles down from two-to-five years to six-to-nine months; in Kraft Jacobs Suchard, to support the introduction of continuous improvement. At Lloyds Bank UK Retail Banking, the challenge was to support increasing customer service levels, and at W. H. Smith News, it was to support enhanced customer focus. These statements of strategic intent were not simply pieces of corporate rhetoric, they were deep-seated views about how these companies will sustain their current competitive advantage. But they become rhetoric if these statements of strategic intent are not supported by people processes which create an understanding of what must be achieved, which provide targeted performance feedback, and which increase skill levels through training and reward targeted on performance.

The challenge these companies face is not the creation of processes to support an ossified business strategy, supporting the way they have always done business, but to create and sustain processes and policies capable of flexing to meet the needs of the future and the changing competitive market in which they operate. But the balance between stability and flexibility is difficult to achieve. Too much change and flex in these processes, and common themes are lost, people become overwhelmed by discontinuities or, as one manager put it, the 'death by a hundred initiatives'; the common integrating message is lost in the barrage of change. Too little flex, and the processes become solidified and ossified, impervious to the changing circumstances.

Across the companies it was clear that much effort had been directed at creating processes which link individual and team objectives to the business plans. However, many were struggling with measuring and rewarding business-focused performance. All the companies had in place processes to measure the 'hard' performance outcomes, such as budgets met or profitability, but few were capable of measuring the 'soft' performance outputs such as team working, innovation, or customer focus. For those for whom these softer elements are critical to the success of the firm, this is a real issue in the quest to link individual performance to business strategy.

In this section we look at those people processes which are strongly linked to business strategy. Across the companies, strength of linkage was strongest for the management of short-term performance and the development of future leaders. Much attention has been focused on linking objectives to business goals and short-term training. The measuring and rewarding of 'softer' performance outcomes (such as customer satisfaction or team skills) was proving more complex, and some of these issues are discussed here.

Objective setting

All these companies had experienced restructuring and many had de-layered, with a resultant emphasis being placed on managerial and employee responsibility. In these companies this devolution had been accompanied by real efforts to create strong linkage between the objectives of individuals, business goals, and outputs. Processes for setting individuals' objectives were a feature of all the companies in the sample. In every company efforts had been made to create and embed processes in which managers and their teams met at least annually to set objectives and agree the targets for the coming year.

As we saw in Chapter 3, two of the companies, Hewlett Packard (with the ten-step process) and Kraft Jacobs Suchard (with their Managing and Appraising People Process), operate with strong strategic linkage and had developed an objective-setting process which links individual objectives to annual business goals in a clear and articulated manner. In both companies joint objective setting was the foundation of a performance management framework which ensured objectives were flexed to meet the changing needs of the business strategy. The processes were well documented, systematically rolled out, supported by trained managers, and the quality was reviewed. As a consequence, of the employees surveyed, the vast majority were aware of the business strategy and how it linked to their performance, had clearly defined work goals, and understood the basis upon which their job performance was appraised. A crucial element of the embedding of the process was that in both companies the objective-setting process had been in place for over a decade, and as a consequence had become part of the way in which individuals saw the company doing business. It was part of the fabric of the culture and an important management discipline.

At Hewlett Packard and Kraft Jacobs Suchard objective setting and performance management were part of the fabric of the business and seen by managers as crucial tools, supported by training and quality monitoring. This was not the case for all of the companies, some of which were struggling to bring objective setting and appraisal into the company, or were doing so against a backdrop of massive organizational change. At W. H. Smith News the concept of systematic objective setting and appraisal was relatively new for the workforce, many of whom were unskilled or semi-skilled. Here we saw pockets of good appraisal taking place where there were highly skilled and motivated managers. At Lloyds Bank UK Retail Banking there had been much effort over the previous couple of years to support the integration of individual objectives and business goals. However, the roll-out of the objective-setting process was taking place against a backdrop of organizational change and realignment. An increasing emphasis on the customer had been accompanied by massive change in the technological base and distribution channels of the retail bank which had created (and would continue to create) significant downsizing. The speed of this change accompanied by the natural inertia of what was a large bureaucracy had created a significant lag between corporate rhetoric and the promises of a performance management process. The perceptions and operationalization of the objective-setting and appraisal systems were lagging behind the new corporate vision. This was reflected in the employee group, some of whom did not fully understand the new vision and were not clear about the contribution they needed to make to realize this vision. They were also sceptical of the need for a new vision, given the strong continuing financial performance of the bank.

Performance metrics

Whilst the linking of objectives to business goals appeared to be an area of leverage across many of the companies, establishing the metrics associated with business goals was proving much more of a challenge. None of these companies had achieved the strongest level of linkage in which the business strategy is reflected in a series of performance measures capturing both 'hard' outcomes (such as financial performance) and 'softer' outcomes (such as customer satisfaction, or the ability of the individual to develop the team) in ways which are reliable and valid, and in which systematic performance feedback is provided.

Whilst the business strategies of these companies frequently referred to customer focus, innovation, or the use of people as a source of competitive advantage, metrics associated with short-term financial targets still predominated. Perhaps then it was not surprising that when people talked in the 'Unwritten Rules of the Game' interviews about their top priorities, the focus was clear and consistent across all of the companies, with comments such as: 'revenue and quota performance are what really count'; 'monitor your budget carefully'; 'the numbers are what really matter'; 'focus on tangible outcomes'; 'focus on the numbers, profit, and/or volume'. From the perspective of the individual, the top priorities in every company were financial. Customers and employees came much further down the list.

As we argued in Chapter 7, if this overemphasis on short-term profitability is to be redressed, and certainly the corporate missions of many of these companies talked of a wider set of priorities and stakeholders, then these other priorities have to become a real part of performance management. The challenge these companies are grappling with is to create metrics that value the 'softer' targets, to realign the metrics away from an overriding emphasis on the short-term to emphasize the role the individual or team is playing in developing longer-term capability. These softer targets such as team development, customer satisfaction, and innovation were for many of these companies part of the objective-setting process. It is the reliable and accurate measurement of the achievement of these objectives which is difficult.

Short-term training

For all the companies, training focused on short-term business needs was seen as a key aspect of their ability to create the flexible and multi-skilled workforce crucial to delivering both short- and longer-term business performance. For a number of them, a key lever was seen to be their ability to maximize the performance of knowledge workers and thus begin to build a learning organization.

For Glaxo Pharmaceuticals UK, Hewlett Packard, and Citibank, on-line and off-line training was seen by employees as making a significant contribution to organizational performance, and the majority believed they had the skills needed to deliver the performance objectives agreed with them. Many also felt the organization encouraged the development of new skills. Interestingly, although these three companies had made significant investments in off-line training (with over 50 per cent of those employees surveyed reporting more than five days training per year), their employees believed that being faced with challenging jobs had played the most significant role in developing their work performance.

Transforming leaders

As we saw in Chapter 4, processes to support the creation of leadership cadres had been a central activity for many of these companies, particularly those requiring international executives capable of operating in a multinational context. Kraft Jacobs Suchard and Citibank both had complex succession processes supported by the early identification of high-potential people, accelerated development of this group, and succession lists and 'backstopping' arrangements. Of the multinationals, only Hewlett Packard had chosen not to systematize a high-potential process. In part this reflects the company's commitment to a meritocracy, where the accelerated development of an elite group would be seen as counter-cultural.

TRENDS ACROSS THE COMPANIES: WEAKLY LINKED PROCESSES

In other areas the link between people processes and business strategy was relatively weak across all of the companies. We focus here on two areas, the creation of a people strategy and the transformation of the workforce.

From a methodological perspective, analysing the processes which support preparation for the future was the greatest challenge for the research team. As we described in Chapter 2, these processes are typically opaque, occurring in small management teams, may not be documented (and if they are the documents are not circulated), and occur on an ad hoc basis. In summary, analysis is complex and circumspect, involving interviews with senior management, document trawls, and questionnaires sent to head office. The piecing together of this rather disparate information began to create a picture of how these companies were preparing for the future and the role people issues played in this preparation. But all is not always as it appears: the existence of a strategic human resource document in one company signified the culmination of a real dialogue about the future and the role of people, while in another company it was a 'dead' document, devoid of meaning. In yet another company there was a lively ongoing debate about the future, but no human resource document.

Creating a people strategy

Here we were looking for examples of processes which supported the creation of a long-term view of the future of the organization and its implications for people. Processes such as scenario planning, models, and simulations have been described as central to the activity of reshaping the view of the organization. None of these companies regularly used these processes, and usage tended to be rather experimental and related to the issues of a single business, or the activities of a particular long-term oriented manager. Most companies were operating with a relatively weak strategic linkage. Cross-functional groups met occasionally to discuss the likely people implications of strategic intent, and these discussions tended to concentrate on current issues. However, they did result in a broad understanding of where the organization should be heading with regard to people.

In each of these companies debates about people followed the development of strategy. As we argued in Chapter 2, in no case did human resource consideration take precedence over business strategy. At Hewlett Packard the alignment was strongest, and as we saw in Chapter 5 the 'HP Way', which informs thinking in the organization, places people as an intrinsic part of the values and culture of the company.

Scanning people trends

This cluster of processes plays a crucial part in preparations for long-term success. They can provide a vehicle to scan the external environment, to identify probable competitive pressures, legal trends, demographic changes, or likely contractual trends. An understanding of these trends can prepare the company for potential skill shortages and help to plan for the impact of work or lifestyle changes. None of these companies engaged in frequent systematic scanning of these trends and as a consequence this information was not used systematically in the development of strategy.

The majority of these companies engaged in ad hoc information gathering about particular areas of concern. For example, the impact of the European directives on Works Councils and the Social Chapter were specific topics of interest. When this information was collected it was likely to remain within the human resource function and therefore had relatively limited impact on the development of wider strategic options.

Workforce development

Whilst high-potential individuals are seen as a key source of longer-term leverage, this view appears not to be held for the general workforce. For many companies, compared to the other processes, the transformation of the workforce was operating at the lowest level of strategic linkage. We would argue that this lack of strategic linkage results from two major factors: profound downsizing and restructuring, which have destroyed the old career paths and the psychological contracts associated with them, and accelerating changes in the technological and competency base of the organization, which require a whole new set of skills. Together these factors had created a real sense of instability for many employees and a lack of understanding of future options for employers.

The first factor, the breakdown of the old career paths and the old notions of the psychological contract, was apparent in all of these companies. In Chapter 4 we discussed the breakdown of the old career paths which had in the past provided on-the-job experience to support (generally in a rather ad hoc way) the longer-term development of experience and knowledge. As these organizations changed, so the paths became obsolete. For some companies, such as Citibank, these new structures had been in place for a sufficient length of time to allow the creation of associated career paths. The creation of task- and project team-based structures and the associated destruction of functional 'silos' was a challenge faced by Glaxo Pharmaceuticals UK. The new structure required an emphasis on ad hoc teams, project teams, and task forces as the predominant structuring mechanisms. This change had destroyed the old career paths and had only begun to create an awareness of what the new paths of experience could be. Under these circumstances it was not surprising that only 18 per cent of the total employees surveyed felt satisfied with their career management.

The move from the old paternalistic psychological contract to a new psychological contract between employer and employee was exemplified by BT Payphones and Lloyds Bank UK Retail Banking. Both are significant UK employers which until relatively recently have operated in a paternalistic, bureaucratic, and hierarchical manner. Historically those joining these companies (generally at the beginning of their career) were assured of a job for life and a relatively clear career structure. This is no longer the case. Since that time these companies have downsized, and refocused their strategy to increase customer focus and product awareness.

The second factor, the profound change in the technological and competency base of the company, also serves to create uncertainty and a lack of focus. For many of these companies the processes required to predict future skill needs were underdeveloped, and therefore there was limited understanding of what work experiences were appropriate to create future-oriented skill sets. Although there were examples of career planning processes (particularly in Hewlett Packard), none had developed systematic portfolios of policies and career planning procedures which would ensure that employees had an opportunity to participate in a series of work experiences which would prepare them for future challenges. Instead those policies and processes in place were primarily serving the current skill and competency needs.

Given this lack of clarity regarding future skill needs and the breaking of the old psychological contract, it was no surprise that the career appraisal processes to collect information about career preferences were viewed with some scepticism. In all companies changes in the organizational structure, delayering, and downsizing had severely reduced employees' opportunities to move vertically, yet processes to encourage or reward horizontal or team-based development were lacking or underdeveloped.

Whilst none of the companies had created horizontal or team-based career paths which had the strength of the old vertical career paths, nevertheless the concept of new career paths was an area of debate and concern. In all of these companies it was understood that future imperatives would require rather different experiences, and in most these implications were under debate in task forces and project teams. So we can see broad directives (for example, to gain multifunctional experience, to develop international awareness, or to gain customer experience), but what is lacking as yet is the translation of these broad directives into clear policies and processes.

The same is true of the psychological contract. All of these companies believed the psychological contract would change, and this was reflected in the career management documents and policy statements which spoke of individual responsibility and the new psychological contract. Just what this meant in practice was less well understood. Attempts had been made to define the new psychological contract with policy statements about 'skill contracts' or employability (a contract to continue to develop the skill base and marketability of employees) and a focus on employee involvement through share schemes and communication. But it was unclear how this employability contract would occur, particularly in a sector such as retail banking where the product knowledge base is highly business-specific and there is no apparent external labour market currently in operation.

DISCUSSION

Embedding people processes and creating strong linkage to business strategy is of enormous importance to any human resource practitioner. In this study we found that some processes seemed more easily embedded than others and that some companies were more skilful at embedding them than other companies. In this discussion we explore why this may be the case.

Differences across the processes

Perhaps the most striking feature of this research is the relatively stronger linkage for short-term people processes and the weaker linkage (with the exception of leadership development) for longer-term oriented processes. We believe this has a number of reasons but is mainly due to the complexity of embedding these processes and the general short-term view of the companies.

Complex interventions

Developing human resource strategies, reshaping the view of the organization, and creating alignment are all processes which are highly complex and on which relatively little has been written. For instance, we looked for examples of processes which supported the creation of a long-term people-oriented vision—using perhaps the scenario planning, models, or simulations described by various commentators (Gratton 1994; Ulrich and Lake 1990; Walker 1980). None of these companies regularly and systematically used any of these processes, and where they had been used it was experimental or related to specific issues, or supported by a particular long-term oriented manager. Cross-functional groups met occasionally to talk about the people implications of strategy but generally the focus was short-term and tactical. We found limited embedding of these processes in a systematic and disciplined manner.

Short-termism

We found that generally the support of the line manager was critical to the successful embedding of people processes and to their quality. Where managers were supportive they were generally appraised on their people management skills and trained to support and deliver the process. But, as we have argued in Chapter 7, a strong counter to the embedding of processes, particularly the long-term processes, was the prevailing short-term drive. In many of these companies the key performance drivers were the maintenance and increase of share price through cost-cutting, emphasizing short-term income. This external pressure has two distinct effects on managers' capacities to deliver these processes. First, managers generally understand both formally, through performance objectives, and informally, through the demands of their bosses, that the main priority is the 'hard stuff', the 'numbers'. The softer people process issues are seen as less significant. Second, managers have (as a result) little incentive to invest in processes, such as reshaping or transforming individuals, which do not have a short-term pay-off.

Differences across the companies

There are clearly differences in the strength of linkage across the processes, with some generally more strongly linked than others. However, the differences in strength of linkage across the companies are equally interesting. Although we have not discussed context as a key aspect in this chapter, the question is central to the longitudinal study taking place during 1996 and 1997.

However, we have developed a number of hypotheses about some of the key factors which influence the organization's ability to create and embed people processes. Before talking of the differences between the companies, the most obvious similarity, which we discussed in the introductory chapter, is the significant downsizing and flattening of structures which all of the companies in this sample had experienced. However, whilst there are commonalities which have had a profound impact (particularly on the long-term development of the workforce), there are striking differences between companies in their ability to create strong linkages. The following are some of our current working hypotheses.

Multinational companies

Generally these had more strongly linked people processes than nationally based companies. Hewlett Packard, Citibank, Glaxo Pharmaceuticals UK, and Kraft Jacobs Suchard all had stronger people processes than BT Payphones, Lloyds Bank UK Retail Banking, and W. H. Smith News. As these companies had moved outside the national boundaries, so the people processes appear to have been more strongly embedded and linked to the strategy, better monitored, and less ad hoc (Adler and Ghoder 1990).

Scale of transformation

The strategic linkage of the processes was generally weakest where the company had recently experienced major catastrophic transformation or change. This was discussed earlier with particular reference to the long-term development of the workforce. But the impact of a major downsizing or refocusing of strategic direction sends shock waves which impact on the basic premiss of all people processes. This was perhaps most marked at BT Payphones and Lloyds Bank UK Retail Banking, where a refocus towards customer orientation had necessitated a fundamental shift in what was appraised, rewarded, and developed. As we described in Chapter 8, in both companies the company rhetoric was still way ahead of the reality and people felt uncomfortable and disoriented as they saw the processes around them changing. Of course change is also part of the corporate agenda for Hewlett Packard and Kraft Jacobs Suchard, but this had been absorbed in an incremental way without the 'catastrophe' and 'unfreezing' experienced in other companies.

Administrative heritage

Our final hypothesis concerns the administrative heritage and discipline within the companies. In those companies where the processes had been in place for many years, and were rolled out in a disciplined and often centralized manner, they were better embedded and supported. For example, the ten-step plan at Hewlett Packard and the MAP process at Kraft Jacobs Suchard had both been in place for more than five years and were not subject to frequent changes in policy. Support and consistency were less apparent where the processes had been recently introduced and where powerful regional managers had blocked their introduction. At W. H. Smith News performance management had been recently introduced and was not seen as part of a wider process of change. At BT Payphones, whilst much effort had been focused on cascading business objectives, a rapid series of initiatives had left employees uncertain and the processes weakly embedded.

This leads us to the complex question of whether strongly linked people processes make for strong corporate business performance. Rather than answering this question directly we would like to make two comments, one about methodology and one about success.

First, with regard to methodology, we have found that it is not unusual for there to be a significant gap between rhetoric and reality, a topic we explore in more detail in the following chapter. For example, one personnel director believed that people understood the basis on which they were appraised, but the reality was that 70 per cent of those employees we surveyed in that company said they did not understand the basis on which they were appraised. The triangulated, multifaceted methodology we used allowed us to differentiate between rhetoric and reality and to comment on the reality. We believe that the gap we observed suggests that this type of triangulated, case-based comparative research is crucial to a real understanding of organizational experiences and can provide a depth and breadth of understanding lacking in studies based exclusively on the comments and conclusions of personnel directors or human resource managers.

Second, with regard to the nature of success, all the companies we considered were at that time within the top five business performers in their sectors. Some had more strongly linked processes than others. For example, BT Payphones and Lloyds Bank UK Retail Banking had recently moved from relatively stable environments to highly turbulent environments. Partly as a consequence the people processes, which had historically been strongly linked to the 'old' strategy, were poorly linked to the 'new' strategy. Without understanding the heritage of BT Payphones and Lloyds Bank UK Retail Banking, and without monitoring these companies over a considerable period of time, it is impossible fully to understand the relationship between their commercial success and their people processes. It is our firm belief that in-depth longitudinal studies will be critical to understanding the relationship between people management practices and profitability. As we write we are embarking on the third iteration of the case study method which will take us to 1999. We believe that this will give us greater insight into the long-term effects of some of the short-term, profit-oriented behaviours we observed in the mid-1990s.

10

The Emerging Themes

In the opening chapter of this book we described what we saw as some of the critical issues for the study of human resource strategy in contemporary organizations. We asked four key questions: what internal and external variables impact on the ability of organizations to devise and deliver a strategic approach to managing people? What is the relationship (if any) between what is intended and what is realized? In what way do human resource interventions impact on the individual? And how does human resource strategy influence everyday managerial behaviour? In the main body of this book we have examined these questions in depth, by considering the role of line management and the human resource function, by providing precise observations about the link between strategy and people processes, and by looking again at the form and reality of the psychological contract. We were also able to comment on the enormous impact of change on the HR agenda.

The aim of this concluding chapter is to give an overview of our study and to consider those themes which we, as a research team, believe to be enormously important. These are not necessarily responses to our initial questions (although some are), rather, they are our lasting impressions, the moments of illumination and clarity. We have chosen to highlight three broad emerging themes. In the first theme we summarize what we have learnt about the nature of human resource strategy in large complex organizations. In doing so we explicitly address the four questions outlined in the Introduction and summarize our findings concerning these four questions. In the second theme we integrate a thread which has run throughout this study—the nature of commitment and trust—and draw together all we have learnt about this crucial outcome. Finally, in the third theme we return to an earlier question about intention and realization and describe the meaning of organizational rhetoric and individual reality. In doing so we bring the focus from the organization to each and every employee.

THEME 1: WHAT HAVE WE LEARNT ABOUT THE NATURE OF HUMAN RESOURCE STRATEGY IN LARGE COMPLEX ORGNAIZATIONS?

In this brief summary we aim to capture our findings about the questions presented at the beginning of this research. Our key learning points about the nature of human resource strategy in large, complex companies are shown below.

The organizational context:

- the profound impact of downsizing.

Linking intended business strategy, intended human resource strategy, and realized human resource interventions:

- the need for a temporal dimension;
- little evidence of a sophisticated HRS process;
- the gap between rhetoric and reality.

The impact of human resource interventions on individual outcomes:

- profound changes in the nature of the employment contract.

How does human resource strategy influence everyday managerial behaviour?

- curtailing the 'architect' role;
- the intention and reality of line management involvement.

The organizational context: the profound impact of downsizing

Throughout this study we have been struck by the profound impact an organization's context and administrative heritage has on its ability to create and deliver a strategic approach to human resource management. The downsizing, restructuring, and cost drivers described in the context section of Chapter 1 have profoundly influenced the way in which people are managed, and consequently the employment relationship in all these organizations is undergoing some form of transition or transformation. In working within a context of downsizing it became clear to us that for every organization we studied, the starting point in the cycle of human resource intervention was crucial. For example, companies such as Hewlett Packard, with a longer history of involving managers in such practices as performance management and career discussions, enjoyed increased managerial buy-in to the importance of these systems, and increased understanding of how they operated. So, at times of downsizing or change they were able to use this managerial understanding to move forward. As we saw in Chapters 7 and 9, those companies operating with the strongest level of integration between business strategy and people processes inevitably did so from a foundation of management commitment and as a way of creating and maintaining continuity and consistency. For example, the performance management processes of both Hewlett Packard and Kraft Jacobs Suchard may have been honed over the years, but at the core they had remained essentially the same.

All the companies we studied operate within their own individual context; they have an intensely idiosyncratic administrative heritage, culture, structure, and competitive environment. It became clear that aspects of this context constrain, at least in the short term, the policies and practices which can be enacted. Our research has shown us the importance of taking into account this contextual diversity when one attempts to understand and interpret the actions and reactions that take place within these companies. But whilst this context is crucial, we observed that these companies are not simply hostages to fortune, blown by the winds of change. All experienced a common external change during the period we observed, then all downsized. Yet the nature of their response was unique to them.

Linking intended business strategy, intended human resource strategy, and realized human resource interventions

The need for a temporal dimension

It became apparent to us that the ways in which we model the concept of intended human resource strategy fail to describe fully the enormous change and flux we saw in these companies. As we explain briefly in Chapter 1, the literature has generally assumed two principal attributes of strategic HRM: a vertical linkage, where there is a clear and deliberate link between the overall strategic objectives of the organization and the strategic objectives established for the management of people, and a horizontal linkage, where the different elements of the people management process (such as the way people are appraised, rewarded, trained, and developed) are mutually reinforcing. One theme running through this book has been the inadequacies of this approach as a way of understanding how these organizations operate in reality. The theoretical inadequacies of the dual typology have already been well rehearsed elsewhere (see Chapter 2 and, for example, Legge 1995b).

From our research, we are able to add a third, temporal dimension, as highlighted in the people process model (Chapter 9), where the lengthened time scales for human capital development are taken into consideration. The dual typology provides no means of understanding how this third dimension can be applied.

Little evidence of a sophisticated HRS process

We described in Chapters 2 and 9 the difficulty we had in really understanding the human resource strategy process in many of these companies. Human

Resource Strategy plans existed in some of the companies but saw limited use, whilst other companies appeared to create some aspects of a strategic approach to managing people without recourse to a separate HRS document. We found that the reality of people management within these companies lags considerably behind the rhetoric expressed within the literature. We found very little evidence in our sample of companies of what might be regarded as sophisticated strategic human resource management practice, and in fact, whilst some of the HR directors in our sample might express their understanding of the need to 'match' the management of people with the overall strategic direction of the organization, in practice they had to operate within the constraints of the administrative heritage of their organizations, and the boundaries to their freedom to develop and implement HR policies imposed by organizational structure and culture. This was reflected in the responses to the employee survey: only 14 per cent of the people who responded felt their HR department had a clear strategy guiding their activities, compared with 61 per cent who thought their organization had a clear corporate strategy.

As regards the issue of horizontal integration or linkage, the problematic nature of this ideal was evident from our study. We found the companies we studied pursued multiple strategies, and had to cater for diverse employee groups which could require totally different forms of management. This was illustrated particularly well in the case of the Chelsea & Westminster Healthcare Trust, which has to cater for a large variety of professional employee groups, each with their own professional representative bodies and requirements, and a partly unionized workforce. Taking the example of the performance management process, the practical difficulties of integration were well illustrated by the companies we studied.

The gap between rhetoric and reality

One principal strand that has run through this entire book is the disjunction between rhetoric and reality in the area of human resource management, between HRM theory and HRM practice, between what the HR function says it is doing and how that practice is perceived by the employees, and between what senior management believe to be the role of the HR function, and the role it actually plays. As we have seen, there are multiple realities in human resource management within all of the organizations we have studied, a complexity which is further exacerbated by contextual factors. For example, as we described in Chapter 4, we observed an overall and gradual shift towards a more transaction-based contract and away from traditional forms of vertical careers within a single organization. Yet, whilst the rhetoric of the companies generally included such concepts as 'employability' and 'lateral careers', we found that the reality experienced by most employees was one of insecurity and anxiety in the face of what were, in effect, diminishing opportunities.

This rhetoric and reality gap was of such an important nature that we consider it in more detail in our final theme. However, with regard specifically to models of HRS, we found a profound difference between rhetoric and reality in another element of the employment relationship, namely the control strategies adopted by the companies. Within the literature (as Chapter 2 shows), a distinction is frequently drawn between management through control and management through commitment—in other words, managing employees by means of tight control mechanisms, as opposed to through measures aimed at eliciting their commitment to organizational objectives. We found that in terms of rhetoric, many of the organizations we studied embraced the tenets of a commitment-based approach, but this stood in sharp contrast to the reality experienced by employees, whose levels of commitment were often low. In fact, as we saw earlier (in Chapter 3), managerial strategies which were ostensibly aimed at increasing employees' internalization of corporate values through responsibility and empowerment may, in fact, achieve the opposite and increase central control.

The impact of human resource interventions on individual outcomes: profound changes in the nature of the employment contract

The notion of employability implies that an individual is not guaranteed a job for life within one organization, but that the employing organization will invest in the development of their skills to broaden the range of potential jobs open to the individual both within the current employing organization and in potential future ones. So, if organizations are embracing the rhetoric of employability, we would expect to see employees being offered tailored training and development opportunities. However, as we saw in Chapter 4, in practice, although the companies were making significant investments in training, most of the training was not from the developmental-humanist stance of training and development for the sake of the employee, but was very much geared towards training individuals to support their current roles, and to underpin the strategic objectives of the organization. In other words, the focus of much of the training provided was organization-centred rather than employee-centred. Access to training opportunities was also, in many cases, limited by line managers' budgets and decisions about the allocation of resources. So, even if training programmes were provided by the organization, there was no guarantee that all employees had automatic access to them.

A further implication of the notion of employability is that possibilities for mobility both within the organization and in the external labour market exist. However, this was by no means universally true. In most of the organizations we studied, there were severe limitations on the amount of mobility available in practice to employees. In the cases of BT Payphones and Lloyds Bank UK Retail Banking, extensive downsizing programmes had truncated internal labour markets, and, in addition, in the banking industry there was little evidence of external labour markets operating. Within the Chelsea & Westminster Healthcare Trust, internal labour markets within the trust were curtailed by professional demarcations.

However, career management for one cadre of employees, the high-potential international cadre, appears to have escaped the shift from paternalism to individualism, from relational to transactional contracts. These employees, on the contrary, had a clearly defined career track carved out for them within the organization, along which they were guided and nurtured. This differentiation between different groups and categories of employee underscores the importance of looking in detail at the practices adopted by organizations when theorizing about human resource management.

How does human resource strategy influence everyday managerial behaviour?

In examining this question it became clear that the ability of managers to deliver on a strategic approach to managing people is enormously influenced by the context and values of the organization.

Curtailing of the architect role

One dimension of strategic HRM is the increased devolution of responsibility for people management from the HR function to the line, accompanied by an increasing strategic or 'architect' role for the HR function itself, and the board level representation of the HR function by the HR director. In common with other studies, we found that the scope for the HR function to play an 'architect' role was curtailed by its limited representation at corporate level. In fewer than half of the organizations we studied did the HR director play an active role in formulating business strategy, and there was only one instance of what might be termed a 'sophisticated' attempt to link business strategy to human resource strategy in the form of a written document. However, as we saw in Chapter 6, our research has shown that it is possible for an organization to manage its people 'strategically', without the HR function itself playing the role of strategist or architect. We have termed this phenomenon 'integrated HRM'. This occurs when people management is viewed as a powerful source of competitive advantage within the mainstream management of the organization, and the line and senior managers incorporate HR processes into their modes of operation without the need for specialist input from the HR department.

Few of the HR functions in our study could be regarded as operating at a 'strategic' level. In fact, what emerged as being most important from the perspective of the line and senior managers, regardless of any aspirations on the part of the HR staff themselves, was the ability of the HR function to deliver platform services on time and to the required standard. This was viewed as more important than the ability to be 'strategic'. What we found was that human resource functions move through a series of stages in their development, and that their starting point along this cycle is very significant in determining how effective they are at any given time.

The intention and reality of line management involvement

As regards the involvement of line managers in HR activities, our research brought to light some important constraints in terms of the ability and the opportunity line managers had to fulfil such a role. We found that the reality of the devolution of HR responsibilities to the line lags behind the rhetoric of the literature, and that such devolution was patchy and inconsistent. As we demonstrated in Chapter 7, we further found that there is an important difference between the intention to give responsibility to the line, and the reality of how this is implemented in practice.

In particular, we found that line manager involvement in HR activities is severely constrained by a number of factors. The most important of these were the formal reinforcement of HR practices (for example, whether line managers were specifically rewarded for implementing HR); the policies and practices of trade unions and professional associations; managerial short-termism (such as the pressures to produce bottom-line results); and de-layering, which meant that managers generally had less time available for such activities. The principle of 'what gets measured gets done' appeared to be overriding. We also found that individual differences between managers affected the way in which policies were implemented. For instance, in some organizations, some managers were using the appraisal system in a defensive way in order to avoid demotivating their staff. The ability of the individual line manager to understand and implement the systems was also a factor. With regard to the area of career management, not all managers embraced the idea of the management of subordinates' careers as being their responsibility, especially in a climate of generally reduced opportunities.

Again, at the organizational level, the starting point on the cycle was crucial: organizations with a longer history of involving managers in such practices as performance management enjoyed increased managerial buy-in to the importance of the system, and increased understanding of how it operated.

However, one major change seems to be occurring in the companies that we studied. Thurley has described a 'credibility gap' that personnel managers experience at work. He writes that 'personnel specialists are caught in a mismatch between a pretentious abstract model of HRM and the reality of a fragmented set of activities carried out with little recognition of their value by other managers' (Thurley 1981: 26). We found contraindications to this. The management of people is seen as important and significant by senior business managers. The complexity of the process is also increasingly recognized at senior levels. (However, the ability to think about people management in a strategic fashion still appears somewhat limited.) At lower levels within the organization there is a greater recognition by line managers that the management of people is important. They also see the role that an effective HR function can play in giving coherence to these activities. Line managers, rather than HR managers, are increasingly playing the role of 'manufacturers of consent' amongst staff. This reflects the devolution of responsibility to the line. These two developments mean that research into 'HRM' or people management in general needs to focus on the activities, attitudes, and perceptions of line and senior managers as well as the HR function.

THEME 2: TRUST AND COMMITMENT

The Leading Edge research has provided a fascinating glimpse into organizational realities in the mid-1990s. It has told us much about the relationship between employees and employers in this time of change and adaptation, as these companies moved from periods of relative stability to the high-velocity environments which will characterize the following decades. During this research we were struck by the manner in which people spoke about their feelings for their company and by the role their work played in their total life. In this section we summarize these feelings and consider the implications for the future.

In the last decade there has been renewed emphasis on the strategic role human resource management can play in creating and delivering business success. Throughout this research we have focused on how this strategic role is played out in reality. In this second emerging theme we look in particular at the rhetoric and reality of creating and sustaining commitment and trust. As we saw in the arguments rehearsed in Chapter 2, there are immense potential gains from a highly committed and inspired workforce. Individuals who are committed to the aims of the organization, and who trust their managers and the organization, have the potential to be self-regulating rather than needing to be controlled by sanctions and external pressures. In essence, they are more likely to be flexible and adaptable, crucial employee characteristics in times of high-velocity changes. In each of the companies we observed, the rhetoric of employee commitment and trust was clear; many of the managers to whom we spoke talked of the importance of commitment. But what of the reality? In Table 4.5 we presented the key commitment variables. At the time of our study, trust in managers was relatively high in Glaxo Pharmaceuticals UK and Hewlett Packard, but it was relatively low in Lloyds Bank UK Retail Banking and BT Payphones, both of which were approaching, or were in the midst of, profound changes. The commitment data is more complex: morale may be low at BT Payphones and at Lloyds, but people want to remain in the company (they will accept any type of job assignment in order to remain working for the company). This ambivalence was also reflected in the interviews, where we heard employees from these companies expressing deep anxiety about the future, which for some individuals was paralysing their ability to change and adapt.

What can we learn about trust and commitment from the companies in this project? Let us look at those factors which have been postulated to create, or indeed destroy, trust and commitment in individual members of the workforce. It has been argued that the human resource activities of an organization can have a potentially profound impact. Those activities which have a potentially positive impact include the provision of self-development and training opportunities, the ability to create and sustain opportunity systems and career paths, the upward and downward communication structures within the organization, and the manner in which performance is appraised and rewarded. Our research would support the view that these factors are indeed important, but it also points to a broader band of variables, which are discussed in the final part of this section.

Self-development and career opportunities

Investment in self-development and career opportunities is seen as a cornerstone of the high-commitment contract, since it implies people are worthy of training and development. Across the companies we examined the rhetoric was clear and, as we saw in Chapter 2, most had created large-scale training initiatives over the preceding couple of years. Yet when we considered the employees' perceptions and feelings about this training and development, it became clear that the impact of these initiatives had not yet been felt. As the survey data in Chapter 2 show, many of the people we surveyed believed they did not receive the training they needed to do their job well.

With an emphasis on self-development comes the notion of career development and the nature of the psychological contract. As we saw in Chapter 4, there have been fundamental changes in the nature of the contract in all the companies we studied, with a shift in career management from the organization to the individual. The 'job for life' was certainly no longer a reality, if it ever had been. This shift from the organization to the individual taking responsibility has the potential to emphasize individual empowerment. However, as we saw in Chapter 4, it was more likely to be associated with limited career opportunity structures. The options for individuals had been severely curtailed by organizational restructuring. In the in-depth interviews the individuals in the downsizing companies talked about the anxiety they felt about the future. For those at Hewlett Packard, change had been a fact of life and the 'HP Way' brought a measure of continuity and consistency underpinning the structural changes they saw. However, for employees at BT Payphones and Lloyds Bank UK Retail Banking the shifts in the organizational fabric had been of earthquake-sized proportions and few structures had been built and embedded which had replaced the old certainties. Here anxiety was high and commitment relatively low.

It became clear to us that whilst managers may rate performance management process as a key point of leverage, for the individual employees it is the developmental processes and opportunity structures which are most critical. There was profound disquiet amongst many of the employees we spoke to about the nature of the psychological contract between themselves and the organization. As we saw in Chapter 2, whilst the rhetoric may centre on employability, the reality is limited opportunity and the creation of a contract which is moving increasingly towards instrumentalism. If companies are truly to move to a contract of employability, then any hope of retaining commitment rests on their ability to deliver the opportunity structures and managerial involvement which support this new contract. Without these structures and involvement the gap between rhetoric and reality becomes intolerable to individual employees.

Beliefs about self-development and career planning may be held by a highly committed group of people, but they run counter to the short-term focus which was prevalent in many of the companies we studied. In Chapter 7 we described some of the dynamics of the managerial short-termism which drove all the companies we observed to varying degrees. The 'Unwritten Rules' interview data revealed clearly this emphasis on short-term financial targets and the 'hard' measures of organizational success. Yet whilst these companies may remain resolutely short-term focused, we know that commitment and trust develop in a workforce which has some belief about the future, and which is prepared to build this trust over a long period of time. Therefore we are faced with something of a dilemma, the short-termism of companies on the one hand and the need to consider longer-term issues such as commitment on the other. In Chapter 8 we described how this longer-term view was vital.

Involving and communicating

We also looked at the involvement people felt with the organization. Whilst over half the employees we surveyed understood what management was trying to achieve, far fewer felt that their voice was heard—upward feedback was barely in place in these organizations. As we saw in the review of performance management (Chapter 3), there were real differences in the control that individuals had over setting their work targets, with BT Payphones and Lloyds Bank UK Retail Banking employees least likely to be solely responsible for or co-determinants of work targets. The involvement of people in the aims of management and the company is predicated in part by involvement of line managers. Yet many of the managers we surveyed and talked to were under severe pressure to deliver in the short term and had little time for people, were operating from a low personal skill and competency base, or were operating in cultures where the management of people was not perceived to be central to the success of the endeavour. As Chapters 7 and 9 show, many line managers play very limited roles in developmental discussions with their teams, and few provide rich and accurate feedback in the performance process. And in some companies, such as BT Payphones, whilst managers were complying with the need to have frequent performance appraisals, they were simply 'going through the motions'. As the interview data revealed, their involvement with performance feedback rested more on organizational compliance than it did on commitment to individuals. So if a company is to place commitment at the heart of its people strategy then there must be a fundamental change to support, reinforce, and value these activities—with reward mechanisms which incorporate people management into the objectives and reward of managers, through the provision of training to create higher skill levels within the company, and by balancing organizational demands for delivery of the 'hard' financial results with the delivery of the 'soft' people aspects.

Trust and commitment are particularly difficult to maintain during times of high-velocity change. At both Lloyds Bank UK Retail Banking and BT Payphones we saw nostalgia about the past and anxiety about the future. As we argued in Chapter 8, we believe that trust in management can be maintained at a higher level if employees can make sense of what is happening to the organization. In the case of Glaxo Pharmaceuticals UK and Hewlett Packard it was evident that the changes, though far reaching, were viewed as incremental and constituted the normal operating procedure of the firm. Both companies were described by their employees as operating in dynamic markets and had implemented a series of changes over recent years which had given the organization competency in handling the change process. As we described in Chapter 8, these changes were well signalled to employees through elaborate communication procedures. So whilst we observed some confusion about the new behaviours required, there was a clear understanding of where the changes would position the company and what the new roles and responsibilities would be like. It is clear that some understanding of why the organization is currently behaving as it is, and how it may behave in the future, is crucial to creating commitment.

Monitoring and tracking employees' trust and commitment

In the organizations we studied the monitoring of employee commitment and trust levels was beginning to be seen as an important organizational process. Many had begun to participate in employee care surveys which were providing insight. However, as we saw in the people process model (Chapter 9), those processes which are concerned with diagnosing current capability, including trust and commitment, are relatively underdeveloped. Without an understanding of the 'state of the system' it becomes impossible to gauge current trust and commitment and the impact of various interventions on these feelings and emotions. If companies are to place commitment at the centre of their organizational strategy then much more must be done to diagnose these emotions in the individual members of the workforce, and to monitor those experiences which appear to enhance commitment and those which destroy it. The experiences of Glaxo Pharmaceuticals UK, reported in Chapter 5, demonstrate the power of this diagnosis, where the employee attitude survey carried out in the early 1990s created an enhanced understanding of the challenges faced by the company and the resources needed to tackle these challenges. However, with the exception of Hewlett Packard, we saw little active use of this type of employee data, which we believe can play a profound role.

Creating just and fair HR practices and procedures

Our in-depth interview data revealed what the employee survey had only hinted at: the deep impression which unfair and unjust human resource practices have on individuals. We found evidence of organizational commitment and trust destroyed in work teams which had been on the receiving end of practices which they perceived to be unjust. These instances of procedural injustice were particularly prevalent in the appraisal and career development procedures. As a consequence of unfairness and injustice the processes failed to have credibility or legitimacy. For example, our in-depth interviews revealed that the variations in appraisal rating procedures, gradings, and target allocation (reported in Chapter 7) created deep feelings of distrust and anger which appeared to have severely damaged the individuals' feelings about the company. However, these feelings of procedural injustice are not limited to the employees: as we described in Chapter 7, managers find it deeply frustrating when no action is taken after they have submitted appraisals. Clearly procedural justice has a crucial role to play in creating a committed workforce, and it is a topic which we have placed centre stage in our continuing longitudinal research.

Conclusions

What insights do these findings bring into the state of trust and commitment in the UK workforce in the mid-1990s? First, they highlight the achievements of Hewlett Packard, which has created the most committed and flexible workforce in our sample of companies. As we describe in Chapter 5, the antecedents of this commitment lie deep within the heritage and culture of this company, the views of the founding partners, and the ownership of people management by each and every line manager, whereby people are seen as a fundamental component of business strategy. We can admire Hewlett Packard, but what it has created rests so deep within the organization that it is almost impossible for other companies to replicate or imitate. It could be argued that the culture of high commitment and trust at Hewlett Packard is one of the company's core competencies, nurtured and developed over many years.

Secondly, these findings brings into sharp relief the context of these companies in the mid-1990s. We observed a group of companies responding to fundamental shifts in the basis of competition. Forces such as deregulation, rapid technological innovation, increased competition, and greater access to information had increased the turbulence of business conditions and commodified the products and services which used to be the foundations of their competitive edge. As we described in Chapter 8, the responses to this change involved both reorienting the strategic context of the companies, with a renewed focus on customer service, and reorienting the structural context, with significant downsizing and decentralization. All the companies we studied had undergone a significant programme of restructuring. This was the result of strategic decisions to privatize, delayer, introduce matrix- and team-based management, or to acquire and merge with other organizations. These changes had led to job losses which ranged from 15 to 50 per cent of the workforce. For example, as we saw in Chapter 2, Lloyds Bank UK Retail Banking was suffering from intensified competition in the wake of changes in the financial services industry and had developed a major programme of restructuring with the centralization of many activities. This was changing the fundamental way in which work was achieved in the company, resulting in a move away from a centralized, paternalistic model where people were promised jobs for life, towards an emphasis on performance management and self-managed careers.

It is our view that it is enormously difficult for companies to maintain high levels of employee commitment and trust during these times of turbulence. The rhetoric behind these downsizing activities may be about decentralizing the organization and giving power to lower-level employees to respond more rapidly to customer needs, but we saw that the reality of downsizing and restructuring can have a profoundly negative impact on the individual's commitment to the company. As we saw in Chapter 8, this was particularly difficult for those companies such as BT Payphones and Lloyds Bank UK Retail Banking which had been operating in markets largely isolated from strong competition and which had developed internal cultures dominated by paternalism, rigid hierarchies, and a strong centralist command and control style. In the past these companies had provided stable employment and a vertical career ladder encouraging a strong relational psychological contract. However, the strength of their organizational identities was such that, when change was needed, the leap to a new form of organization was very hard for employees to make. As we saw in Chapter 8, disbelief at the changes and nostalgia for the old ways of working had a profound impact on people's trust in management.

In Chapter 7 we saw how downsizing had been a contributing factor in creating managerial short-termism and therefore reducing the time spent by line managers in actively managing people. In our review of career management practices (Chapter 4) we argued that downsizing and structural changes had destroyed well-established developmental opportunity structures and, by putting little in their place, had created many opportunities for procedural injustice.

As we postulated in Chapter 7, our findings raise important questions about the possibilities for high-commitment models of employment in the context of industrial adjustment through downsizing and re-engineering. Companies operating in the high-velocity environments described in Chapter 3 face a particular challenge to manage trust and commitment as the organization transforms. The Leading Edge study places in sharp relief some of the fundamental philosophical paradoxes faced by the companies we studied. These paradoxes are particularly apparent in attitudes to creating and maintaining a high-commitment workforce.

The first paradox concerns the role of the manager in creating a highly committed workforce and the organizational structures needed to reinforce such activities. As we argue in Chapter 7, this scenario of reward and measurement runs contrary to the spirit of 'developmental humanism' which underlies many of our notions of the empowering manager, unleashing the hitherto untapped potential of his or her staff. Rather than managers being empowering, they risk being caught up in an increasingly bureaucratic web of human resource policies and procedures in which they not only implement policies but also have their own implementation of those policies monitored, evaluated, and rewarded. The challenge is to create a 'light hand' capable of supporting these activities without embroiling managers in a web of bureaucracy.

The second paradox concerns the notion of developmental humanism placed against the tide of downsizing and the organizational short-termism which we observed. Perhaps, as we postulated in Chapter 7, the notion of developmental humanism which underlies our understanding of human resource management naïvely underestimates the extent to which short-term pragmatism is embedded within the enterprise. In such circumstances, managers find it difficult to follow blindly the apparently logical assumption that a committed workforce can contribute to mutual gains for both the employer and the employee.

As we argue in Chapter 2, an emphasis on financial return and short-term performance was inevitable in the economic climate of the mid-1990s. However, as these firms move to a post-recessional period and seek to grow their markets, rather than downsizing themselves, then the interests of individual employees must receive more attention. Our study has shown the tensions and contradictions between a rhetoric of high commitment and developmental humanism and a reality experienced by employees of tight strategic direction towards organizational goals. As we argue in Chapter 7, if these companies wish to promote the notion of high commitment then they need to address some of the wider problems in contemporary business such as management training, managerial short-termism, and the tendency to treat employees as *resources* rather than as *people*. Through this study we have begun to create a deeper understanding of commitment in these companies and a clearer view of the challenges they face in nurturing and building this commitment.

Our own insights into enhancing commitment would suggest that the heritage is critical, as the Hewlett Packard case described in Chapter 5 has so clearly demonstrated. But this insight is of limited use to companies such as BT Payphones and Lloyds Bank UK Retail Banking who are in the midst of profound change. Given their situation, our study would point to a number of key factors which could play a role in enhancing commitment: a closer monitoring and tracking of the attitudes and commitment of individual employees; a longer-term focus; an individual and career development process which goes beyond the mere rhetoric of employability; line managers who have interpersonal and teams skills and who are supportive of their team; and finally, embedded human resource practices and processes which are seen to be just and fair.

THEME 3: MAKING SENSE OF ORGANIZATIONAL INITIATIVES—THE GAP BETWEEN ESPOUSED THEORY AND THEORY-IN-USE

For organizations to succeed, it is the management of their human capital, rather than their physical capital, which is seen to be the essential ingredient. Much depends therefore on the ability of organizations to convey their intentions to employees and to ensure that employees absorb and are motivated by these aims. However, this research has shown that the alignment between what the organization espouses in terms of its aims, policies, and processes, and their interpretation by employees is far from easy. Consider some examples from the previous chapters. In career management (Chapter 4), career progression based on regular vertical moves in a highly defined internal labour market has been replaced in a number of cases by a promise of employability—the promise that while the firm cannot guarantee opportunities for career advancement within the firm, they can offer to provide skills to make the employee highly valued on the external labour market. This notion was viewed by some employees as a rationalization of an essentially one-sided employment contract, with employees taking the burden which was once the organization's responsibility. That is, what was intended as a new take on the career process was interpreted by some managers as a cop-out by the organization. In performance management (Chapter 3), the introduction of new value statements in BT Payphones concerning the importance of teamwork in performance was undermined by the reality of a pay process which rewarded employees on an individual basis. In other words, there was no supporting process to embed the new initiative, and so it encountered problems in terms of employee buy-in. Similarly, in Chapter 7, the rhetoric surrounding the role of line managers in human resource practices, typically urging their greater involvement, came up against a series of barriers including the pressures of delivering short-term business results, a lack of incentives, and an overall lack of training in HR activities.

These examples illustrate the gap between what the organization intends and how this is interpreted by employees or, more theoretically, the distinction between theory espoused and theory-in-use (Argyris and Schon 1978). In spite of the importance of this issue for the concept of organization/employee alignment, the determinants of such a gap have received little attention. What has been written has usually diagnosed the issue either as a failure of communications or as poor operationalization of the content of the initiative, or else has identified characteristics of the situation which have hampered the flow from the source of the initiative to its recipient (Szulanski 1995). Although these approaches have identified the content and the context of the initiative as affecting how it is received by employees, what is missing in such accounts is the importance of managerial *cognition* in the process of interpreting organizational intentions.

Analysing interpretations

The programmes, initiatives, innovations, and values which are set in motion by senior management when implementing change are interpreted and accorded meaning by employees. Understanding managerial cognition is therefore crucial in the examination of change processes in general and the alignment of organizational initiatives and employee actions in particular.

In this section, we focus on the response of middle managers to change events instigated by senior management. Our underlying assumption is that within organizations, there are multiple and possibly conflicting interpretations as to the content of organizational change events and that no one group's interpretation represents an objective reality (Bartunek 1984). In effect there are a number of 'realities'. A key question, however, is whose reality is going to be attended to? There are two reasons why senior management's view carries a high level of legitimacy: first, senior management usually determines the corporate purpose and is in the best position to determine how the corporate purpose is to be interpreted, and secondly, the position and authority of the senior management team makes it the most important source of cues about the organization's purpose and direction.

Our methodology allowed us to gather in-depth data not only on senior management initiatives (both through interviews and through extensive secondary data collection) but also on how initiatives were received by managers, in particular using the Unwritten Rules of the Game approach. As we described in Chapter 1, the ethnographic method of the 'Unwritten Rules' allowed us to probe the perceptions of employees and gather data on how they were interpreting organizational initiatives.

We analysed the gap between the espoused and enacted realities in organizations by examining the effects of content, context, and cognition on how organizational changes are defined. We have identified multiple sources of the gap and here we argue that under certain circumstances, the lack of alignment may give rise to a number of negative consequences—the failure of strategy implementation, resistance to change initiatives, the creation of an 'us and them' culture, and the phenomenon of 'mixed messages' which can disrupt the employment relationship through the setting up of inconsistent expectations between employer and employee. However, we have also identified positive effects from a lack of alignment, namely the encouragement of stretch goals which can facilitate change and the provision of space for the pursuance of entrepreneurial activity.

Briefly summarized, the research data revealed that there are a number of factors which enable or constrain the reception of organizational initiatives. These can be broadly divided into three groups. The first are content factors: whether the initiative is salient to its intended target, or is ambiguous, or is perceived as a threat or opportunity, and the degree to which it conforms to existing organizational norms or organizational identity. The second group concerns organizational contextual effects, such as size, the degree of bureaucracy, the presence of supporting processes, the level of political activity, the legitimacy of senior management, and the nature of the firm's rules of the game. The third group are cognitive factors, including sense-making, selective perception, organizational experience, and absorptive capacity. Fig. 10.1

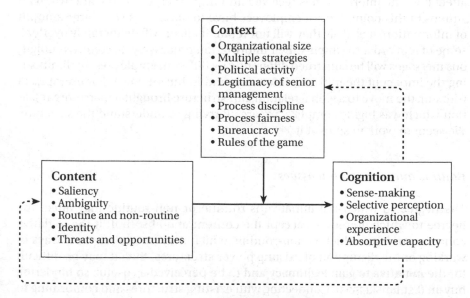

Fig. 10.1. An emergent model of initiative transfer within organizations

presents these variables in a schematic diagram of the theoretical framework. The dotted lines represent feedback loops; we believe that though most initiatives are top-down in character, change occurs through the interaction of content, context, and cognition. In other words, managerial interpretations of change initiatives help shape the elements of those initiatives and alter the context for future initiatives.

Factors concerning content

Saliency

The degree to which an organizational initiative is tailored to meet the interests of employees will influence its absorption. Large, complex organizations have a high level of internal differentiation in terms of structure, culture, goals, and values. This diversity within complex organizations can mean that employees view initiatives from the point of view of their own department rather than of the business as a whole. If the initiative is not seen as appropriate to this level of meaning, then it may be ignored or changed.

Ambiguity

The extent to which the organizational initiative is complex and ambiguous will affect how the information is received and implemented. There are two main strands to this point. First, if employees have to make sense of a large amount of information, it is likely they will not retain it all, or will deliberately overlook some of it in order to simplify their information processing. Secondly, ambiguous messages will be construed differently by different employees, so diminishing the impact of the initiative (Morrison and Robinson 1997). For example, at Citibank the move to a global relationship structure brought a matrix organization which was highly complex: 'we are all trying to understand the structure. We seem to work in spite of it.'

Routine and non-routine issues

The degree to which the initiative is routine or non-routine may affect the degree to which employees accept the content and absorb it. If the initiative concerns an issue which is non-routine, which may necessitate new ways of working or the disruption of existing power structures, then it may be difficult for the initiative to gain legitimacy and to be perceived as useful, so hindering buy-in (Szulanski 1995). Connecting with existing structures and conforming to existing organizational norms may reduce cognitive dissonance and avoid violating interpretations of organizational identity.

Identity issues

The role of identity schemata has also been invoked to examine why change efforts do not succeed. Organizational identity includes those features of an organization which its employees regard as central, distinctive, and enduring. Resistance to organizational initiatives may occur because beliefs about the organization's identity constrain understanding and create cognitive opposition to radical moves. The downsizing at Lloyds Bank and the restructuring of the branch network seemed to some to tear up the former identity of the organization, previously thought of as a highly secure employer. Though the passage of time has ensured that downsizing is now seen as a useful and even necessary initiative (by default, we asked only survivors of the workforce reduction), the method of the downsizing process is still questioned.

Threats and opportunities

Another factor which affects the impact of organizational initiatives is that some major change initiatives are viewed as threats. When an initiative is perceived to have potentially negative or harmful effects on the interests of a group or individual, this leads to a set of responses which tends to become less varied (Staw *et al.* 1981). As Griffin *et al.* argue, 'groups tend to respond to threatening situations rigidly by becoming less open to change, less accepting of new ideas and more uniform in their behaviours, attitudes and beliefs' (1995: 1710). This phenomenon was clearly seen in companies which had undergone major restructuring, particularly downsizing, where concern for the survival of employee groups was paramount. However, some initiatives were seen as opportunities, notably the new emphasis placed on innovation at Kraft Jacobs Suchard and the introduction of new technology to speed up patient referrals at the Chelsea & Westminster Healthcare Trust. This framing, too, will affect the impact of organizational initiatives, facilitating buy-in.

Factors concerning context

Organizational size

Organizational context can have a powerful influence on employee cognitions, particularly where the absorption of initiatives is concerned. Large organizations have complex structures, differentiated units, and a high degree of internal diversity. Large organizations tend to create strong inertial forces which limit the degree to which new information or initiatives may be accepted. Size is usually accompanied by difficulties in communication; as the size of an organization increases, the number of potential communication networks increases exponentially. With an increase in communication linkages, communication between levels becomes more difficult. Large organizations will also tend to have greater differentiation in terms of organizational structure and hierarchy. Organizational initiatives will, in this type of environment, pass through various levels of the corporate hierarchy and across the variegated structure. Differences in interpretation and implementation from managers at different levels will affect how the initiative is actually manifested to employees. Both problems were acute at BT before the creation of the Payphones business: one manager said, 'the sheer scale of trying to achieve change in an organization this size is bewildering. It's like turning a supertanker. You have to take everyone with you but you can't hope to reach everyone.' The setting up of the Payphones business helped to alleviate some of these problems. Its smaller size, flattened structure, and clear branding to bring greater identity to the business were factors in getting organizational initiatives across.

Multiple strategies and values

Within organizations, there may be competing legitimate strategies and goals and values, and managers may be forced to make choices between them. Certainly the case companies had diverse and competing aims and wide product market variations. Such diversity has led the companies to follow multiple strategies and to establish a number of values. The 'Unwritten Rules of the Game' data revealed this fact clearly. For example, in the case of Kraft Jacobs Suchard, the demands of delivering short-term financial goals were combined with the goal of managerial innovation, while at W. H. Smith News, emphasis on satisfying customers was made in a context of organizational demands for severe cost constraints. Managers are faced with the choice of following alternative organizational goals and so the lack of absorption of an initiative may reflect not resistance to its aim, but the pursuance of other legitimate organizational initiatives (Brower and Abolafia 1995; Fenton-O'Creevy 1996).

Political activity

Organizations represent environments where individuals and coalitions seek to impose their views on organizational issues and to effect control over decision-making. As a result, a high degree of political activity may distort the impact of organizational initiatives as various groups attempt to protect their own interests. At Lloyds Bank UK Retail Banking, branch managers sought to protect their staff by filtering out information on change initiatives in order to preserve morale and motivation. At W. H. Smith News the warehouse managers, who held considerable power in the organization, resisted changes in working practices and demands from the Group to encourage employee involvement because of the threat to their traditional power base.

The legitimacy of senior management

When the source of organizational initiatives was expert and trustworthy, it was likely that the message would be accepted by managers. The legitimacy, therefore, of senior management affected the degree to which initiatives were received and accepted. At Glaxo Pharmaceuticals UK, the internal merger of Allen and Hanbury's and Glaxo Laboratories necessitated a change in the senior management team. One manager said, 'when the new top team came in, they were seen as experimenting. Why did we need to change? Some people took a lot of convincing.' The change process at Lloyds Bank UK Retail Banking was not helped by the branch managers' perceptions of senior management as remote, even dubbing the headquarters 'planet Bristol' because of its perceived other-worldliness. The personal commitment of senior managers to the initiatives they proposed was also highly important to lower-level managers.

Process discipline

The likely success of organizational initiatives being implemented in their intended fashion will be influenced by the nature of the processes and practices within the organization which will serve to embed the initiative. Part of this will involve the nature of the communication channels themselves, their efficiency and effectiveness. There have to be systems in place to ensure that the plans and policies of the organization are being implemented and to show where there may be problems which could lead to their revision and improvement. Clear standards for the new plans, consistent incentives and sanctions to reinforce the initiative, and formal opportunities to provide feedback characterize a good discipline environment (Ghoshal and Bartlett 1994). Lack of motivation on the part of the recipients of the organizational initiatives is an important part of resistance to change. Incentives are key to this process, as too are training and development support. There may be a need, therefore, to address multiple organizational systems in order to effect the embedding of change initiatives (Nadler and Tushman 1989). At Kraft Jacobs Suchard, for instance, the new organizational focus on innovation was not aligned with the reward system, which continued to measure short-term, process-driven goals. Such a situation may undermine middle managers' faith in the commitment of senior management to the initiative (Fenton-O'Creevy 1996).

Process fairness

The procedural justice of the decision-making process can affect the relationship between senior management and lower-level employees and so influence their receptiveness to organizational initiatives. Process fairness (or procedural justice) has been shown to affect outcome satisfaction, commitment, trust, and social harmony. It can be argued that greater attention to procedural justice would be reflected in employees' greater willingness to absorb organizational initiatives. At W. H. Smith News, the legacy of paternalism and the absence of competition had left the company relatively inexperienced in monitoring and paying for performance and with a history of top-down implementation which meant that explanations of decisions and processes were often not forthcoming to employees. The new competitive environment and the intention to give employees greater responsibility and discretion has ensured that these former problems—poor supporting processes and insufficient process fairness—are being remedied.

Bureaucracy

The degree of bureaucracy can constrain the interpretation of organizational initiatives. Excessive bureaucracy or bureaucratic constraints can lead to passive mindsets and inertia. If the initiative is concerned with empowering employees, encouraging innovation activity and creativity, then an organization with a history of excessive bureaucracy will encounter resistance. At Lloyds Bank UK Retail Banking, the bureaucracy had created a 'process' culture, with decisions having to go up multiple levels and sign-offs requiring numerous signatures. Even companies as fast-paced as Kraft Jacobs Suchard and Hewlett Packard have experienced this problem. A major trend seen in the Leading Edge research has been companies seeking to reduce their level of bureaucracy and decentralizing decision-making power, and employees urged to take on greater responsibility and discretion (see Chapter 8).

The rules of the game

The rules of the game are in the assumptions, values, and understandings of employees, normally implicit, about how to behave and how to succeed in their organization, and about how to interpret activity within their organization. These rules are products of the firm's history and culture and they determine to a large extent the boundaries of strategic decision-making and organizational responses to competitors' moves. They are strongly bound up with the concept of organizational identity and to this extent they represent a force constraining large-scale change. The concept also has affinities with the concept of the psychological contract. In those terms, the former 'deal' at BT Payphones, Lloyds Bank UK Retail Banking, and W. H. Smith News was one of job security and career advancement based on tenure. The rules of the game were to be deferential to one's boss and to deliver one's (short-term) targets. These rules are currently changing, as the old deal no longer holds. The new deal is job security for high performers and the promise of employability for those who have the capacity to manage their own careers. Such a break with the past has proved very difficult for some, whose absorptive capacity is reduced by the expectancies and experiences they have built up over the years at these companies.

Factors concerning cognition

Sense-making

The employees of organizations actively create the environments within which they work (Weick 1979). This assumption means that within an organization there may be a multiplicity of interpretations of the 'reality' of that organization—different views of the way the organization operates. Employees use framing—cognitive sense-making of events and actions—in order to interpret information. They use past experiences to interpret new information and process it into meaningful categories. This inevitably involves a simplification of the information and can lead to systematic differences in the perception of an organizational initiative (Tversky and Kahnemann 1974).

Selective perception

An important cognitive filter is selective perception, the phenomenon that managers only attend to the information in a situation which relates specifically to the activities of their department. Such practice is a sub-optimal information processing strategy and militates against organization-wide initiatives. At BT Payphones, the restructuring which accompanied the downsizing programme meant considerable shifts in power, with consequent winners and losers. Managers were concerned not with the effects of the workforce reductions on BT's profitability and growth, but with the consequences for their unit or department.

Organizational experience

The degree of organizational experience employees have is related to how they interpret organizational initiatives. Specifically, the longer their tenure, the more likely they are to defend the status quo (Friedrickson 1985). This relates both to the desire not to upset group norms, status, and hierarchy (Miller and Rice 1967) and also to the desire to stave off anxiety (Argyris 1970). In the Chelsea & Westminster Healthcare Trust, long-serving clinicians had been initially hostile to efforts to move towards trust status, fearing that the introduction of a general management cadre would disrupt traditional ways of working and the established hierarchy. At W. H. Smith News, one member of the HR staff said, 'we're waiting for the old guard to leave and then we can really get things moving'.

Absorptive capacity

The capacity of an employee to understand the content of an organizational initiative may depend on their level of prior related knowledge. Such knowledge will affect their 'absorptive capacity' (Cohen and Levinthal 1990). As Szulanski states, 'a recipient that lacks absorptive capacity will be less likely to recognize the value of new knowledge, less likely to assimilate that knowledge and less likely to apply it successfully to commercial ends' (1995: 438). At BT Payphones, many employees we interviewed had been working for BT since before privatization. For some of them, adapting to the performance culture and the speed of change had been bewildering. For some Glaxo Pharmaceuticals UK sales managers, being asked to behave like 'mini-chief executives' over their sales regions had caused a great deal of anxiety since they only had experience of reporting upwards.

Types of gap and their implications

Our research findings confirmed the importance of interpretation in determining how information that is transmitted within the firm either detracts from or enhances integration. Against the dominant trend of much of the literature on organizational initiatives, which highlights failure of implementation as the major cause of lack of integration, we find that a cognitivist approach is necessary for a full understanding of the factors leading to the integration of organizational initiatives. Within our research we found that the four cognitive factors interacted with variables from both the organizational context and the content of the initiative, and from the analysis of the data we identified three major kinds of gap between espoused and enacted reality. The first is what we call 'slip-up'. This refers to simple breakdowns in communication, oversights in implementation, and the usual run of errors which can accompany the dissemination of any new initiative. The second we have called 'structural', where organizational characteristics and the characteristics of employees' cognitive processes make the absorption of initiatives problematic. The third we have termed 'stretch', where organizations actively seek to create a mismatch between intention and action in order to increase motivation and, in many cases, promote organizational change.

Slip-up

Undoubtedly, failures of implementation play a significant part in determining the integration of organizational initiatives. In terms of context, a lack of supporting structures and processes to reinforce the initiatives will hamper its integration. Providing appropriate incentive schemes and organizational structures, according high priority to the initiative, and a clearly articulated need will influence the degree of acceptance organizational initiatives receive. Concerning the content, the poor framing of the initiatives, leading either to ambiguity or to a lack of saliency for particular groups, will affect its absorption. For some of the organizations in our sample, ambiguity over the extent of downsizing, in particular how many jobs would be cut and at what levels, increased stress amongst employees and reduced morale dramatically, affecting the relationship between the institution and managerial- and technical-level employees. Ambiguity produces equivocality in employees; information is equivocal when 'multiple and conflicting interpretations exist' (Daft and Lengel 1986: 556). As Kanter argues, organizations should ensure that they 'make more information available to more people through more devices' (1989b: 5). But it is not just quantity of information that is required, but quality and appropriateness. In cognitive terms, if the initiative exceeds the conventional organizational norms, or disrupts the dominant logic by extending organizational identity too far, this represents poor framing and will adversely affect the integration of the initiative. Better framing of initiative so that employees can understand and interpret information to suit their own environment is an important process. The initiative must be specific, accessible, and desirable if employees are to be motivated by it. A directive which is not seen as useful or as somehow adding value will be bypassed. Greater attention to procedural justice in the implementation of initiatives may also gain employees' buy-in to new directives and is a positive step in increasing the potential for aligning employers and employees.

Structural

Better implementation or framing may help to mitigate against the slip-up factors, but there remain more hard-wired or structural issues. At the contextual level, organizational size increases the number of employees, the number of hierarchical levels, and the internal differentiation. The number of filters through which an initiative has to permeate may distort the message. Large organizations tend to pursue multiple strategies, which also increases the potential for mixed messages. In terms of content, new organizational content will usher in a new organizational context, and there will be an element of uncertainty surrounding the content and how it may fit into this new context (Szulanski 1995). In cognitive terms, framing is an inescapable feature of employees' sense-making activity, which entails multiple interpretations and simplifying meanings to fit individual cognitive schemas. Political activity, too, is said to be inherent in organizations (Cyert and March 1963), and this too increases the potential for the distortion of messages and for increased resistance to initiatives.

As the number of employees increases, along with the hierarchical levels, the scope of the firm, and its internal differentiation, greater attention to the choice of communication media becomes crucial. Increased use of feedback loops will also help to reduce the impact of hierarchical-level filters and to reduce the distance between the cognitive schemata of senior management and lower-level employees. The degree of change can be a source of much anxiety for employees. A clear end point for change, wide consultation, and sensitive handling of former power configurations will increase the receptivity to the organizational initiative (Jick 1993). The problem of multiple strategies is difficult to handle, but accepting trade-offs will be important and the use of the balanced scorecard, as used in BT Payphones, Lloyds Bank UK Retail Banking, and Citibank, may be one way to institutionalize this process.

Because the implementation of initiatives depends on the relationship between giver and receiver, this relationship should be as harmonious and close as possible. The source of the initiative should be perceived as credible and legitimate and should have the trust and confidence of employees. Increased senior management visibility and interaction with lower-level employees, perhaps using informal as well as formal communication channels, may increase understanding of the organization and its aims and also increase the level of trust between senior management and employees.

To reduce the impact of the effects of sense-making and its potential to dilute or distort the interpretation of organizational initiatives, greater attention should be paid to the differentiation amongst employee groups when designing change events. There is clear evidence that departmentalization, or segregating organizational attention on discrete units, can enhance learning by simplifying the information and making it more relevant (Levinthal and March 1993). Further, increased use of socialization may reduce the gap between the interpretations of employees and the interpretations of senior management concerning organizational issues. Greater use of feedback in performance and the use of two-way communication processes will also serve the same end.

An important step is to realize that, in large organizations, commitment tends to have different focuses and different bases. If commitment is sought between employee and supervisor or between employee and business unit, rather than to the organization as a whole, this may produce better performance and increase the receptivity of organizational initiatives (compare Becker 1992). The promotion of BT Payphones as an autonomous business unit, with minimal links to BT as a whole, certainly promoted a strong unit identity and commitment to the business. The issue of power within the organization is a complex subject. The minimization of political activity—for example, a lack of tolerance for coalition forming—may help reduce conflict and so help reduce the distortion of initiatives due to self-interested behaviour. The easing out of trade union influence is one strategy organizations have pursued to facilitate this end.

Stretch

A third set of examples showed organizations deliberately creating a gap between intention and action for the purpose of introducing stretch goals and encouraging managerial discretion. It is this third set which shows that the gap between espoused theory and theory-in-use might in fact, contrary to received wisdom, be a good thing, and actively encouraged by organizations. Perfectly aligned organizations may lack the responsiveness to adapt to new situations and challenges and may actually inhibit change. As organizations face changing environmental conditions, the need for flexibility and adaptation is paramount. Companies are experimenting with new ways of working and new structural forms, and facing constantly changing customer demands. The need to maintain a gap between intention and reality is therefore important—as Ghoshal and Bartlett put it, to create an environment where 'individuals voluntarily stretch their own standards and expectations' (1994: 98). Secondly, the gap may provide for what Burgelman (1983) calls 'autonomous strategic behaviour' on the part of managers—activity which goes beyond what is espoused, pushing the boundaries of organizational activity, experimenting with processes and new ways of working, and contributing new ideas and new directions for the organization. In other words, the gap may encourage entrepreneurial behaviour on the part of lower-level employees, which can help the organization to unlearn old habits and facilitate learning and change. At Hewlett Packard, managers at the front line of customer service saw that the traditional demarcation between computer products and computer services was becoming increasingly blurred. Their feedback led senior management to instigate a merger between the two internal divisions. At Glaxo Pharmaceuticals UK, the traditional geographic structure was seen to be unwieldy by sales staff as it no longer matched how the NHS, GP UK's largest customer, was configured. Again, this information was crucial in triggering organizational restructuring.

Over time, organizations build a sense of identity, a notion of what is central and enduring about them, which provides for security and continuity for employees and acts as a guide to 'the way things are done around here'. Since the existing organizational identity is usually well embedded and relatively inflexible, shifting from the status quo can be difficult. To introduce stretch goals, therefore, the organization must move far enough to overcome inertia, but not so far as to break completely with the old identity, which would increase anxiety and lead to resistance and cynicism.

CONCLUSION

In the fast-changing circumstances which all the Leading Edge organizations face, the effective management of human capital is vital in order to secure competitive advantage. If there is a large disjunction between the aims of the organization and the interpretations of those aims by employees, this may have negative consequences, suggesting that something is amiss with the communication processes and belief formation processes in general. We have seen examples where simple failures of implementation can lead to poor organizational efficiency. However, the gap between rhetoric and reality takes a number of forms and may in certain cases confer important benefits. In order to improve organizational learning and unlearn old habits, some degree of freedom is required for managers to be creative and to stretch the boundaries of customary thinking. Among the Leading Edge companies, building in space for employee discretion is now virtually a norm and the encouragement of risk-taking behaviour is increasingly important. Sometimes, the mismatch between the blueprint and the finished article may illustrate constructive differences, differences which can add to learning and the encouragement of greater exploration.

The themes of this final chapter capture the spirit of this endeavour, the belief that the competencies, aspirations, and inspirations of people are central to organizational success. In this book we have held a mirror to those nine organizations which were prepared to look closely at what they saw. In the reflections we presented they saw the hopes and concerns of employees, the challenges which managers faced, and the true state of policies and systems. In their courage they were prepared not only to face up to reality, but also to share that reality with others. We hope that this spirit of openness and sharing will mark a new step along the development of our understanding of human resource management, that it will lead to a more realistic view of organizational life, and a clearer understanding of the complexities of organizations and the challenges they face.

We believe absolutely that people are central to organizations, and through our research we hope to discard much of the hyperbole and rhetoric of human resource management and allow us all a clearer view of its realities.

REFERENCES

ADLER, N. J., and GHODER, F. (1990). 'Human Resource Management: A Global Perspective', in R. Pieper (ed.), *Human Resource Management: An International Comparison*. Berlin: De Gruyter.

ADLER, W. J., and JELINEK, M. (1986). 'Is Organizational Culture Culture-Bound?', *Human Resource Management*, 25/1: 73–90.

ALPANDER, G. C., and BOTTER, C. H. (1981). 'An Integrated Model of Strategic Human Resource Planning and Utilization', *Human Resource Management*, 20/1: 189–203.

ANTHONY, P. (1986). *The Foundation of Management*. London: Tavistock.

—— (1994). *Managing Culture*. London: Sage.

ARGYRIS, C. (1970). *Personality and Organization: The Conflict between Systems and the Individual*. New York: Harper & Row.

—— (1977). 'Double Loop Learning in Organizations', *Harvard Business Review*, Sept.–Oct., 55/5: 115–25.

—— and SCHON, D. A. (1978). *Organizational Learning: A Theory in Action Perspective*. Reading, Mass.: Addison-Wesley.

ARMSTRONG, P. (1984). 'Competition between the Organizational Professions and the Evolution of Managerial Control Strategies', in K. Thompson (ed.), *Work, Employment and Unemployment*. Milton Keynes: Open University Press.

BACH, S. (1994). 'Restructuring the Personnel Function: The Case of NHS Trusts', *Human Resource Management Journal*, winter, 4/2: 99–115.

BAIRD, L., and MESHOULAM, I. (1988). 'Managing Two Fits of Strategic Human Resource Management', *Academy of Management Review*, 13/1: 116–28.

BARNEY, J. (1991). 'Firm Resources and Sustained Competitive Advantage', *Journal of Management*, Mar., 17/1: 99–120.

BARTLETT, C. A., and GHOSHAL, S. (1989). *Managing across Borders: The Transnational Solution*. London: Hutchinson.

BARTUNEK, J. M. (1984). 'Changing Interpretive Schemes and Organizational Restructuring: The Example of a Religious Order', *Administrative Science Quarterly*, 29: 355–72.

—— and RINQUEST, J. L. (1989). 'Enacting New Perspectives through Work Activities during Organizational Transformation', *Journal of Management Studies*, 26: 541–60.

BASSETT, G. (1994). 'The Case against Job Satisfaction', *Business Horizons*, 37/3: 61–8.

BASSETT, P. (1994). 'Total Union Numbers at Lowest Level since 1946', *The Times*, 9 June.

BEATTY, R. W. (1989). 'Competitive Human Resource Advantage through the Strategic Management of Performance', *Human Resource Planning*, 12/3: 179–94.

—— and ULRICH, D. O. (1993). 'Re-engineering the Mature Organization', in T. D. Jick (ed.), *Managing Change: Cases and Concepts*. Homewood, Ill.: Richard D. Irwin.

BEAUMONT, P. B. (1992). 'The US Human Resource Management Literature: A Review', in G. Salaman (ed.), *Human Resource Strategies*. London: Sage.

BECKER, T. E. (1992). 'Foci and Bases of Commitment: Are they Distinctions Worth Making?', *Academy of Management Journal*, 35: 232–44.

BECKHARD, R. (1992). 'A Model for the Executive Management of Transformational Change', in G. Salaman (ed.), *Human Resource Strategies*. London: Sage.

BEER, M. S., and SPECTOR, B. (1985). *Readings in Human Resource Management*. New York: Free Press.

———— and LAWRENCE, P. R. (1984). *Managing Human Assets*. New York: John Wiley & Sons.

———————— MILLS, D. Q., and WALTON, R. E. (1985). *Human Resource Management: A General Manager's Perspective*. New York: Free Press.

———— EISENSTAT, A., and SPECTOR, B. (1990). 'Why Change Programmes Don't Produce Change', *Harvard Business Review*, Nov.–Dec., 68/6: 158–66.

BETTIS, R. A., and HILL, M. A. (1995). 'The New Competitive Landscape', *Strategic Management Journal*, 16 (special issue, summer): 7–9.

BEVAN, S., and HAYDAY, S. (1994). *Helping Managers to Manage People*. Brighton: Institute of Manpower Studies, BEBC Ltd.

BOURGEOIS, L. J., and EISENHARDT, K. M. (1988). 'Strategic Decision Processes in High Velocity Environments: Four Cases in the Micro-computer Industry', *Management Science*, 34: 816–35.

BOYAZTIS, R. (1982). *The Competent Manager: A Model for Effective Performance*. New York: John Wiley & Sons.

BREWSTER, C., and HEGEWISCH, A. (1994). *Policy and Practice in European Human Resource Management*. London: Routledge.

BROWER, R. S., and ABOLAFIA, M. Y. (1995). 'The Structural Embeddedness of Resistance among Public Managers', *Group and Organization Management*, 20: 149–66.

BURGELMAN, R. I. (1983). 'Corporate Entrepreneurship and Strategic Management: Insights from a Process Study', *Management Science*, 29/12: 1349–64.

BUTLER, J. E., FERRIS, G. R., and NAPIER, N. K. (1991). *Strategy and Human Resource Management*. Cincinnati: South Western Publishing.

CASEY, C. (1995). *Work, Self and Society: After Industrialization*. London: Routledge.

CHILD, J. (1972). 'Organizational Structures, Environment and Performance: The Role of Strategic Choice', *Sociology*, 6: 1–22.

———— (1974). 'Managerial and Organizational Factors Associated with Company Performance', *Journal of Management Studies*, 11/2: 173–89.

———— (1984). *Organizations*. London: Harper & Row.

———— and PARTRIDGE, B. (1982). *Lost Managers*. Cambridge: Cambridge University Press.

CLARK, J. (1993). 'Line Managers, Human Resource Specialists and Technical Change', *Employee Relations*, 15/3: 22–8.

COATES, G. (1994). 'Performance Appraisal as Icon', *International Journal of Human Resource Management*, 5/1: 167–91.

COHEN, W. M., and LEVINTHAL, D. (1990). 'Absorptive Capacity: A New Perspective on Learning and Innovation', *Administrative Science Quarterly*, 35: 128–52.

CYERT, R. M., and MARCH, J. G. (1963). *A Behavioral Theory of the Firm*. Englewood Cliffs, NJ: Prentice-Hall.

DAFT, R. L., and LENGEL, R. M. (1986). 'Organizational Information Requirements, Media Richness and Structural Design', *Management Science*, 32/15: 554–71.

DEAN, J. W., and SNELL, S. A. (1993). 'Integrated Manufacturing and Job Design: The

Moderating Effect of Organizational Inertia', *Academy of Management Journal*, 36: 776–804.

DE GEUS, A. P. (1988). 'Planning as Learning', *Harvard Business Review*, Mar.–Apr. 66/2: 70–4.

DEMIRAG, I., TYLECOTE, A., and MORRIS, B. (1994). 'Accounting for Financial and Managerial Causes of Short-Term Pressures in British Corporations', *Journal of Business Finance and Accounting*, Dec. 21/8: 1195–213.

DESS, G., and BEARD, D. (1984). 'Dimensions of Organizational Task Environments', *Administrative Science Quarterly*, 29: 52–73.

DEVANNA, M. A., FOMBRUN, C. J., TICHY, N. M., and WARREN, L. (1982). 'Strategic Planning and Human Resource Management', *Human Resource Management*, spring, 21/1: 11–17.

—————— (1984). 'A Framework for Strategic Human Resource Management', in C. J. Fombrun, N. M. Tichy, and M. A. Devanna (eds.), *Strategic Human Resource Management*. New York: John Wiley & Sons.

DOZ, Y. L., and THANHEISER, H. H. (1993). 'Regaining Competitiveness: A Process of Organizational Renewal', in J. Hendry, G. Johnson, and J. Newton (eds.), *Strategic Thinking: Leadership and the Management of Change*. Chichester: John Wiley & Sons.

———— (1996). *Embedding Transformational Capability*. ICEDR Research Report. Lexington, Mass.: ICEDR.

DRUCKER, P. (1992). 'The New Society of Organizations', *Harvard Business Review*, Sept.–Oct. 70/5: 95–104.

—— (1993). *Post-capitalist Society*. Oxford: Butterworth-Heinemann.

DUNHAM, R. B., and SMITH, F. J. (1979). *Organizational Surveys*. Chicago: Scott, Foresman.

DUTTON, J. E., and DUKERICH, J. M. (1991). 'Keeping an Eye on the Mirror: Image and Identity in Organizational Adaptation', *Academy of Management Journal*, 34: 517–54.

DYER, L. (1984). 'Linking Human Resource and Business Strategies', *Human Resource Planning*, 7/2: 79–84.

—— (1985). 'Strategic Human Resource Management and Planning', in K. M. Rowland and G. Ferris (eds.), *Research in Personnel and Human Resource Management*. Greenwich, Conn.: JAI Press.

The Economist (1994). 'The Anorexic Corporation', 3–9 Sept., 332/7879: 17–18.

EDWARDS, P. K. (1987). *Managing the Factory: A Survey of General Managers*. Oxford: Basil Blackwell.

EDWARDS, R. (1979). *Contested Terrain*. New York: Basic Books.

EISENHARDT, K. M. (1989). 'Making Fast Decisions in High Velocity Environments', *Academy of Management Journal*, 32: 543–76.

ETZIONI, A. (1975). *The Comparative Analysis of Complex Organizations*. New York: Free Press.

EVANS, P. A. L. (1986). 'The Strategic Outcomes of Human Resource Management', *Human Resource Management*, 25/1: 149–67.

FENTON-O'CREEVY, M. (1996). 'Employee Involvement and the Middle Manager: A Multi-level, Cross-company Study of their Role in the Effectiveness of Employee Involvement Initiatives', Ph.D. thesis. London: London Business School.

FIOL, C. M. (1991). 'Managing Culture as a Competitive Resource: An Identity-Based View of Sustainable Competitive Advantage', *Journal of Management*, 17/2: 191–211.

FLETCHER, C., and WILLIAMS, R. (1985). *Performance Appraisal and Career Development*. London: Hutchinson.

FOMBRUN, C. J., TICHY, N. M., and DEVANNA, M. A. (eds.) (1984). *Strategic Human Resource Management*. New York: John Wiley & Sons.

FREEMAN, R. E. (1985). 'Managing in Turbulent Times', in M. Beer and B. Spector (eds.), *Readings in Human Resource Management*. New York: Free Press.

FRIEDRICKSON, J. W. (1985). 'Effects of Decision, Motive and Organizational Performance Level on Strategic Decision Processes', *Academy of Management Journal*, 4: 821–43.

GHOSHAL, S., and BARTLETT, C. A. (1994). 'Linking Organizational Context and Managerial Action: The Dimensions of Quality of Management', *Strategic Management Journal*, 15 (special issue, summer): 91–112.

GOLDEN, K. A., and RAMANUJAM, V. (1985). 'Between a Dream and a Nightmare: On the Integration of Human Resource Management and Strategic Business Planning Processes', *Human Resource Management*, 24/4: 429–52.

GOMEZ-MEJIA, L. R., and WELBOURNE, T. M. (1990). 'The Role of Compensation in the Human Resource Management Strategies of High Technology Firms', in M. A. Von Glinow and S. A. Mohrman (eds.), *Managing Complexity in High Technology Organizations*. New York: Oxford University Press.

GOOLD, M. C., and CAMPBELL, A. (1987). *Strategies and Styles: The Role of the Centre in Managing Diversified Corporations*. Oxford: Basil Blackwell.

GRATTON, L. (1994). 'Implementing Strategic Intent: Human Resource Process as a Force for Change', *Business Strategy Review*, 5/1: 47–66.

GRIFFIN, M. A., TESLUK, P. E., and JACOBS, R. R. (1995). 'Bargaining Cycles and Work-Related Attitudes: Evidence for Threat–Rigidity Effects', *Academy of Management Journal*, 38: 1709–25.

GRINT, K. (1993). 'What's Wrong with Performance Appraisals? A Critique and a Suggestion', *Human Resource Management Journal*, 3/3: 61–77.

GUEST, D. E. (1987). 'Human Resource Management and Industrial Relations', *Journal of Management Studies*, 24/5: 503–21.

—— (1989). 'Human Resource Management: Its Implications for Industrial Relations and Trade Unions', in J. Storey (ed.), *New Perspectives on Human Resource Management*. London: Routledge.

—— (1992). 'Right Enough to be Dangerously Wrong: An Analysis of the "In Search of Excellence" phenomenon', in G. Salaman (ed.), *Human Resource Strategies*. London: Sage.

—— (1995). 'Human Resource Management, Trade Unions and Industrial Relations', in J. Storey (ed.), *Human Resource Management: A Critical Text*. London: Routledge.

—— and MACKENZIE, K. (1996). 'Don't Write off the Traditional Career', *People Management*, Feb., 2/4: 22–5.

HAMBRICK, D. C., and SNOW, C. C. (1989). 'Strategic Reward Systems', in C. C. Snow (ed.), *Strategy, Organizational Design and Human Resource Management*. Greenwich, Conn.: JAI Press.

HAMEL, G., and PRAHALAD, C. K. (1989). 'Strategic Intent', *Harvard Business Review*, May–June, 67/3: 63–76.

—— —— (1990). 'The Core Competence of the Corporation', *Harvard Business Review*, May–June, 68/3: 79–91.

HANNAN, M. T. & FREEMAN, J. (1989). *Organizational Ecology*. Cambridge, Mass.: Harvard University Press.

HENDRY, C., and PETTIGREW, A. (1986). 'The Practice of Strategic Human Resource Management', *Personnel Review*, 15/3: 3–8.

—— —— (1990). 'Human Resource Management: An Agenda for the 1990s', *International Journal of Human Resource Management*, 1/1: 17–44.

HENDRY, J., and HOPE, V. (1994). 'Cultural Change and Competitive Performance', *European Management Journal*, Dec., 12/4: 401–6.

HERRIOT, P. (1995). 'The Management of Careers', in S. Tyson (ed.), *Strategic Prospects for HRM*. London: IPD.

——and PEMBERTON, C. (1995). 'A New Deal for Middle Managers', *People Management*, 4/12: 32–5.

HOFSTEDE, G. (1991). *Culture and Organizations: Software of the Mind*. London: McGraw-Hill.

HOPE, V. (1993). 'The Wrong Kind of Attitude? A Study of Control and Consent in HRM', Ph.D. thesis. Manchester: University of Manchester.

——(1994). 'HRM and Corporate Cultural Control: The Limits to Commitment', *Proceedings of the Annual Conference of the British Academy of Management*. Lancaster: Lancaster University.

——and HENDRY, J. (1995). 'Corporate Cultural Change: Is it Still Relevant for the Organization of the '90s?', *Human Resource Management Journal*, 5/4: 61–73.

HOPE HAILEY, V. (1997). 'The Chameleon Function', *Human Resource Management Journal*, 7: 5–18.

HREBINIAK, L. G., JOYCE, W. F., and SNOW, C. C. (1988). 'Strategy, Structure and Performance: Past and Future Research', in C. C. Snow (ed.), *Strategy, Organizational Design and Human Resource Management*. Greenwich, Conn.: JAI Press.

HUFF, A. S., and REGER, R. K. (1987). 'A Review of Strategic Process Research', *Journal of Management*, 13/2: 211–36.

HYMAN, J., and CUNNINGHAM, I. (1995). 'Change in Employee Relations: Can Line Managers Deliver?', in *Proceedings of the Employment Research Unit Annual Conference: Organizing Employment for High Performance*. Cardiff: Cardiff University.

JACKSON, S. E., SCHULER, R. S., and RIVERO, J. C. (1989). 'Organizational Characteristics as Predictors of Personnel Practices', *Personnel Psychology*, winter, 42/4: 727–86.

JAEGER, J. A., and BALIGA, B. R. (1985). 'Control Systems and Strategic Adaptation: Lessons from the Japanese Experience', *Strategic Management Journal*, 16: 115–329.

JICK, T. D. (1979). 'Mixing Qualitative and Quantitative Methods: Triangulation in Action', *Administrative Science Quarterly*, 24/3: 602–11.

——(1993). 'Implementing Change', in T. D. Jick (ed.), *Managing Change: Cases and Concepts*. Homewood, Ill.: Richard D. Irwin.

JOHNSON, G., and SCHOLES, K. (1986). *Exploring Corporate Strategy*. London: Prentice Hall.

JUDGE, W. Q., and MILLER, A. (1991). 'Antecedents and Outcomes of Decision Speed in Different Environmental Contexts', *Academy of Management Journal*, 34: 449–63.

KAMOCHE, K. (1994). 'A Critique and a Proposed Reformulation of Strategic Human Resource Management', *Human Resource Management Journal*, 4/4: 29–43.

KANTER, R. M. (1989a). 'The New Managerial Work', *Harvard Business Review*, Nov.–Dec., 67/6: 85–92.

——(1989b). *When Giants Learn to Dance: Mastering the Challenge of Strategy, Management and Careers in the 1990s*. London: Routledge.

KEENOY, T. (1990). 'Human Resource Management: Rhetoric, Reality and Contradiction', *International Journal of Human Resource Management*, 1/3: 363–84.

——and ANTHONY, P. (1992). 'Metaphor, Meaning and Morality', in P. Blyton and P. Turnbull (eds.), *Reassessing Human Resource Management*. London: Sage.

KEEP, E. (1989). 'Corporate Training Strategies: The Vital Component?', in J. Storey (ed.), *New Perspectives on Human Resource Management*. London: Routledge.

KERFOOT, D., and KNIGHTS, D. (1992). 'Planning for Personnel? Human Resource Management Reconsidered', *Journal of Management Studies*, 29/5: 651–68.

KHANDWALLA, P. N. (1973). 'Effect of Competition on the Structure of Top Management Control', *Academy of Management Journal*, 16: 285–95.

KIRKPATRICK, I., DAVIES, A., and OLIVER, N. (1992). 'Decentralization: Friend or Foe of HRM?', in P. Blyton and P. Turnbull (eds.), *Reassessing Human Resource Management*. London: Sage.

KOCHEN, T. A., and DYER, L. (1993). 'Managing Transformational Change: The Role of Human Resource Professionals', *International Journal of Human Resource Management*, 4/3: 569–90.

—— —— (1995). 'HRM: An American View', in J. Storey (ed.), *Human Resource Management: A Critical Text*. London: Routledge.

KUNDA, G. (1992). *Engineering Culture: Control and Commitment in a Hi-tech Firm*. Philadelphia: Temple University Press.

LATHAM, G. P. (1984). 'The Appraisal System as a Strategic Control', in C. J. Fombrun, N. M. Tichy, and M. A. Devanna (eds.), *Strategic Human Resource Management*. New York: John Wiley & Sons.

—— and LOCKE, E. A. (1991). 'Self-Regulation through Goal Setting', *Organizational Behaviour and Human Decision Processes*, 50: 212–95.

LAWLER, E. E. (1990). *Strategic Pay*. San Francisco: Jossey Bass.

LAWRENCE, P. R., and LORSCH, J. W. (1967). *Organization and Environment*. Cambridge, Mass.: Harvard University Press.

LEGGE, K. (1978). *Power, Innovation and Problem Solving in Personnel Management*. London: McGraw-Hill.

—— (1989). 'Human Resource Management: A Critical Analysis', in J. Storey (ed.), *New Perspectives on Human Resource Management*. London: Routledge.

—— (1995a). 'HRM: Rhetoric, Reality and Hidden Agendas', in J. Storey (ed.), *Human Resource Management: A Critical Text*. London: Routledge.

—— (1995b). *Human Resource Management: Rhetorics and Realities*. London: Macmillan.

LENGNICK-HALL, C. A., and LENGNICK-HALL, M. L. (1988). 'Strategic HRM: A Review of the Literature and a Proposed Typology', *Academy of Management Review*, 13/3: 454–70.

—— —— (1990). *Interactive Human Resource Management and Strategic Planning*. Westport, Conn.: Quorum Books.

LEVINTHAL, D. A., and MARCH, J. G. (1993). 'The Myopia of Learning', *Strategic Management Journal*, 14 (special issue, winter): 95–112.

LEWIN, K. (1973). *Field Theory in Social Science*. New York: Harper & Row.

LONGENECKER, C. O., GIOLA, D. A., and SIMS, H. P. (1987). 'Behind the Mask: The Politics of Employee Appraisal', *Academy of Management Executive*, 1/1: 183–94.

LOWE, J. (1992). 'Locating the Line: The Front Line Supervisor and Human Resource Management', in P. Blyton and P. Turnbull (eds.), *Reassessing Human Resource Management*. London: Sage.

LUNDBERG, C. C. (1985). 'Towards a Contextual Model of Human Resource Strategy: Lessons from the Reynolds Corporation', *Human Resource Management*, 24/1: 91–112.

LUNDY, O. (1994). 'From Personnel Management to Strategic Human Resource Management', *International Journal of Human Resource Management*, 5/3: 687–720.

MABEY, C., and SALAMAN, G. (1995). *Strategic Human Resource Management*. Oxford: Basil Blackwell.

McGOVERN, P., HOPE HAILEY, V., and STILES, P. (1998). 'The Managerial Career after Downsizing. Case Studies from the "Leading Edge"', *Work, Employment and Society*, 12/3: 457–477.

McGREGOR, D. (1960). 'Theory X and Theory Y', in D. S. Pugh (ed.), *Organization Theory: Selected Readings*. London: Penguin.

MacNEILL, I. (1985). 'Relational Contract: What we Do and Do Not Do', *Wisconsin Law Review*, 485–525.

MAHONEY, T. A., and DECKOP J. R. (1986). 'Evolution of Concept and Practice in Personnel Administration/Human Resource Management', *Journal of Management*, 12/2: 223–41.

MARSH, P. (1990). *Short-Termism on Trial*. London: International Fund Managers Association.

MAYO, A. (1995). 'Economic Indicators of HRM', in S. Tyson (ed.), *Strategic Prospects for HRM*. London: IPD.

MENTO, A. J., STEEL, R. P., and KARAN, R. J. (1987). 'A Meta-analytic Study of the Effect of Goal Setting on Task Performance: 1966–1984', *Organizational Behaviour and Human Decision Processes*, 39: 52–83.

MIGLIORE, R. H. (1982). 'Linking Strategy, Performance and Pay', *Journal of Business Strategy*, 3: 90–4.

MILES, R. E., and SNOW, C. C. (1978). *Organizational Studies, Structure and Process*. Kogakusha: McGraw-Hill.

——— (1984). 'Designing Strategic Human Resource Systems', *Organizational Dynamics*, summer, 13/1: 36–52.

MILKOVICH, G. T., and BOUDREAU, J. W. (1991). *Human Resource Management* (6th edn.). Homewood, Ill.: Richard D. Irwin.

MILLER, E. J., and RICE, R. K. (1967). *Systems of Organization*. London: Tavistock.

MILLER, P. (1987). 'Strategic Industrial Relations and Human Resource Management: Distinction, Definition and Recognition', *Journal of Management Studies*, 24/4: 347–61.

MILLWARD, N. (1994). *The New Industrial Relations?* London: PSI Publishing.

——— STEVENS, M., SMART, D., and HAWES, W. R. (1992). *Workplace Industrial Relations in Transition: The Ed/ESRC/PSI/ACAS Surveys*. Aldershot: Gower.

MINTZBERG, H. (1973). *The Nature of Managerial Work*. New York: Harper & Row.

——— (1983). *Structure in Fives: Designing Effective Organizations*. Englewood Cliffs, NJ: Prentice-Hall.

——— (1994). *The Rise and Fall of Strategic Planning*. New York: Free Press.

MOHRMAN, A. M., MOHRMAN, S. A., and WORLEY, C. G. (1990). 'High Technology Performance Management', in M. A. Von Glinow and S. A. Mohrman (eds.), *Managing Complexity in High Technology Organizations*. New York: Oxford University Press.

MORRISON, E. W., and ROBINSON, S. L. (1997). 'When Employees Feel Betrayed: A Model of How Psychological Contract Violation Occurs', *Academy of Management Review*, 22/1: 226–56.

MOVERY, D. C., OXLEY, J. E., and SILVERMAN, B. S. (1996). 'Strategic Alliances and Interim Knowledge Transfer', *Strategic Management Journal*, 17: 77–91.

MOWDAY, R. T., STEERS, R. M., and PORTER, L. W. (1978). 'The Measurement of Organizational Commitment', *Journal of Vocational Behaviour*, 14/2: 224–49.

MUMFORD, E. (1971). 'Job Satisfaction: A Method of Analysis', *Personnel Review*, 1/3: 11–19.

NADLER, D. A., and TUSHMAN, M. L. (1989). 'Organizational Frame-Bending: Principles for Managing Re-orientation', *Academy of Management Executive*, 3: 194–204.

NATHAN, B. R., MOHRMAN, A. M., and MILLIMAN, J. (1991). 'Interpersonal Relations as a Context for the Effects of Appraisal Interviews on Performance and Satisfaction: A Longitudinal Study', *Academy of Management Journal*, 34: 352–69.

NICHOLSON, N. (1996). 'Career Systems in Crisis: Change and Opportunity in the Information Age', *Academy of Management Executive*, 10/4: 40–51.

NICHOLSON, N. and WEST, M. (1988). *Managerial Job Change: Men and Women in Transition.* Cambridge: Cambridge University Press.

NONAKA, I. (1988). 'Toward Middle–Up–Down Management: Appreciating Information Creation', *Sloan Management Review,* spring, 29/3: 9–18.

NOON, M. (1992). 'Human Resource Management: A Map, Model or Theory?', in P. Blyton and P. Turnbull (eds.), *Reassessing Human Resource Management.* London: Sage.

NORTHCOTE, J. (1991). *Britain in 2010: The PSI Report.* London: Policy Studies Institute.

OECD (1991–2). *Economic Survey, UK.* Paris: Organization for Economic Cooperation and Development.

—— (1993). *Economic Survey, US.* Paris: Organization for Economic Cooperation and Development.

—— (1994). *Economic Survey, US.* Paris: Organization for Economic Cooperation and Development.

—— (1996). *Economic Survey, UK.* Paris: Organization for Economic Cooperation and Development.

OGBONNA, E. (1990). 'Corporate Strategy and Corporate Culture: The View from the Checkout', *Personnel Review,* 19/4: 9–15.

PAAUWE, J. (1995). 'Personnel Management without Personnel Managers', in P. Flood *et al.* (eds.), *Managing without Traditional Methods.* London: Addison-Wesley.

PACKARD, D. (1995). *The HP Way: How Bill Hewlett and I Built Our Company.* New York: Harper Business.

PENLEY, L., and GOULD, S. (1988). 'Etzioni's Model of Organizational Involvement: A Perspective for Understanding Commitment to Organizations', *Journal of Organizational Behaviour,* Jan., 9/1: 43–59.

PETERS, T. J. (1992). *Liberation Management.* London: Macmillan.

—— and WATERMAN, R. H. (1983). *In Search of Excellence: Lessons from America's Best Run Companies.* New York: Harper & Row.

PETTIGREW, A. M. (1985). *The Awakening Giant.* Oxford: Basil Blackwell.

—— (1992). 'On Studying Managerial Elites', *Strategic Management Journal,* 13 (special issue, winter): 163–82.

—— and WHIPP, R. (1991). *Managing Change for Competitive Success.* Oxford: Basil Blackwell.

PHILPOTT, L., and SHEPPARD, L. (1992). 'Managing for Improved Performance', in M. Armstrong (ed.), *Strategies for Human Resource Management: A Total Business Approach.* London: Kogan Page.

PRIETO, C. (1993). 'The Management of the Workforce: A Sociological Criticism of Prevailing Fashions', *International Journal of Human Resource Management,* 4/3: 611–30.

PURCELL, J. (1989) 'The Impact of Corporate Strategy on Human Resource Management', in J. Storey (ed.), *New Perspectives on Human Resource Management.* London: Routledge.

—— (1993). 'The Challenge of Human Resource Management for Industrial Relations Research and Practice', *International Journal of Human Resource Management,* 4/3: 511–27.

—— (1995). 'Corporate Strategy and its Link with Human Resource Management Strategy', in J. Storey (ed.), *Human Resource Management: A Critical Text.* London: Routledge.

—— and AHLSTRAND, B. (1994). *Human Resource Management in the Multi-divisional Company.* Oxford: Oxford University Press.

—— and SISSON, K. (1983). 'Strategies and Practice in the Management of Industrial

Relations', in G. Bain (ed.), *Industrial Relations in Britain: Past Trends and Future Prospects*. Oxford: Basil Blackwell.

QUINN, J. B. (1989). *Strategies for Change: Logical Incrementalism*. Homewood, Ill.: Richard D. Irwin.

QUINN MILLS, D. (1985). 'Planning with People in Mind', *Harvard Business Review*, July–Aug., 63/4: 97–105.

RAELIN, J. (1985). 'The Basis for the Professional's Resistance to Managerial Control', *Human Resource Management*, 24/2: 147–76.

RANDELL, G. (1989). 'Employee Appraisal', in K. Sisson (ed.), *Personnel Management in Britain*. Oxford: Basil Blackwell.

RAY, C. A. (1986). 'Corporate Culture: The Last Frontier of Control?', *Journal of Management Studies*, 23/3: 287–97.

ROBERTSON, P. J., ROBERTS, D. R., and PORRAS, J. I. (1993). 'Dynamics of Planned Organizational Change: Assessing Empirical Support for a Theoretical Model', *Academy of Management Journal*, 36: 619–34.

ROBINSON, L., and ROUSSEAU, D. M. (1994). 'Violating the Psychological Contract: Not the Exception but the Norm', *Journal of Organizational Behaviour*, 15/3: 245–61.

ROSENBAUM, J. E. (1979). 'Tournament Mobility: Career Patterns in a Corporation', *Administrative Science Quarterly*, June, 24/1: 220–41.

ROUSSEAU, D. M. (1996). *Psychological Contracts in Organizations*. Thousand Oaks, Calif.: Sage.

SALANCIK, G. (1977). 'Commitment is too Easy', *Organizational Dynamics*, summer, 6/2: 62–80.

SCASE, R., and GOFFEE, R. (1989). *Reluctant Managers: Their Work and Lifestyles*. London: Unwin Hyman.

SCHEIN, E. (1984). 'Coming to a New Awareness of Organizational Culture', *Sloan Management Review*, winter, 25/2: 3–16.

SCHOONHOVEN, C. B., and JELINK, M. (1990). 'Dynamic Tension in Innovative High Technology Firms: Managing Rapid Technological Change through Organizational Structure', in M. A. Von Glinow and S. A. Mohrman (eds.), *Managing Complexity in High Technology Organizations*. New York: Oxford University Press.

SCHULER, R. S., and JACKSON, S. E. (1987). 'Linking Competitive Strategies with Human Resource Management Practices', *Academy of Management Executive*, 1/3: 207–19.

—— and MACMILLAN, I. C. (1984). 'Gaining Competitive Advantage through Human Resource Management Practices', *Human Resource Management*, 23/3: 241–55.

SCOTT-MORGAN, P. (1994). *The Unwritten Rules of the Game*. New York: McGraw-Hill.

SENGE, P. (1990). *The Fifth Discipline: The Art and Practice of the Learning Organization*. New York: Century Business.

SIMONS, R. (1994). 'How Top Managers Use Control Systems as Levers of Strategic Renewal', *Strategic Management Journal*, 15/1–4: 169–89.

—— (1995). *Levers of Control*. Boston: Harvard Business School Press.

SISSON, K. (ed.) (1989). *Personnel Management in Britain*. Oxford: Basil Blackwell.

—— (1995). 'The Personnel Function', in J. Storey (ed.), *Human Resource Management: A Critical Text*. London: Routledge.

SNELL, S. A. (1992). 'Control Theory in Strategic Human Resource Management: The Mediating Effect of Administrative Information', *Academy of Management Journal*, 35: 292–327.

—— and DEAN, J. W. (1992). 'Integrated Manufacturing and Human Resource Management: A Human Capital Perspective', *Academy of Management Journal*, 35: 467–504.

SNOW, C. C., and THOMAS, J. B. (1994). 'Field Research Methods in Strategic Management: Contributions to Theory Building and Testing', *Journal of Management Studies*, 31/4: 457–80.

SPARROW, P. (1996). 'Transitions in the Psychological Contract in the UK Banking Sector', *Human Resource Management Journal*, Nov., 6/4: 75–92.

STACE, D. A., and DUNPHY, D. (1990). 'A New Paradigm: Human Resource Strategies and Organizational Transformation in Australian Service Industries', *Research in Personnel and Human Resource Management Supplement*, 2: 37–51.

STAW, B. M., SANDELANDS, L. E., and DUTTON, J. E. (1981). 'Threat–Rigidity Effects in Organizational Behaviour: A Multi-level Analysis', *Administrative Science Quarterly*, 26: 501–24.

STEWART, A. (1989). *Team Entrepreneurship*. Newbury Park, Calif.: Sage.

STEWART, R. (1989). 'Studies of Managerial Jobs and Behaviour: The Way Forward', *Journal of Management Studies*, 26/1: 1–10.

STOREY, J. (1987). 'Developments in the Management of Human Resources: An Interim Report', *Warwick Papers on Industrial Relations*, 17, Nov., School of Industrial and Business Studies, University of Warwick.

—— (1989). 'From Personnel Management to Human Resource Management', in J. Storey (ed.), *New Perspectives on Human Resource Management*. London: Routledge.

—— (1992). *Developments in the Management of Human Resources*. Oxford: Basil Blackwell.

—— (1995). 'Human Resource Management: Still Marching on, or Marching out?', in J. Storey (ed.), *Human Resource Management: A Critical Text*. London: Routledge.

—— and SISSON, K. (1989). 'Looking to the Future', in J. Storey (ed.), *New Perspectives on Human Resource Management*. London: Routledge.

—— —— (1993). *Managing Human Resources and Industrial Relations*. Milton Keynes: Open University Press.

STREECK, W. (1987). 'The Uncertainties of Management in the Management of Uncertainty: Employers, Labor Relations and Industrial Adjustment in the 1980s', *Work, Employment and Society*, 1/3: 281–308.

SULLIVAN, J. J. (1986). 'Human Nature, Organizations and Management Theory', *Academy of Management Review*, 11/3: 534–49.

SZULANSKI, G. (1995). 'Unpicking Stickiness: An Empirical Investigation of the Barriers to Transfer Best Practice in the Firm', *Academy of Management Journal*, Best Papers Proceedings: 437–41.

TANNENBAUM, A. (1968). *The Social Psychology of Work Organizations*. Belmont, Calif.: Brookes-Cole.

THURLEY, K. (1981). 'Personnel Management in the UK: A Case for Urgent Treatment?', *Personnel Management*, Aug., 24/8.

TICHY, N. M., FOMBRUN, C. J., and DEVANNA, M. A. (1982). 'Strategic Human Resource Management', *Sloan Management Review*, 23/2: 47–61.

TORRINGTON, D. (1989). 'Human Resource Management and the Personnel Function', in J. Storey (ed.), *New Perspectives on Human Resource Management*. London: Routledge.

TOWNLEY, B. (1989). 'Selection and Appraisal: Reconstituting "Social Relations"', in J. Storey (ed.), *New Perspectives on Human Resource Management*. London: Routledge.

TRUSS, C. J., and GRATTON, L. (1994). 'Strategic Human Resource Management: A Conceptual Approach', *International Journal of Human Resource Management*, Sept., 5/3: 663–86.

Tsui, A. (1988). 'Activities and Effectiveness of the Human Resource Department: A Multiple Consultancy Approach', in R. S. Schuler, A. A. Youngblood, and V. L. Huber (eds.), *Readings in Personnel and Human Resource Management*. St Paul, Minn.: West.

Tversky, A., and Kahnemann, D. (1974). 'Judgement under Uncertainty: Heuristics and Biases', *Science*, 185: 1124–31.

Tylecote, A. (1995). 'Policy Revitalisation: Managerial Objectives, Short-Termism and Innovation', in *Proceedings of the British Academy of Management Annual Conference*. Sheffield.

Tyson, S. (1987). 'The Management of the Personnel Function', *Journal of Management Studies*, Sept., 24/9: 523–32.

—— (1995a). *Human Resource Strategy*. London: Pitman.

—— (ed.) (1995b). *Strategic Prospects for HRM*. London: IPD.

—— and Fell, A. (1986). *Evaluating the Personnel Function*. London: Hutchinson.

Ulrich, D. (1987). 'Organizational Capability as a Competitive Advantage: Human Resource Professionals as Strategic Partners', *Human Resource Planning*, 10/4: 169–84.

—— (1997). *Human Resource Champions: The Next Agenda for Adding Value and Delivery Results*. Boston: Harvard Business School Press.

—— and Lake, D. (1990). *Organizational Capability: Competing from the Inside out*. New York: John Wiley & Sons.

Walker, J. W. (1980). *Human Resource Strategy*. New York: McGraw-Hill.

—— (1994). 'Integrating the Human Resource Function into the Business', *Human Resource Planning*, 17/2: 59–77.

Wall Street Journal (1994). 'Job-Cutting Medicine Fails to Remedy Productivity Ills at Many Companies', Tuesday, 7 June.

Walsh, J. P., and Seward, J. K. (1990). 'On the Efficiency of Internal and External Corporate Control Mechanisms', *Academy of Management Review*, 15: 421–58.

Walton, R. E. (1985a). 'Towards a Strategy of Eliciting Employee Commitment Based on Policies of Mutuality', in R. E. Walton and P. R. Lawrence (eds.), *HRM Trends and Challenges*. Boston: Harvard Business School Press.

—— (1985b). 'From Control to Commitment in the Workplace', *Harvard Business Review*, Mar.–Apr., 63/2: 77–84.

Waterman, R., Waterman, B., and Collard, B. (1994). 'Towards a Career-Resilient Workforce', *Harvard Business Review*, July–Aug., 72/4: 87–95.

Watson, T. (1977). *The Personnel Managers: A Study in the Sociology of Work and Employment*. London: Routledge.

Watson, T. J. (1994). *In Search of Management*. London: Routledge.

Weick, K. (1979). *The Social Psychology of Organizing*. Reading, Mass.: Addison-Wesley.

Whipp, R., Rosenfeld, R., and Pettigrew, A. M. (1989). 'Culture and Competitiveness: Evidence from Two Mature UK Industries', *Journal of Management Studies*, 26: 561–86.

Whittington, R. (1992). 'Putting Giddens into Action: Social Systems and Managerial Agency', *Journal of Management Studies*, 29/6: 693–713.

—— (1993). *What is Strategy and Does it Matter?* London: Routledge.

Willmott, H. (1993). 'Strength is Ignorance, Slavery is Freedom: Managing Culture in Modern Organizations', *Journal of Management Studies*, 30/4: 515–52.

Wood, S. (1995). 'The Four Pillars of HRM: Are they Connected?', *Human Resource Management Journal*, 5/5: 49–59.

—— (1996). 'High Commitment Management and Unionization in the UK', *International Journal of Human Resource Management*, 7/1: 41–58.

WRIGHT, P., McMAHAN, G., and McWILLIAMS, A. (1994). 'Human Resources and Sustained Competitive Advantage: A Resource Based Perspective', *International Journal of Human Resource Management*, 5/2: 301–26.

YEUNG, A., BROCKBANK, W., and ULRICH, D. (1994). 'Lower Cost, Higher Value: Human Resource Function in Transition', *Human Resource Planning*, 17/3: 1–16.

INDEX

Abolafia, M. Y. 218
accountability 12, 59, 74, 169, 175
acquisitions 33–4, 53, 65, 127–8, 150, 153, 166, 211
adaptability 11, 41, 55, 225
Adler, N. J. 197
Adler, W. J. 6
administration 11–12, 61
administrative heritage 6, 20, 25, 31, 197–8, 200–2, 210, 213
Ahlstrand, B. 42, 44, 48, 54, 120
Allen and Hanbury 168, 219
Alpander, G. C. 41
ambiguity and content of change 215, 223
Anthony, P. 11, 12, 101, 104, 118
anti-trust issues 24
appraisal:
    commitment 207, 209, 210
    culture management 114
    HRM 201, 205
    'new careers' 84, 99
    people processes 172, 175–6, 185, 190, 194, 196–8
    performance management 61–4, 68–9, 73, 76–7
    performance, policies and practices 135–9, 141, 145–6, 148–9
    transformation 163–4
architect role of HR 12, 51, 80–2, 84–91, 118–19, 129, 200, 204–6
archival data 17–19
Argyris, C. 64, 175, 214, 221
Armstrong, P. 11, 118
attitudes 68, 84, 91, 105–6, 133, 162, 210, 212–13, 217

Bach, S. 145
Baird, L. 5, 7, 41, 44
Baliga, B. R. 61
Barney, J. 11, 170, 171, 178
Bartlett, C. A. 25, 219, 225
Bartunek, J. M. 154, 214
Bassett, G. 44
Bassetst, P. 25
Beatty, R. W. 59, 157
Beaumont, P. B. 42
Becker, T. E. 224

Beckhard, R. 103
Beer, M. S. 7, 41, 59, 103, 118
behaviour:
    commitment 209
    contextual diversity 123
    culture management 102–7, 112, 114–16
    line management 133–4
    management 200
    methodology 16, 18
    'new careers' 84
    people processes 170–3, 176
    performance management 61, 67–8, 73, 76–7
    sense-making 217, 220
    soft–hard models of HRM 41
    strategy 5, 7, 11–14
    transformation 154, 162–5, 168–9
best practice 116–17, 121, 145
Bettis, R. A. 24
Bevan, S. 13, 135
biotechnology, influence of 28, 60, 155
Botter, C. H. 41
bottom-up change 103, 166
Boudreau, J. W. 6
Bourgeois, L. J. 60
Boyaztis, R. 61
Brewster, C. 120
British Telecom 153
Brower, R. S. 218
Brutsche, Ernst 66
BT Payphones:
    commitment 206–9, 211, 213
    context 20–6, 32–3
    HRM 203
    'new careers' 79, 86, 89–97
    people processes 194, 197–8
    policies and practices 137, 140–2, 144, 147–9
    sense-making 213, 218, 220–2, 224
    soft–hard models of HRM 46–50, 52, 55–6
    transformation 154, 156, 158, 161, 164–6
bureaucracy 60–1, 69, 77, 102–3, 108, 114, 117–18, 126, 131, 152, 162, 166, 190, 194, 212, 215, 220
Burgelman, R.I. 225
'burn-out' 94, 99
Buse, Rodney 2
business process engineering 32
business strategy:

business strategy (*cont.*):
  HRM and 3, 5, 7–10, 18, 43–4, 51, 53–5, 105, 118–19, 127, 129, 131, 133–4, 204, 210
  interventions 200–4
  people processes 170–6, 179, 187–93, 195
  performance 174–5
  performance management 66
business units:
  contextual diversity 120, 122–4, 127, 132
  culture management 103, 108, 112
  'new careers' 79, 91, 93
  people processes 175
  performance management 59
  sense-making 224
  soft–hard models of HRM 51
  transformation 155, 161–2
Butler, J. E. *et al.* 7, 44, 177, 180

Campbell, A. 146
capability, current 173, 179, 180, 183, 185–6, 188, 209
capacity, absorptive 215, 220–1
capital, human 47, 64, 171, 178, 201, 213, 225
career:
  development 27, 107, 114, 147–9, 186, 200, 202, 210, 213, 220
  management 48–9, 51, 57, 164, 204–5, 213
  paths 168, 193–4, 207, 211
  planning 178–9, 194–5
careers, 'new' 35–6, 79–100
case study, use of 14, 18–19, 198
Casey, C. 104
centralization 28, 30, 54, 65, 74, 76, 94, 129, 168
  de-centralization 59, 61, 66, 79, 108, 119–20, 122, 128, 132, 153, 161–2, 175, 211, 220
change:
  agents 120
  commitment 207, 209, 211, 213
  environment 34
  HRM and 199, 201
  management 153–4, 173, 177, 179–80, 1845
  methodology 2
  people processes 190, 197–8
  sense-making 214–22, 224–5
  trust and commitment 206
Chelsea and Westminster Healthcare Trust:
  context 21, 25–7, 32–3
  contextual diversity 131–2
  HRM 202, 204
  'new careers' 86, 88–90, 92, 95–7
  policies and practices 137–8, 140–2, 144–9
  sense-making 217, 221
  soft–hard models of HRM 46, 49–50, 52, 54–6
  transformation 153–6, 164, 166
Child, J. 20, 104, 134, 175
Citibank:
  context 20–4, 27, 32
  contextual diversity 122, 128–31, 132
  data collection 18
  'new careers' 85–6, 88–90, 92–8
  people processes 188, 191–2, 194, 197
  performance management 64–8, 70–2, 76
  policies and practices 137–8, 140–2, 144, 147–9

sense-making 216, 224
soft–hard models of HRM 46–50, 52–6
transformation 153, 155, 157, 161, 164–6
Clark, J. 135
coaching 64, 71, 76–7, 165, 178–9
Coates, G. 59
cognition and management 154, 214–16, 221–4
Cohen, W. M. 222
cohesion 125, 172, 186
commitment:
  contextual diversity 125
  culture management 101, 104, 109, 114
  as emergent theme 199–200, 203, 206–13
  'new careers' 83–4, 93–5, 99–100
  people processes 179
  performance management 66, 77–8
  policies and practices 150
  sense-making 219, 224
  soft–hard models of HRM 41–5, 49, 51, 54, 56–8
  strategy 8, 11–12
  transformation 165
communication 13, 41, 49–50, 55, 66, 69, 77, 103, 105–6, 135, 145, 165, 168, 179–80, 208–9, 217–19, 223–5
competency:
  competitive advantage 172–3, 177, 178
  culture management 107, 115
  management 208
  'new careers' 80, 82
  people processes 183, 193–4, 194
  performance management 61, 63, 67–9, 71, 73
  policies and practices 135
  strategy and 11–13
  transformation 163–4, 169
competition:
  context and 23–4, 26, 28, 32–3, 201
  contextual diversity 127
  culture management 103, 105, 108
  HR strategy 9
  'new careers' 80
  performance management 59–60, 64–5
  policies and practices 150
  soft–hard models of HRM 54
  transformation 153, 154–5, 168
competitive advantage:
  contextual diversity 127
  HR strategy 11–12, 204
  people processes 38, 170–98
  sense-making 225
  soft–hard models of HRM 41, 43, 47–8, 56–7
  transformation 154, 157, 169
conduct of appraisal 138–9
confidentiality 19
consent 83
consistency 62, 76, 110–11, 118, 136, 146, 167, 197, 201, 207
constraints, policies and practices 136, 139–51
content and sense-making 214–17, 222–3
context:
  commitment 211
  culture management 102, 115–16
  diversity and role and practice of HR 117–32

HRM 200–2, 204
  methodology 19–33
  'new careers' 83
  people processes 188, 196
  performance management 71
  sense-making 214–21, 222–3
  strategy 3–6
  transformation 154–62
continuity 76, 186, 201, 207, 225
continuous improvement 62, 127–8, 161, 188
contract:
  employment 2, 12, 45, 82–4, 94, 99, 168, 179,
    193–5, 199–200, 203–4, 207–8, 211, 213, 220
  managerial 119, 131
control:
  commitment 208
  financial 147
  HR function 53–4
  labour 102–4, 116
  managerial 42–3, 45, 175
  'new careers' 97–8
  performance management 59–60, 77
  policies and practices 134
  strategies 49–58, 203
  transformation 168
core workers 79–80, 91, 93, 100, 174
cost-cutting 7, 23, 27, 32, 45, 47, 79, 90, 127, 135,
  196, 200, 218
counselling 64, 71, 76–7, 84, 165
creativity 62–5, 67, 69, 73, 77, 220, 226
credibility 50, 139, 205, 210, 224
critical theory 118, 121
cross-country mobility 90
cross-functional working 65, 67, 70, 79–80, 90,
  115, 158, 163, 165, 186, 192, 196
culture:
  change 47, 53–4, 57, 153–5, 163, 165, 168
  commitment 210–11
  context 201–2, 220
  context and methodology 15–16, 20, 25, 27–
    30, 36
  contextual diversity 123–6, 127
  management 101–16
  'new careers' 93–4
  people management 208
  people processes 190, 193
  performance 59, 76, 222
  sense-making 216
  strategy 3, 6, 8, 11
Cunningham, I. 13, 135
customer service 28, 54, 71, 79–80, 153, 155–61,
  163–6, 170–3, 188, 190–1, 197, 211, 218, 225
Cyert, R.M. 76, 223

Daft, R. L. 223
De Geus, A. P. 185, 186
de-layering 48, 97, 100, 139–40, 149–51, 161, 169,
  189, 194, 205, 211
Dean, J. W. 62, 63, 64, 69
decision making 8, 12, 105, 218–20
Deckop, J. R. 42, 60, 172, 173, 183
Demirag, I. et al. 146
demographics 5

departmentalization 224
deregulation 23–4, 32, 60, 154, 211
descriptive model of HRM 121
Devanna, M. A. et al. 7, 8, 9, 41
development:
  career 27, 107, 114, 147–9, 186, 200, 202, 210,
    213, 220
  change 201
  commitment 207–9
  culture management 114
  employability 203
  management 219
  organization 180, 182, 186, 187
  people processes 171, 173, 177, 178, 197
  performance management 62, 64–5, 68, 70–
    6, 78
  personal and 'new careers' 82–4, 88, 90, 93,
    97–100
  policies and practices 135
  short-termism 148
  soft–hard models of HRM 42, 45, 47–9, 53–4,
    56–7
  strategy and 13
  transformation 163, 165
developmental-humanism 40–1, 45, 49, 57, 152,
  203, 212
devolution of responsibility 13, 18, 48, 54, 76,
  94, 133–6, 151–3, 163–5, 168, 189, 204–7
dimensions of linkage of People Process Map
  172–3
discussion, career 97
diversity:
  contextual and practice of HR 117–32
  and control 104
divestments 32–3
documents, HR 192
'dominant coalition' 9
downsizing:
  commitment 211–12
  context 23–4, 27, 30–2
  contextual diversity 129
  culture management 109, 111
  impact of 200–1, 203
  'new careers' 79, 83, 90, 94, 99–100
  people processes 190, 193–4, 196–7
  policies and practices 140, 149–51
  sense-making 217, 221, 223
  soft–hard models of HRM 48–9
  transformation 161–2
Doz, Y. L. 154, 169
Drucker, P. 104
Dukerich, J. M. 20
Dunham, R. B. 42
Dunphy, D. 8
Dutton, J. E. 20
Dyer, L. 44, 118, 120, 172, 187

economic change 5, 20
education 5, 13, 135
Edwards, P. K. 134
Edwards, R. 134
effectiveness 78, 118, 171, 176, 179
efficiency 77

Eisenhardt, K. M. 60
embeddedness:
    identity 225
    practice 154, 165, 169, 213
    process 170–1, 173, 186, 189–90, 195–7, 213, 219
emergent culture change 102–4, 115–16
emergent strategies 44
emotional–rational alignment 103, 162–3
employability 80–2, 85, 88, 90–1, 94, 98–100,
    195, 202–3, 208, 213, 220
empowerment 48, 57, 103, 152, 162, 169, 203,
    207, 212, 220
entrepreneurialism 84, 112, 114, 163, 215, 225
environment:
    change 154–5, 177
    context 20, 31, 33
    methodology 3, 5–6, 8–9
    people processes 180, 183, 193
    performance management in high-velocity
        59–78, 212
    sense-making 218, 221, 225
    soft–hard models of HRM 54, 57
equality 63, 69–70, 74–6, 82, 99
espoused strategy 5
espoused theory and theory-in-use gap 213–25
espoused values 102, 114
ethnographic interviews 15–16
Etzioni, A. 83
European Quality Award 161
Evans, P. A. L. 7
evolution:
    business 7–8
    cycle of HR function 18, 118–19, 122–9
    strategy 44
expectancy theory 63
expectations 59, 61, 65, 76, 215
experience, organizational 215, 221
'experienced relevant business conditions' 5
expertise 13, 128
external–internal variables and context 4, 6,
    31–3, 117–18, 155, 169, 199

feedback:
    commitment 208–9
    contextual diversity 123
    'new careers' 84
    people processes 175–6, 180, 182–6, 188, 190
    performance management 68, 73
    sense-making 216, 219, 223–5
    transformation 165–6
Fell, A. 12, 41, 51, 174
Fenton-O'Creevy, M. 218, 219
field study, use of 14
financial services 23, 27, 54, 65, 103, 211
Fiol, C. M. 154
flattening of organizational structure 48, 76,
    150–1, 163, 194, 196, 218
Fletcher, C. 139
flexibility:
    commitment 206, 210
    culture management 110, 115–16
    'new careers' 79, 98
    people processes 179, 186, 188–9, 191

performance management 61, 63–5, 67–9,
    73–4, 76–7
sense-making 225
soft–hard models of HRM 41, 43–5, 54–6
focus groups, use of 15–16, 19
Fombrun, C. J. et al. 7, 41, 59, 118
forecasting 178, 183
freedom 67, 102–3, 108, 112, 116, 123
Freeman, R. E. 5, 20
frequency of appraisal 137–8
Friedrickson, J. W. 221
functional flexibility 44–5

gap:
    analysis 180, 183, 184, 185, 188
    implications of, and sense-making 222–5
    rhetoric/reality 200
Ghoder, F. 197
Ghoshal, S. 25, 219, 225
Giordarno, Richard 28
Glaxo Pharmaceuticals UK:
    commitment 206, 209, 210
    context 20–2, 24, 27–8, 32–3
    culture management 105–8, 114–16
    data collection 17–18
    'new careers' 79, 86, 88–90, 92, 95–7
    people processes 188, 191, 194, 197
    performance management 64–71, 73, 75–6
    policies and practices 137, 140–2, 144, 147–9
    sense-making 219, 222
    soft–hard models of HRM 46, 49–56
    transformation 153, 155, 157–8, 161–8
Global Finance Europe 27, 128–9
globalization 20, 24, 27, 80, 153, 216
Goffee, R. 12, 134
Golden, K. A. 44, 55
Gomez-Mejia, L. R. 63
Goold, M. C. 146
Gould, S. 83, 101
grading 113, 138–9, 210
Griffin, M. A. et al. 217
Griffiths Inquiry (1983) 27
Grint, K. 139
Guest, D. E. 40, 41, 42, 43, 44, 57, 82, 99, 101, 118,
    133, 134, 143, 145, 172, 179, 187

Hamal, G. 173, 183
Hambrick, D. C. 176
Hannan, A. 20
Hayday, S. 13, 135
health care 23, 26, 158, 163, 188
Hegewisch, A. 120
Hendry, C. 7, 41, 42, 152, 173
Hendry, J. 101
Herriot, P. 82, 84, 99
Hewlett, Bill 23, 28, 29, 162
Hewlett Packard:
    change 2
    commitment 206–7, 209–11, 213
    context 20–4, 28–9, 32–3, 200–1
    contextual diversity 122–4, 130–1
    culture management 108–16
    'new careers' 85–6, 88–90, 92–3, 95–8

people processes 188–92, 193–4, 197
performance management 64–8, 70–1, 74, 76
policies and practices 137–8, 140–2, 144–5, 147–51
sense-making 220, 225
transformation 153, 155, 159, 161–2, 164–8
high-potential employees 83, 91, 93, 100, 178, 192–3, 204
high-velocity environment and performance management 35, 59–78, 206, 209, 212
Highton, David 27
Hill, M. A. 24
history, organizational 20, 119, 154, 205, 220
Hofstede, G. 104
HP Way (Hewlett Packard) 28, 53, 67, 76, 108–12, 115–16, 122–3, 193, 207
HR function:
  control 53–4
  management 204–6
  methodology 16, 18
  'new careers' 85, 88
  policies and practices 136, 148, 152
  role of 12–13, 199
  strategic role 117–18, 120–3, 125–32
  theory and practice 202
Hrebiniak, L. G. et al. 10
Huff, A. S. 59
human relations movement 41
Hyman, J. 13, 135

identification with organization 59
identity, organizational 153–4, 165, 167–9, 211, 215–18, 220, 223–5
image 153, 162
incentives 136, 140–3, 147–8, 151, 214, 219, 222
individualism:
  commitment 213
  culture management 112–14
  HRM 128
  methodology 3, 5
  'new careers' 79, 81–5, 91–3, 98–9
  outcomes 11
  performance management 73, 76–7
  soft–hard models of HRM 42–3, 45, 47–9, 55–7
  workforce development 179
industrial relations 118–19, 130–1, 145
information 65–6, 85, 90, 98–100, 154, 166, 211, 216, 221–3
information technology 5, 32
innovation 7, 42, 71, 73, 76, 84, 102–3, 108, 112, 114–16, 123, 163, 170–1, 190–1, 217, 219–20
institutional theory 20
institutionalization of management role 140–1, 143, 151–2
instrumentalism 40–1, 45, 57, 208
integration 7, 42–5, 51–2, 55, 59, 71, 129–31, 204, 222–3
interpretation of change 154, 163–6, 169, 214–16, 218, 220–5
interventions:
  change 155–60
  commitment 209

complex 195–6
culture management 102–3, 106
individual 199
methodology 18
outcomes 200, 203–4
performance management 59, 64
realized 201–3
strategy and 5, 7, 10–11, 13
systemization 118
transformation 163
interviews, use of 14–18
involvement 97, 135–7, 143, 149, 151, 208–9, 213
Involving Everyone (BT Payphones) 47–8

Jackson, S. E. 7, 14, 43, 172, 174
Jaeger, J. A. 61
Jelinek, M. 6, 60
Jick, T. D. 14, 161, 224
job:
  classification 48, 63
  description 140–1
  experience 178–9, 194
  role 163–4, 168–9
  security 25–6, 51, 83, 93–4, 99–100, 124, 202–3, 217, 220, 225
Johnson, G. 101, 162
Judge, W. Q. 60
justice 210, 212, 215, 219–20, 223

Kahnemann, D. 221
Kamoche, K. 42, 44, 152
Kanter, R. M. 12, 104, 223
Keenoy, T. 44, 101, 104
Keep, E. 64
Kerfoot, D. 120
Key Result Areas 176
Khandwalla, P. N. 77
Kirkpatrick, I. et al. 13, 135, 151
Knights, D. 120
knowledge workers 104
Kochen, T. A. 120, 187
Kraft Jacobs Suchard:
  context 20–2, 24, 29, 32–3, 201
  contextual diversity 122, 124–8, 131–2
  'new careers' 87–98
  people processes 188–90, 192, 197
  policies and practices 137–8, 140–2, 144, 147–9
  sense-making 217–20
  soft–hard models of HRM 46–53, 55–6
  transformation 153, 155, 159, 161, 164–5
Kunda, G. 102, 104

labour:
  culture management as control 102–4, 116
  market 20, 25–6, 79–82, 85, 94, 98–9, 195, 203–4, 213
Lake, D. 162, 174, 176, 179, 183, 186, 196
Latham, G. P. 59, 62
Lawler, E. E. 176
Lawrence, P. R. 104
leadership 9, 67, 91, 163, 178, 180–2, 185–6, 187, 189, 191–2, 195

learning 34, 63–4, 71, 163, 173, 175, 183, 191, 224–6
  lifelong (Hewlett Packard) 85, 88
Legge, K. 8, 11, 40, 41, 42, 43, 49, 101, 118, 120, 121,
  127, 133, 135, 137, 201
Lengel, R. M. 223
Lengnick-Hall, C. A. and M. L. 7, 10, 41, 44
Levinthal, D. 222, 224
Lewin, K. 155
liberalization of markets 20, 23–4, 26
life cycle 7
lifetime employment 54, 79–80, 93, 111, 115, 150,
  179, 194, 203, 207, 211
line management:
  commitment 208–9, 210–11, 213
  contextual diversity 118, 122, 125–6, 129, 130–1
  culture management 114
  intention and reality 200, 205–6
  'new careers' 80–1, 84–5, 88, 90–1, 94–100
  people processes 176, 196
  performance management 68, 71, 76
  policies and practices 133–43
  responsibility 18
  role in HRM 133–6, 199, 204
  sense-making 213
  soft–hard models of HRM 43, 48, 50, 53
  strategy and 5, 11–14
  transformation 162, 165–6
Little, Arthur D. 16
Lloyds Bank UK Retail Banking:
  commitment 206–9, 211, 213
  context 20–2, 24, 29–30, 32–3
  contextual diversity 131
  HR strategy 203
  'new careers' 80, 85, 87–8, 90, 92–7
  people processes 188, 190, 194, 197–8
  performance management 64–8, 70–1, 76
  policies and practices 137–44, 147–9
  sense-making 217–20, 224
  soft–hard models of HRM 46–52, 54–6
  transformation 153, 155, 157, 160–1, 164–6
Locke, E. A. 62
long-termism 171, 173, 177–85, 187–8, 191–7, 208,
  213
Longenecker, C. O. et al. 77
Lorsch, J. W. 104
Lowe, J. 13, 134, 135, 151
loyalty 83, 94–5, 124
Lundberg, C. C. 6, 9
Lundy, O. 42, 170

Mabey, C. 62, 64
McGovern, Patrick 37, 133–52
McGregor, D. 41, 42
Mackenzie, K. 82, 99
MacMillan, I. C. 10
MacNeill, I. 82
Mahoney, T. A. 42, 60, 172, 173, 183
managed culture 104
management:
  commitment 210, 212
  contextual diversity 127–9
  future development 185–6
  HRM 5, 11–14, 199–200, 203, 204–6
  multiple 79–80

people processes 175, 178, 190
performance management 59, 62, 64–9, 71,
  73, 76–8
policies and practices 139–51, 150–1
sense-making 225
strategy 3
training of employees 203
transformation 162, 164–5, 169, 218, 221
March, J. G. 76, 223, 224
market 8, 13, 20, 28, 30, 54–5, 59–60, 70, 105,
  108, 111, 115, 150, 155, 157, 166, 168, 187, 188,
  211
Marsh, P. 146
matrix management 93, 119–20, 122, 128–9, 150,
  211, 216
Mayo, A. 82
Mento, A. J. et al. 62
mentoring 71, 76–7, 97, 179
Mercury 23
mergers 26, 28, 33–4, 150, 211, 219, 225
Meshoulam, I. 5, 7, 41, 44
messages, mixed 171, 215, 223
methodology:
  aims 3–4
  data collection and analysis 17–19, 22
  development 14–17
  philosophy 2–3
  questions and measure 4–14
middle management 90, 145, 154, 165–7, 169,
  214, 219
Migliore, R. H. 59
Miles, R. E. 7, 41
Milkovich, G. T. 6
Miller, A. 60
Miller, E. J. 221
Miller, P. 44, 56
Millward, N. 120, 143
Mintzberg, H. 12, 15, 18, 44, 134, 183
mission 8, 158, 161, 165, 171, 191
mobility 48–9, 81–2, 85, 90, 93, 99, 203–4, 213
modern–hermeneutical man 42–3, 57–8
Mohrman, A. M. et al. 60, 61–2
Monopolies and Mergers Commission 24, 31,
  33, 155, 157
morale 94–5, 109, 165, 206, 218, 223
Morrison, E. W. 216
motivation 53, 61, 69, 103, 115, 125, 143–4, 151, 171,
  178–9, 183, 185, 213, 218–19, 223
motivators, enablers and triggers of unwritten
  rules interviews 16
Movery, D. C. et al. 33
Mowday, R. T. 51
multi-divisional companies 7
multinationals 20, 24, 115, 162, 197
Mumford, E. 48

Nadler, D. A. 219
Nathan, B. R. et al. 78
nature, human 42–3, 57
networks 69, 79–80, 93, 166, 171
NHS reform, influence of 23, 26, 65, 105–6, 146,
  153, 155, 168, 225
Nicholson, N. 84–5, 98, 99, 134
Nonaka, I. 178

Noon, M. 42, 43, 45, 187
normative model of HRM 9, 40, 117, 119, 121
Northcote, J. 24
numerical flexibility 44–5

objective setting:
   people processes 172–3, 175–7, 180, 185–6, 187,
      189–91, 197
   performance management 61–2, 64–9, 71–6
objectives:
   culture management 111–14
   linkage 201
   organization 212
   performance 139–43, 151
   sense-making 214, 216, 218
   soft–hard models of HRM 41
   strategy 11
   training 203
Ogbonna, E. 120
Open Learning Centres (Lloyds Bank UK Retail
      Banking) 71, 85, 88
opportunism 128
opportunities, career 48, 56, 81, 90, 93, 98, 100,
      202, 205, 207–8, 212–13
Organizational Commitment Questionnaire 51
outcomes:
   contextual diversity 123
   culture management 102
   organizational 162–5, 169
   performance 83–4
   performance management 59, 61, 63, 67, 71
   soft–hard models of HRM 44
   strategy 10–11
output and performance management 61, 67,
      69, 73, 77
outsourcing 79–80
ownership and change 101–3

Packard, Dave 23, 28, 29, 67, 162
partnerships 33–4
Partridge, B. 134
paternalism:
   BT Payphones 26, 194
   change 168
   culture 104
   evolution cycle 118–19, 130
   Glaxo Pharmaceuticals UK 66
   Hewlett Packard 108, 110
   high-potential employees 91, 93, 204
   individualism and 81–2, 85, 94
   Lloyds Bank UK Retail Banking 30, 48, 66,
      76, 211
   WH Smith News 31, 54, 124–6, 131, 153, 220
Pauuwe, J. 119, 132
pay:
   flexibility 25, 44–5
   performance related 54, 63, 68–71, 73, 75–6,
      125, 145, 152, 176–7, 213
Pemberton, C. 83
Penley, L. 83, 101
people management:
   commitment 208–9, 210–11
   contextual diversity 117–18, 120, 123, 125, 129–
      30

culture management 109–12
   HRM 199, 201–2, 204–6
   line management 134
   'new careers' 84, 98
   people processes 172–3, 196, 198
   policies and practices 140, 147–8, 150
   soft–hard models of HRM 43, 51, 53–4, 56
   strategy 1–2, 5, 7, 10, 12–14, 20
People Process Map 170, 172–85
people processes and competitive advantage
      38, 170–98
people strategy 180, 184–6, 188, 192–3, 199, 201,
      209
performance:
   business 170, 172–3, 176
   career development 207
   context and 32
   culture management 101–2, 107, 109, 111–15
   financial 212
   HRM 7
   line management 133, 135
   people processes 171–2, 174–6, 181
   sense-making 220, 224
   soft–hard models of HRM 56–7
   strategy and 10–11
performance management 35, 43, 54, 59–78,
      122, 128, 154, 163–5, 169, 172, 189–91, 197,
      200–1, 205, 208–9, 211, 213
performance measurement 59, 61–3, 68–75, 77–
      8, 109, 113–14, 127, 141, 180, 185–6, 187–91
periphery workers 79–80
personnel management 12, 84, 101, 111–12, 117–
      26, 129–31, 133–5, 139–41, 146, 149, 152, 205
Peters, T. J. 59, 82, 101, 104
Pettigrew, A. M. 7, 18, 26, 41, 42, 152, 154, 173, 179
Philip Morris Organization 29
philosophy of HR 14
Philpott, L. 59
policies:
   HR 112–13
   'new careers' 79, 91
   and practices 15, 18, 37, 41, 44–5, 57, 133–52
political activity 20, 215, 218, 223–4
political change 5
population ecology 20
Porter, L. W. 51
power 6, 9, 166, 168, 221, 224
practices:
   fair 210
   of HR and contextual diversity 117–32
   management and 205
   'new careers' 79, 84
   policies and 15, 18, 37, 41, 44–5, 57, 133–52
Prahalad, C. K. 173, 183
prescriptive model of HRM 9, 40, 101, 103, 117,
      119–21, 137, 152
Prieto, C. 44, 45
privatization 23, 26, 32, 150, 154, 211
process:
   discipline 215, 219
   fairness 215, 219–20
   HR as 4, 8–9, 11, 200–2
   integration 222
   methodology 15

process (*cont.*):
  people 38, 170–98
processual strategy 8, 44
professional associations 139–40, 143–6, 151, 202, 205
professionalism 88, 121
profitability 11, 59, 101, 108, 191, 198, 221
project groups 66, 82, 88, 90, 98, 106–7, 113, 163, 194–5
psychological contract 2, 12, 82–4, 168, 179, 193–5, 199, 207–8, 211, 220
Purcell, J. 42, 43, 44, 48, 51, 54, 120, 132, 175, 177, 183

qualitative research 17, 121
quality 7, 43–4, 46–7, 54–5, 69, 71, 136–7, 151, 161, 169
quantitative research 17, 121
questionnaires, use of 17–19, 22
Quinn, J. B. 166
Quinn Mills, D. 174

Raelin, J. 146
Ramanujan, V. 44, 55
Randell, G. 139
Ray, C. A. 104
re-engineering 32, 67, 90, 161, 169, 212
recession 20, 23, 25, 28, 31–2, 212
Reed, John 27
Reger, R. K. 59
relational contract 82–3, 204
reliability of measurement 176
reporting lines 161–4
resources 11–12, 69, 82, 170, 173, 212
responsibility 12, 76, 82, 84–5, 91, 93–4, 97, 105, 113, 118, 136–7, 140, 146, 150–2, 175, 195, 203–6, 220
  see also devolution of responsibility
restructuring:
  commitment 207, 211
  context and 23–4, 26, 30, 32, 34
  contextual diversity 127
  'new careers' 79–80, 90
  people processes 189, 193–4
  performance management 59, 65, 76
  policies and practices 149–51
  sense-making 217, 221, 225
  soft–hard models of HRM 54, 57
  strategy 200
  transformation 153, 155, 161–2, 164, 169
reward:
  commitment 207, 209
  culture management 105
  effort–reward 145
  measurement 212
  methodology 16
  'new careers' 83
  people processes 171–3, 175–8, 180, 185–6, 187–9, 197
  performance management 59, 61, 63–4, 67, 69–70, 72–6
  sense-making 213, 219
  soft–hard models of HRM 48, 54

startegy 201
transformation and 163–5
rhetoric–reality:
  appraisal 137
  commitment 206, 208, 211–12
  gap between 225–6
  HRM 201–3
  'new careers' 36, 79–100
  organization and individual 199–200
  people management 1–3, 8, 11
  people processes 174, 197–8
  soft–hard models of HRM 47, 55–8
  strategy 14–16
Rice, R. K. 221
Rinquest, J. L. 154
Robertson, P. J. *et al.* 163
Robinson, L. 82, 179
Robinson, S. L. 216
role of HRM 36–7, 117–32, 162–3, 206
Rosenbaum, J. E. 179
Rousseau, D. M. 82, 83, 99, 168, 1790
routine issues and content of change 215–16
rules of the game and context of change 215, 220–1

Salaman, G. 62, 64
Salancik, G. 83
sales and performance management 64–5
saliency and content of change 216, 223
scanning people trends 180, 184, 185, 188, 193
Scase, R. 12, 134
scenario planning 186, 192, 195–6
Schein, E. 102
Scholes, K. 101, 162
Schon, D. A. 214
Schoonhoven, C. B. 60
Schuler, R. S. 7, 10, 43, 172, 174
Scott-Morgan, Peter 16, 123, 171
secondments 71, 76, 90
security, job 25–6, 51, 83, 93–4, 99–100, 124, 202–3, 217, 220, 225
selective perception 215, 221
self-assessment 68
self-development 71, 76–7, 113, 178, 207–8
self-management 48, 57, 80–4, 90–4, 98–9, 211
self-regulation 42, 206
semi-structured interviews 15, 19
Senge, P. 183
senior management:
  context 215, 219
  contextual diversity 123–8
  culture management 103–6, 108, 111–13
  HRM 202
  'new careers' 91, 93, 99
  sense-making 214, 224–5
  soft–hard models of HRM 50, 53
  strategy 204–6
  transformation 166
sense-making 15, 162, 171–2
  as emergent theme 213–25
Seward, J. K. 61
Sheppard, L. 59
short-termism:

career 208
  commitment 211–12
  context 218
  contextual diversity 127
  devolution of responsibility 13
  managerial 148, 205, 214
  'new careers' 84, 98–9
  people processes 171, 173, 175–81, 183, 185,
    187–9, 191, 195–6
  performance management 69, 77
  policies and practices 135, 139–40, 146–9,
    151–2
  transformation 165
Simons, R. 59, 76
simulation models 186, 192, 195–6
Sisson, K. 8, 41, 59, 61, 62, 120, 152, 177
size of organization and context of change 215,
    217–18, 223
skills:
  competitive advantage 171, 173, 177,
    178–9
  employment 203, 213
  management 12–13, 124, 141–3, 208–9, 213
  'new careers' 79–85, 88, 90, 98
  people processes 183, 188, 190–1, 193–5
  performance management 61, 64, 69–71, 77
  policies and practices 135
  soft–hard models of HRM 47, 57
  technological 24
slip up gap 222–3
Smith, F. J. 42
Snell, S. A. 60, 61, 62, 63, 64, 69, 77
Snow, C. C. 7, 14, 41, 176
social change 5, 8, 20
socialization 224
soft–hard models of HRM 13, 34–5, 40–58, 135,
    147, 151, 176, 189–91, 196, 209
Sparrow, P. 84
specialist management 130, 136–7
Spector, B. 7
stability 168, 189, 193, 206, 211
Stace, D. A. 8
stakeholders 5–6, 9
start-up businesses 7
Staw, B. et al. 217
Steers, R. M. 51
Stewart, A. 12
Stewart, R. 134
stock market 30, 108, 147
Storey, J. 7, 8, 9, 10, 12, 40, 41, 41–2, 43, 49, 57,
    59, 61, 62, 118, 119–20, 132, 133, 134, 143, 145
strategic choice theory 20
strategy:
  commitment 210
  control 49–58
  culture management 101
  fit 41, 43–4, 57, 154
  HR complex organisations 199–206
  methodology 5–14
  multiple 215, 218, 223–4
  organizational 117–21, 125, 127
  performance management 59, 63–4, 66, 73
  planning 183

transformation 154–63, 168–99
Streeck, W. 145
strength of linkage of process and business
    strategy 170–7, 179–82, 184–5, 288–98
stretch gap 222, 224–5
stretch goals 215
structural gap 222–4
structure 3, 6, 13, 105, 153–5, 201–2, 211–12, 216,
    218, 222–3, 225
style, management 6–7, 13
succession 90, 178, 192
Sullivan, J. J. 42
supervisors 134–5
surveys, use of 14, 17, 19
systemic strategy 8, 44
Szulanski, G. 214, 216, 222, 223

Tannenbaum, A. 60
targets:
  allocation 210
  behaviour 116
  financial 29, 31, 127, 147, 180
  management 143
  performance 61, 66–9, 73, 77, 113–14
  soft–hard models of HRM 53, 55
task:
  alignment 103
  forces 113, 158, 163, 168, 194–5
Taylorism 109, 114
team management 211
teamwork 62, 65, 67–8, 70, 73–4, 77, 79–80, 84,
    110, 128, 164–5, 179, 191, 210, 213
technology:
  change 5, 20, 24, 32, 154–5, 190, 194, 211, 217
  people processes 170, 173, 177
  performance management 60, 64–5
  temporal linkage 170, 173–4, 186
tensions of soft–hard models of HRM 40–5, 57
Thanheiser, H. H. 154, 169
Thomas, J. B. 14
threat, change as 215, 217
360° appraisal 70, 73, 84
Thurley, K. 205
Tichy, N. M. et al. 5, 41, 44, 172
time 171, 173, 200–1
top-down change 8, 76, 102–4, 106, 115–16, 165,
    216, 220
Torrington, D. 118
Total Quality Management 32, 161
Townley, B. 139
training:
  change 201
  commitment 207, 207–9
  contextual diversity 126
  employability 203
  management 13, 212, 214, 219
  'new careers' 81–3, 85, 88–9, 98–100
  people processes 172, 175, 177–8, 180, 185, 187–
    91, 196
  performance management 62, 64–5, 70–6
  policies and practices 135, 139–41, 150–2
  soft–hard models of HRM 42, 45–8, 53, 56–7
  transformation 163–5

transactional contract 82–3, 94, 99, 202, 204
transformation:
    at leading edge 37, 153–69
    contextual diversity 117–18, 121, 125, 131
    downsizing 200
    people processes 170–1, 173, 179–80, 183,
        185–6, 193, 197
transparency 77, 164, 169
trend analysis 180
triangulation methodology 14–15, 18
trust 12, 41–3, 49–50, 55, 94–5, 199, 224
    as emergent theme 206–13
Tsui, A. 5, 6
Tushman, M. L. 219
Tversky, A. 221
Tyson, S. 12, 41, 42, 51, 118, 119, 120, 129, 131, 174

Ulrich, D. 12, 84, 157, 162, 174, 176, 179, 183, 185,
    196
unemployment 20, 23, 25
unions 25, 125, 127, 137, 139–40, 143–6, 151–2, 202,
    205, 224
unitarism 8, 59
universalism 8, 83, 100, 117–19, 121, 132
unwritten rules of the game interviews 6, 16,
    19, 69, 109, 123, 125, 147–8, 191, 208, 214, 218
utilitarian–instrumentalism 40–1, 45, 57, 208

validity of measurement 176
values:
    commitment 213
    culture management 102–7, 109–10, 112, 114–
        16
    Hewlett Packard 193
    management 204
    performance management 67–8, 74, 76
    sense-making 215–16
    transformation 158, 161–4, 169
    WH Smith News 126
vertical–horizontal linkage:
    integration 7, 201–2

people processes 170, 172, 174
performance management 71
structures and 'new careers' 79–81, 85, 99
Voluntary Severance Pay (Hewlett Packard)
    108, 122, 150

Walker, J. W. 10, 12, 174, 177, 178, 180, 186, 196
Walsh, J. P. 61
Walton, R. E. 41, 42
Waterman, R. et al. 81, 82
Waterman, R. H. 59, 101
Watson, T. 11, 118, 134
Weick, K. 154, 168, 221
Welbourne, T. M. 63
welfare 118–19, 125, 127
Wellcome 27, 33, 166
West, M. 134
WH Smith News:
    context 20–2, 24, 30, 32–3
    contextual diversity 122, 124–6, 130–1
    'new careers' 87, 89, 92, 94–7
    people processes 188, 190, 197
    policies and practices 137–42, 144–5, 147–9
    sense-making 218, 220–1
    soft–hard models of HRM 44–7, 49–52, 54–6
    transformation 153, 155, 157, 160–1
Whipp, R. 26, 154, 179
Whittington, R. 8, 44, 104
Williams, R. 139
Willmott, H. 83, 101, 103, 104
Wood, S. 40, 41
workforce development 178, 9–80, 182, 184, 187–
    8, 192–5, 197
working, change in ways of 163, 169
workshops 71, 85, 88
    methodological 18–19
worth of employee 82
Wright, P. et al. 170, 171, 172, 178
Wriston, Walter 27

Yeung, A. et al. 12